THE ULTIMATE
EVERYTHING KIDS'®
FAIRY TALE BOOK

THE ULTIMATE EVERYTHING KIDS' FAIRY

TALE BOOK

Get to know enchanted princesses, fairies, and majestic horses

Calla Timmerman, Charles Timmerman,
Sheryl Racine & Kathi Wagner

Avon, Massachusetts

Contains materials adopted and abridged from *The Everything Kids'
Fairies Puzzle and Activity Book*, *The Everything Kids' Horses Book*,
and *The Everything Kids' Princess Puzzle and Activity Book*

Published by
Adams Media, an F+W Media Company
57 Littlefield Street
Avon, MA 02322
www.adamsmedia.com

ISBN 10: 1-60550-098-4
ISBN 13: 978-1-60550-098-0

Printed in United States of America.

J I H G F E D C B A

This publication is designed to provide accurate and authoritative information with regard to the sub-ject matter covered. It is sold with the understanding that the publisher is not engaged in rendering legal, accounting, or other professional advice. If legal advice or other expert assistance is required, the services of a competent professional person should be sought.
—From a *Declaration of Principles* jointly adopted by a Committee of the American Bar Association and a Committee of Publishers and Associations

Many of the designations used by manufacturers and sellers to distinguish their product are claimed as trademarks. Where those designations appear in this book and Adams Media was aware of a trademark claim, the designations have been printed with initial capital letters.

Cover illustrations by Dana Regan.
Interior illustrations and puzzles by Charles Timmerman.
Chapter opener art by Kurt Dolber.

This book is available at quantity discounts for bulk purchases.
For information, please call 1-800-872-5627.

Contents

Introduction

Fairy tales always have happy endings. But first there must be a challenge, something to test the main character. For example, Cinderella had to live with her mean stepmother and stepsisters before she met the prince at the ball. In Pinocchio's case, he changed into a real boy only after he learned to treat his father with respect. Good things happened to Cinderella and Pinocchio after they proved that they were worthy. In this book you will be challenged, but in a fun way. Are you ready?

Amusing math and logic puzzles will tickle your brain and try to trip you up. Clever word puzzles like crosswords, word searches, and rhyming games will do their best to stump you. Mysterious mazes and other picture puzzles will attempt to stop you in your tracks. Along the way you will meet all kinds of fairies, princesses, and noble steeds who seem to have jumped off the pages of your favorite fairy tales—right into this book!

So grab your magic wand (or pencil), sprinkle some fairy dust around the room, and engage your brain as we start this journey through a fairytale of puzzles. May you have fun and live happily ever after!

PART 1
Princess Puzzles

Chapter 1

Cinderella

Mixed-up Kitchen

Cinderella's stepmother was very mean and made Cinderella work long hours in the kitchen. Can you help Cinderella find everything in this mixed-up kitchen by unscrambling these letters? The items are all displayed in the pictures on these two pages.

1. etkelt _____
2. ekfni _____
3. onev _____
4. evsto _____
5. onpso _____
6. rfko _____
7. wobl _____
8. letap _____
9. phcrtei _____
10. pto _____
11. pcu _____
12. pna _____
13. bleta _____

See if you can fit all of the unscrambled words into this clueless crossword puzzle. Each word is used only once, and must fit exactly into the number of boxes.

The Magic Wand

Cinderella's fairy godmother used her magic wand to turn a pumpkin into a carriage. In these puzzles you will change words just by dropping letters.

For example, drop the first letter from this:

and turn it into a nighttime bird with big eyes.
The answer is: **BOWL & OWL**.

Drop the first letter from...

...and turn it into drops from the sky.
_ _ _ _ _ & _ _ _ _

Drop the last two letters from...

...and turn it into the event where Cinderella and the Prince meet.
_ _ _ _ _ _ & _ _ _ _

Drop the first two letters from...

...and turn it into gorillas.
_ _ _ _ _ _ & _ _ _ _

Drop the first letter from this...

...and turn it into something heartfelt.
_ _ _ _ _ & _ _ _ _

Drop the first letter from these...

and turn it into something cold
_ _ _ _ & _ _ _

Drop the first letter from a...

...and turn it into a garden tool.

_ _ _ _ & _ _ _ _

Drop the last letter from...

...and turn it into a drink made with leaves.

_ _ _ _ & _ _ _

Drop the last letter from this...

...and turn it into a baby bear.

_ _ _ _ & _ _ _

Drop the first letter from...

...and turn it into what you breathe.

_ _ _ _ & _ _ _

Drop the first two letters from a...

...and turn it into a creative work.

_ _ _ _ _ & _ _ _

Drop the first letter from these...

...and turn them into noisemakers

_ _ _ _ _ _ & _ _ _ _ _

Riding to the Ball

Find the path for Cinderella's carriage so that she can get to the ball. The prince is waiting!

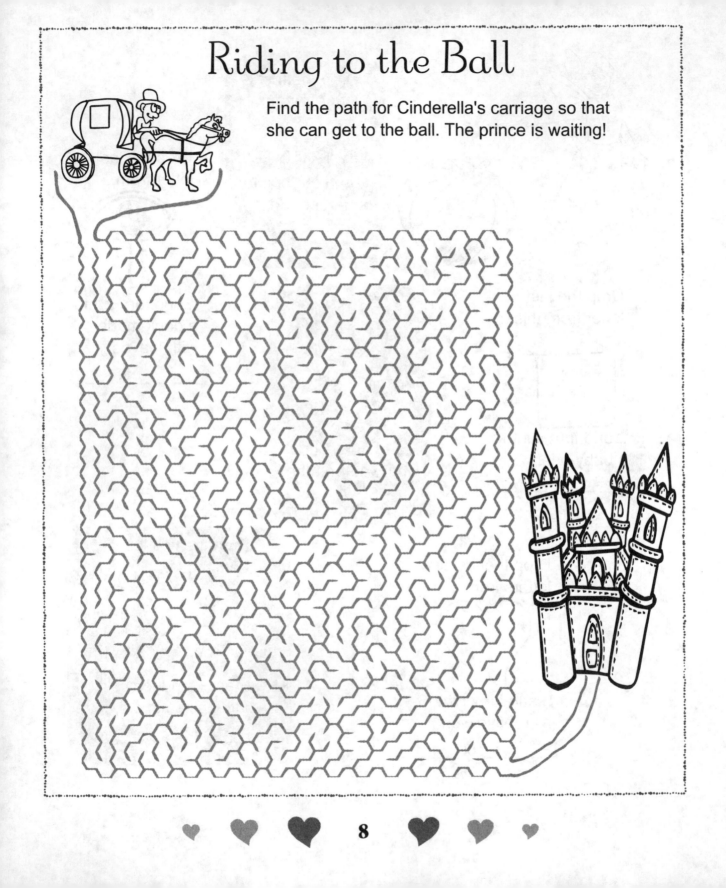

Dancing by the Numbers

Dancing at the ball requires some fancy footwork!
What numbers should go in the boxes to complete the equations?

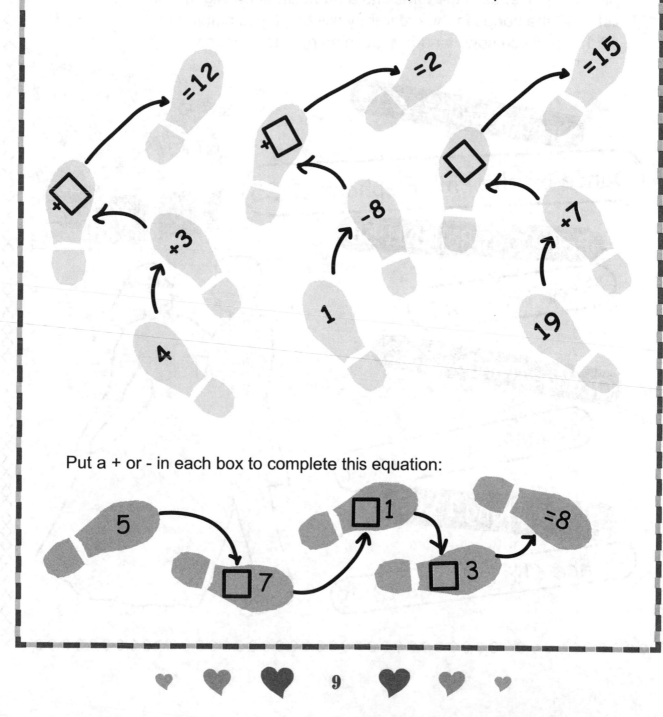

Put a + or - in each box to complete this equation:

The Last Dance

Cinderella must leave after what song? She wants to dance with the prince as long as possible, and doesn't want to leave in the middle of a song. Her carriage turns into a pumpkin at midnight! Here is a list of all the songs in the order they will be played starting at 10:15pm. Each song length is given as minutes:seconds.

Dream Waltz 15:13

Dance of the Pink Elephant 17:35

Polka Dot Polka 11:58

Foxy Trot 16:47

Orange Tango 18:22

Momma Mambo 14:31

Swing Thing 13:03

Prince Cha Cha Cha 12:49

The Confused Prince

The prince tried the slipper on every young lady in the kingdom. But things are not always as they seem! Can you help the prince figure out these optical illusions?

Which center dot is bigger?

Which horizontal line is longer?

Which horizontal line is longer?

If the Shoe Fits, Wear It!

Draw a line from each footprint to a shoe of the same size. Use a ruler if you need help. Can you figure out which footprint belongs to Cinderella? It is the one that will fit the slipper in the star.

Example of a shoe that fits a footprint:

12

Wedding Seating

Everybody will be at the wedding to see Cinderella and the Prince get married. You are in charge of deciding who sits where! These four people must sit in the front row:

The Duchess of Duncan

The Earl of Eaton

The Countess of Calypso

The Marquis of Macadamia

Due to royal protocol, the following rules must be followed:
1. An Earl cannot sit next to a Marquis.
2. A Duchess cannot sit next to a Countess.
3. A Marquis cannot sit next to a Duchess.

And of course, The Earl of Eaton must have the Countess of Calypso to his right.

The front row has only four chairs. Write the names of each person below the chair where they shall sit:

_____ _____ _____ _____

Wedding Cake

What shadow exactly matches this silly Cinderella and her goofy prince on their wedding day?

Cryptic Conclusion

Decode this final message. Clue: every letter had been shifted up or down by one. For example, B could be coded as either A or C.

BME UIDZ MJWDC GBQOJMX FWDS BESDQ...

Chapter 2

Pocahontas

My Real Name

The world knows me as Pocahontas, but that was just my nickname. Solve this puzzle to find out my real name. This is the name that was used within my tribe.

1. The first letter in my name is in beam but not bear.
2. The second letter in my name is in eagle and mountain.
3. The third letter in my name is the 20th in the alphabet.
4. The fourth letter in my name is in canoe but not cane.
5. The fifth letter in my name is in animal twice.
6. The sixth letter in my name is in oak but not oar.
7. The seventh letter in my name has already been used twice.

___ ___ ___ ___ ___ ___ ___
1   2   3   4   5   6   7

Where I'm From

My father was Powhatan, a powerful chief of the Algonquian Indians. To find out what state our lands are in, cross out all of these letters from the grid: ESM

EMVSIMSE
REMSGIMS
MENSMIAE

The Time Machine

Pocahontas was born around the year 1595. At that time the printing press and toothpaste had been invented, but not the microscope. Pretend that Pocahontas can fly through time and space. Do you know what she will find?

The year is 1700, what has not yet been invented:
- ☐ pencil
- ☐ lightning rod
- ☐ toilet

The year is 1800, what has not yet been invented:
- ☐ lawn mower
- ☐ steam engine
- ☐ piano

The year is 1850, what has not yet been invented:
- ☐ batteries
- ☐ zipper
- ☐ Morse code

The year is 1900, what has not yet been invented:
- ☐ telephone
- ☐ light bulb
- ☐ antibiotics

The year is 1950, what has not yet been invented:
- ☐ Internet
- ☐ television
- ☐ computer

The year is 1990, what has not yet been invented:
- ☐ cell phone
- ☐ pocket calculator
- ☐ DVD movies

The Path to Jamestown

Pocahontas made frequent trips to visit the colonists. Can you find a path from the Indian village to Jamestown where the colonists lived?

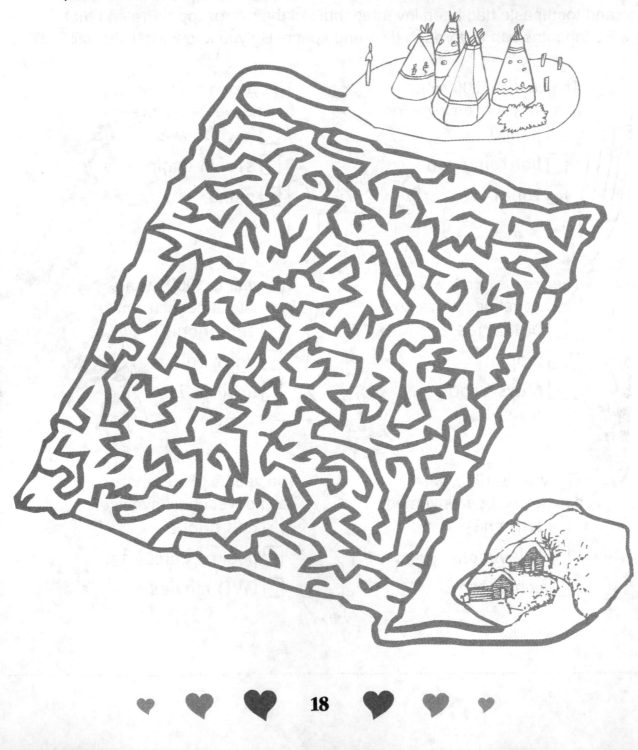

Fair Trades

Pocahontas helped improve relations between the colonists and the Indians. Can you help Pocahontas determine which trades between the two groups are fair? Put an equal sign, greater than sign, or less than sign in each box.

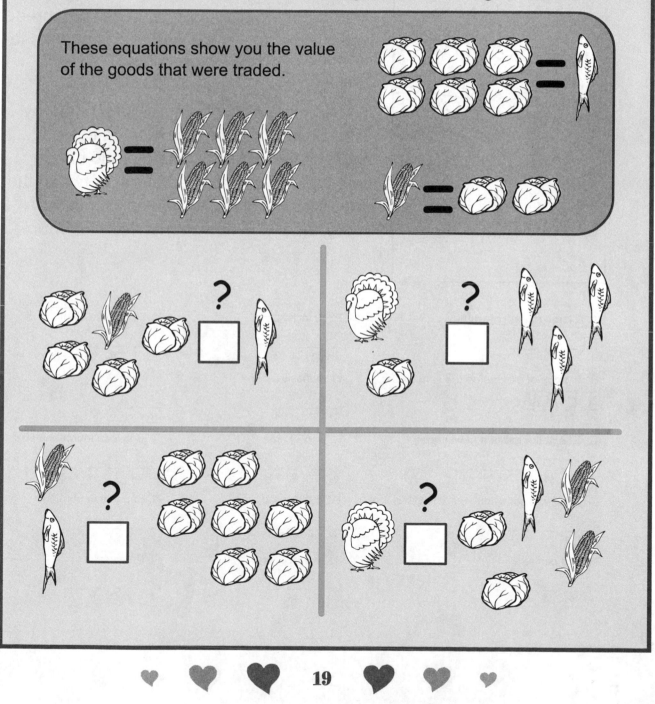

John Smith and Pocahontas

Legend has it that Pocahontas saved the life of John Smith, a colonist who was captured by the Indians. His life was spared thanks to Pocahontas's impassioned plea.

In this puzzle you will figure out a quote by John Smith. Answer the clues on this page and also fill the letters into the grid on the next page. Work back and forth between the clues and the grid until you figure out the quote. One clue has been solved for you.

A. A large stream of water.

— — — — —
17 22 63 27 6

B. A group of players on the same side.

T E A M
4 24 39 13

C. Title at the top of a newspaper.

— — — — — — — —
11 60 48 43 28 29 42 31

D. What you get when you boil water.

— — — — —
54 21 36 41 23

E. Ten cents.

— — — —
40 51 15 53

F. 12 inches.

— — — —
20 56 16 25

G. Opposite of low.

— — — —
26 62 66 47

H. Bird's home.

— — — —
52 12 55 34

I. Do it at a red light.

— — — —
9 10 32 49

J. To turn over.

— — — —
30 61 64 50

K. Stay out of sight.

— — — —
59 8 37 46

L. Not no.

— — —
18 38 3

M. Between fourth and sixth.

— — — — —
33 2 57 44 45

N. Capable of burning.

— — —
35 19 58

O. Bees make it.

— — — — —
1   5 65 14 7

Pocahontas was a young girl when she rescued John Smith. Solve this crazy formula to determine her age:

$$\begin{array}{l} \text{number of hours in a day} \\ -\ \text{number of kings in a deck} \\ +\ \text{number of cups in a pint} \\ -\ \text{number of days in a week} \\ -\ \text{number of feet in a yard} \\ \hline =\ \text{age of Pocahontas when she rescued John Smith } ? \end{array}$$

1O	2M	3L	4B T	5O	6A	7O	■	8K	9I	■	■
10I	11C	12H	■	13B M	14O	15E	16F	17A	18L	■	■
19N	20F	■	21D	22A	23D	24B E	,	25F	26G	27A	■
28C	29C	30J	31C	■	32I	33M	■	34H	35N	36D	■
37K	38L	39B A	40E ,	■	41D	42C	43C	■	44M	45M	46K
47G	48C	49I	50J	51E	52H	53E	54D	55H	■	56F	57M
58N	59K	60C	■	61J	62G	63A	64J	65O	66G	■	.

Missing Flowers

John Smith has sent Pocahontas flowers!
Which piece will complete the bouquet?

A.

B.

C.

D.

E.

F.

A Vase for Pocahontas

Can you find a vase for Pocahontas?
It must have all of these characteristics:

1. No zigzag stripe
2. One heart

3. One star
4. No flower

Mathematical Teepee

Indians often painted designs on their teepees. Can you complete this mathematical teepee? For each empty square, enter the sum of the two numbers beneath it on either corner. One of the examples is already done (3+7=10). Complete all of the squares to the very top.

A Corny Pyramid

Can you help Pocahontas turn these corn pyramids upside down? Move only the given number of ears. It might help to try to solve this puzzle on a table using coins for the ears of corn.

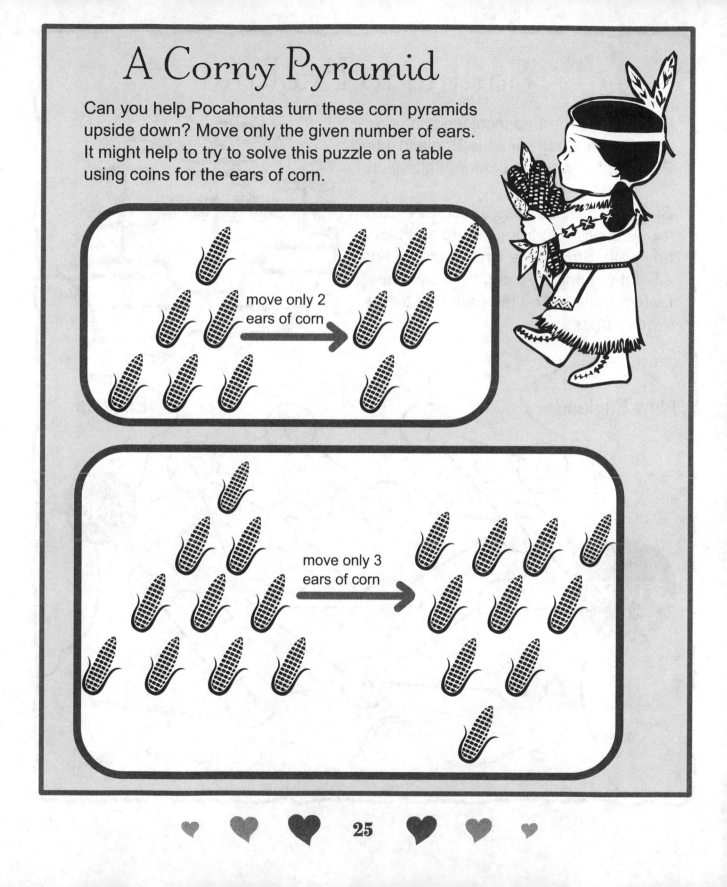

move only 2 ears of corn

move only 3 ears of corn

Sailing to England

Pocahontas married a colonist named John Rolfe. They sailed to England, where Pocahontas was the center of attention.

Can you chart the fastest course across the Atlantic? Go from start to end along any path. Stop at the circles and add up all of the numbers along the way. The fastest route will be the path with the lowest total.

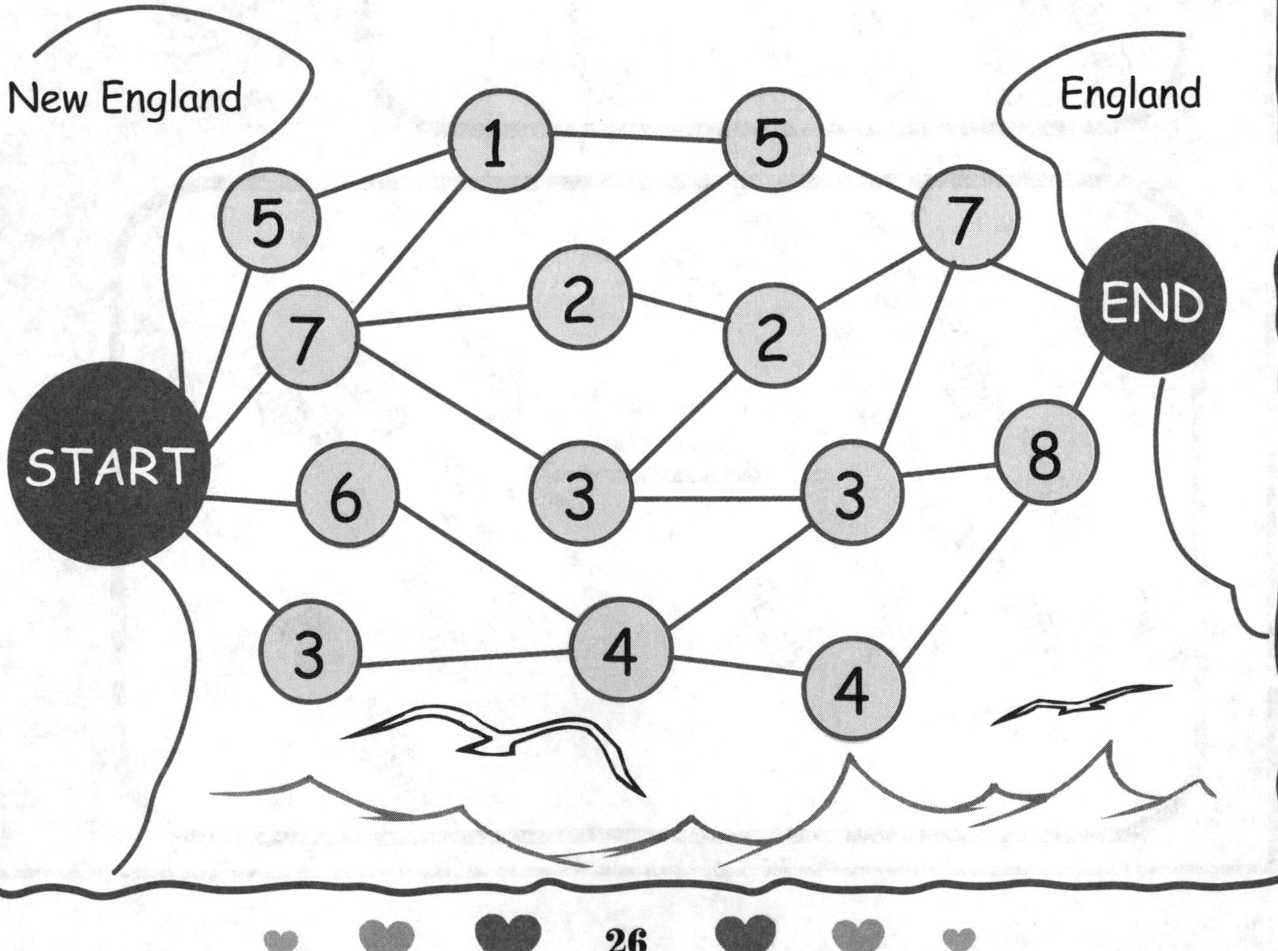

New England

England

START

END

5
1
5
7
7
2
2
6
3
3
8
3
4
4

Mermaids: Princesses of the Sea

Interesting Combinations

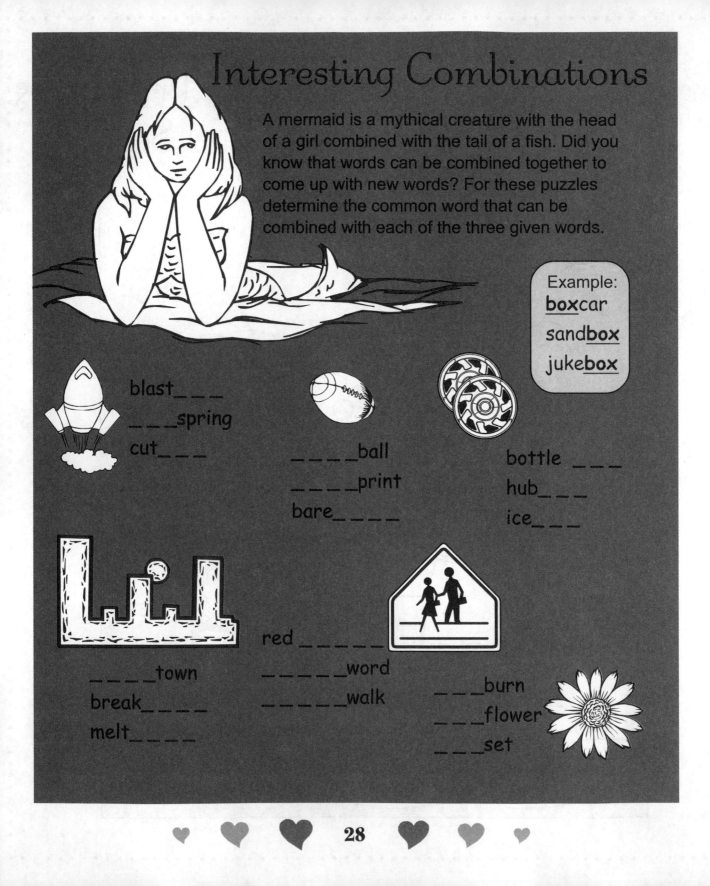

A mermaid is a mythical creature with the head of a girl combined with the tail of a fish. Did you know that words can be combined together to come up with new words? For these puzzles determine the common word that can be combined with each of the three given words.

Example:
boxcar
sand**box**
juke**box**

blast_ _ _
_ _ _spring
cut_ _ _

_ _ _ _ball
_ _ _ _print
bare_ _ _ _

bottle _ _ _
hub_ _ _
ice_ _ _

_ _ _ _town
break_ _ _ _
melt_ _ _ _

red _ _ _ _ _ _
_ _ _ _ _word
_ _ _ _ _walk

_ _ _burn
_ _ _flower
_ _ _set

_ _ _ _stand
side_ _ _ _
_ _ _ _ball

camp_ _ _ _ _ _ _
under_ _ _ _ _ _
_ _ _ _ _ _floor

saw_ _ _ _
_ _ _ _pan
_ _ _ _storm

bus_ _ _ _
_ _ _ _watch
door_ _ _ _

_ _ _ _ _house
winter_ _ _ _ _
ever_ _ _ _ _ _

rail_ _ _ _
_ _ _ _runner
_ _ _ _block

_ _ _ _ _house
_ _ _ _ _weight
flash_ _ _ _ _

outer _ _ _ _ _
parking _ _ _ _ _
_ _ _ _ _ _shuttle

Mathmagic Mermaid

Some mermaids have magical abilities. This mermaid can work magic with math. Her favorite number is seven. Follow these instructions and she will work magic with your favorite number.

1. Pick a favorite number between 1 and 9.

2. Double the number.

3. Add 7 to the result.

4. Multiply this sum by 5.

5. Now subtract 28.

The lowest digit of your answer is the mermaid's favorite number.
The highest digit of your answer is your favorite number.
How did the mermaid do this?

Transform

It is a common theme in mermaid stories for the mermaid to turn into a human.

Can you change one word into another word in these puzzles? Each step must be a real word and differ from the previous word by only one letter. There are many possible solutions, but try to use only the given number of steps.

Example:
BOY to MAN

B O Y

B A Y

M A Y

M A N

BIRD to BEAR

B I R D

_ _ _ _

_ _ _ _

_ _ _ _

B E A R

CAT to DOG

C A T

_ _ _

_ _ _

D O G

COW to PIG

C O W

_ _ _

_ _ _

P I G

MOON to MARS

M O O N

_ _ _ _

_ _ _ _

M A R S

HAND to FOOT

H A N D

_ _ _ _

_ _ _ _

_ _ _ _

F O O T

Fishy Friends

Letters are missing from the names of the mermaids' fishy friends. Complete each name by adding one letter. Then find all of the names in the grid of letters on the next page. Look up, down, across, backward, and diagonally. Some letters may appear in more than one name.

Hint: If you're not sure what letter to add, first find the given part of the name in the grid and then you can determine the missing letter.

S_ARK	FLOUN_ER	PIK_
DAR_ER	YELLO_TAIL	MAR_IN
GUPP_	GOL_FISH	GRUN_ON
BLU_GILL	CAT_ISH	G_OUPER
FLU_E	MINN_W	H_RRING
C_APPIE	ALBAC_RE	BA_S
C_UB	SO_E	PER_H
GOB_	TU_A	STURGE_N
_OD	CA_P	BARRACU_A
	HALI_UT	BULLH_AD
	WALLE_E	TRO_T
	_ADDOCK	MA_KEREL
	ANCH_VY	SN_PPER
	S_LMON	SA_DINE
	GU_TARFISH	M_SKIE
	AN_EL	PA_ROTFISH

```
E K I P R E D N U O L F Y H R
Y Y V O H C N A M U S K I E K
E N I D R A S L E I P P A R C
L T R O U T N E C H U B H R O
L N J A N F A R L S L S S I D
A G D L O I P E O I I L T N D
W O B B M S P K H F A P U G A
D L L A L H E C R T T N R B H
A D U C A R R A B O W O G A Q
R F E O S E T M Y R O I E E C
T I G R P I A B P R L N O K L
E S I E U R O N P A L U N U E
R H L G L G R O U P E R R L C
H A L I B U T Q G T Y G O F T
M I N N O W S H A R K S S A B
```

Predictions

Mermaids appear in stories from all parts of the world. In many of these stories mermaids can predict the future. Can you predict which bubble will come after the first two?

1.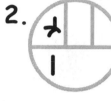

2.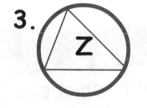

3.

4.

5.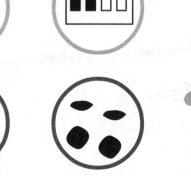

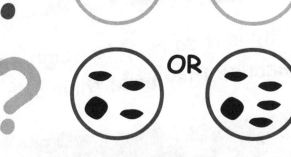

Mermaid Riddles

Mermaids love to tell riddles about fish!
Use the pictures to help solve these riddles.

What fish is the most valuable?

+

Why are fish so smart?
Because they live in...

What fish likes bubble gum?

+

What fish is the most famous?

+

Why is it so easy to weigh a fish?
Because they have their own...

Where is My Prince?

This mermaid dreams of becoming human and meeting the prince. She found these scraps of paper in the ocean that have the address of the prince. Help the mermaid by copying each scrap into the corresponding area of the box so that the address will be revealed.

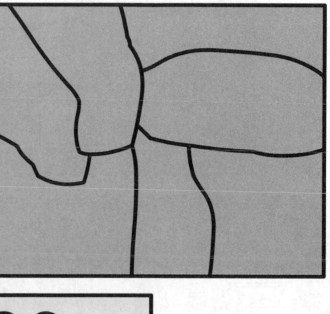

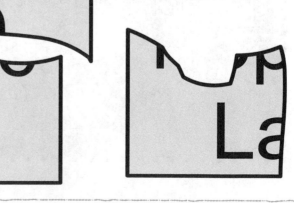

Treasure Watcher

This mermaid keeps an eye on her undersea treasure. Can you find ten things in the top picture that are missing from the bottom picture?

38

Chapter 4

Sleeping Beauty

Good Fairies

Eight fairies came to see the young princess. Seven were good fairies and brought gifts. One of the fairies was mean and cast an evil spell. Use these clues to figure out which one is the mean fairy:

> Only the good fairies have wings. The mean fairy sits on a cloud and does not have a star on her wand.

Fairy Gifts

Can you piece together the gifts from the seven good fairies? Each gift is a personal quality that is valued.

What's in a Name?

Using letters in the name SLEEPING BEAUTY, you can make the words LEAP and NAP and many others. Can you find at least twenty words contained in the name SLEEPING BEAUTY?

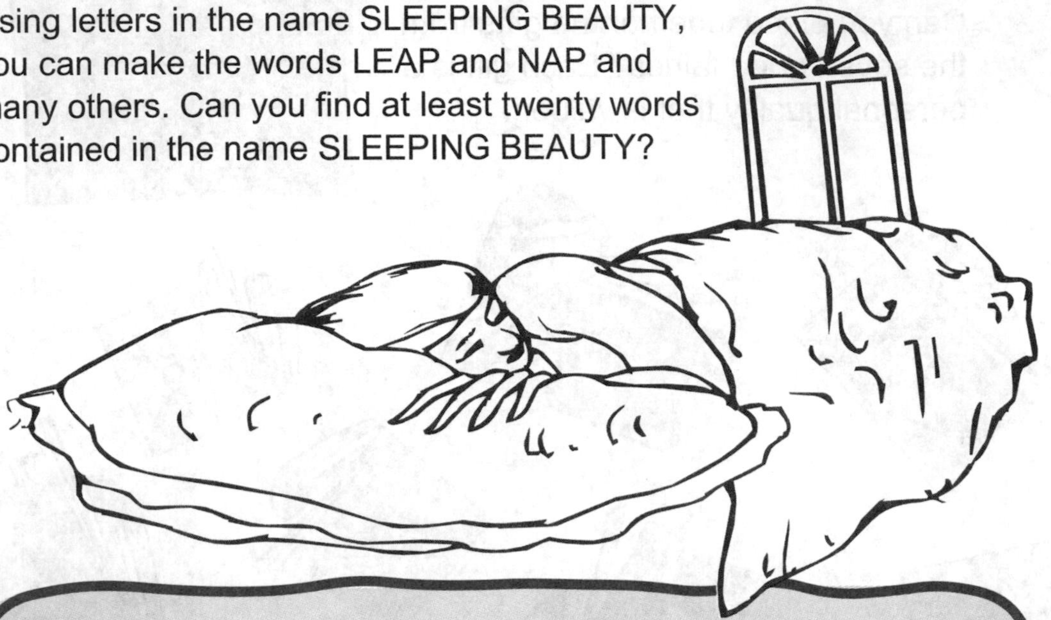

1. _____
2. _____
3. _____
4. _____
5. _____
6. _____
7. _____
8. _____
9. _____
10. _____

11. _____
12. _____
13. _____
14. _____
15. _____
16. _____
17. _____
18. _____
19. _____
20. _____

Spinning Wheel Spell

These spinning wheels have a hidden message for the princess. To read the message, put the letter at the top of each wheel in the first blank. Then move clockwise around and transfer every other letter from the wheel to the blanks until words are formed. The first letters are completed to get you started.

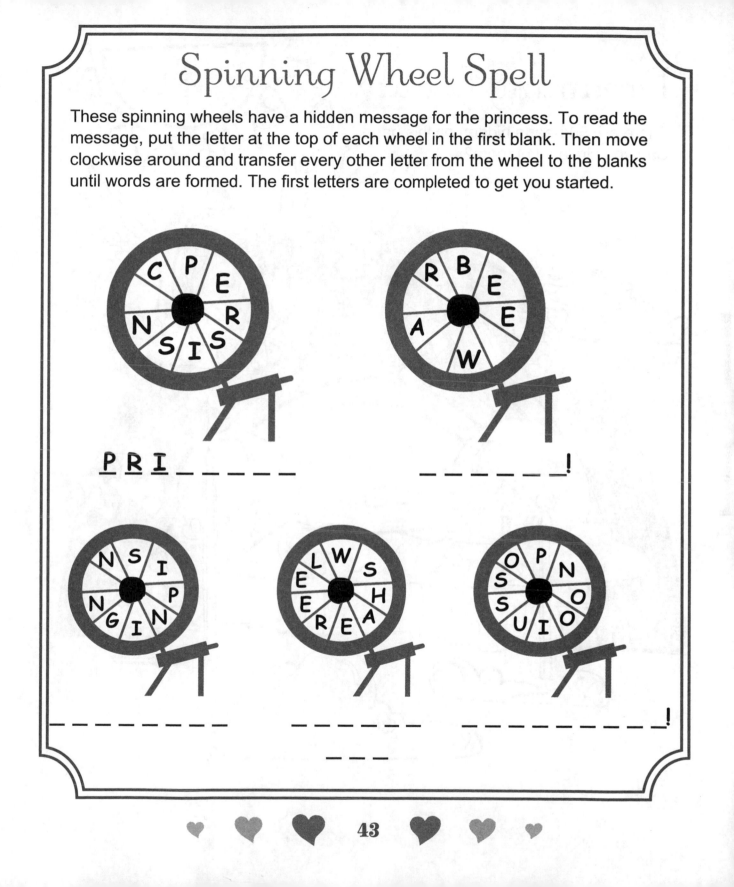

P R I _ _ _ _ _ _

_ _ _ _ _ _ _!

_ _ _ _ _ _ _

_ _ _ _ _ _

_ _ _ _ _ _ _!

_ _ _

Dreaming Beauty

There are 50 hearts hidden on this page.
Can you circle all of them?

One Hundred Years

Sleeping Beauty slept for one hundred years. Find all of the columns and rows in this castle wall where the numbers add up to exactly one hundred. One of the answers has already been found.

25	18	16	10	21	7	18
7	20	23	10	9	24	4
8	27	7	0	15	12	12
25	3	4	22	24	5	17
16	5	12	18	11	9	22
7	4	27	10	9	20	23
12	10	15	0	11	24	5

Double E

Just like Sl<u>ee</u>ping Beauty, everything on these two pages has a double E. Can you fill in all of the blanks with letters so that each item is named?

_ E E _ _ _ _

_ E E _ _ _ _

_ E E

_ _ E E

_ _ E E _

_ _ E E _

_ E E _

_ E E _ _

_ _ E E _

_ _ E E _ _

_ E E _ _

_ E E _ _

_ _ E E _ _ _ _ _

47

The Path to Sleeping Beauty

Can you help the prince find the correct path to sleeping beauty's castle? The prince should follow the path that has all 14 letters in SLEEPING BEAUTY.

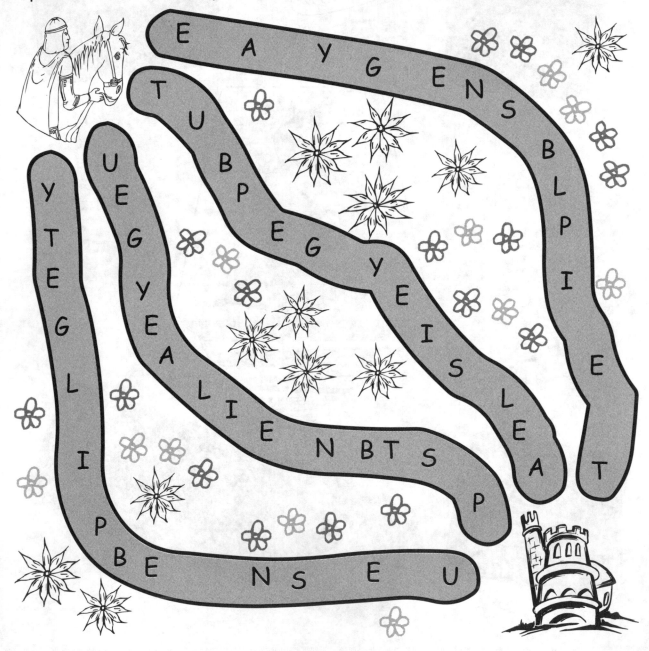

The prince has found the castle! Can you help him find a path through the castle to Sleeping Beauty?

Castle Maze

START

A Message from the Prince

Sleeping Beauty awoke after the prince kissed her. The prince immediately sent a secret message back to the king and queen. Help them figure out the message by putting the letters into the grid. Each letter has a symbol and a number to tell you where it should go in the grid. One letter has already been entered.

$7 \diamond = E$

$5 \heartsuit = V$

$1 \diamond = M$

$4 \heartsuit = A$

$2 \diamond = Y$

$2 \spadesuit = O$

$3 \spadesuit = V$

$6 \heartsuit = E$

$1 \spadesuit = L$

$4 \clubsuit = N$

$3 \clubsuit = U$

$5 \diamond = R$

$4 \diamond = T$

$5 \clubsuit = D$

$3 \heartsuit = H$

$1 \heartsuit = I$

$1 \clubsuit = F$

$2 \clubsuit = O$

$6 \diamond = U$

$4 \spadesuit = E$

	1	2	3	4	5	6	7
♥							
♣				N			
♦							
♠							

Chapter 5

Snow White

Mirror, Mirror

The queen was furious when her talking mirror said that Snow White was the fairest in the land! Can you find ten differences between these mirror images of Snow White working in the kitchen?

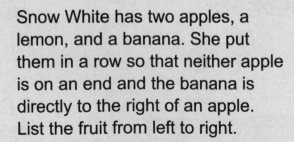

Snow White has two apples, a lemon, and a banana. She put them in a row so that neither apple is on an end and the banana is directly to the right of an apple. List the fruit from left to right.

Snow White has three forks and two knives. She put them in a row so that no fork was next to another fork. List the order of forks and knives from left to right.

The Secret Answer

The Queen asked, "Mirror, mirror, on the wall, who is the fairest one of all?" Knowing the answer would anger the queen, the mirror displayed the answer in code. Can you figure out the answer? A substitution code is used where 1=A, 2=B, and so on.

19 14 15 23   23 8 9 20 5

9 19   1

20 8 15 21 19 1 14 4

20 9 13 5 19   6 1 9 18 5 18

20 8 1 14   25 15 21 !

Twisty Walk

Snow White fled through the forest to escape the evil queen.
Can you find the path to the dwarfs' cottage?

START

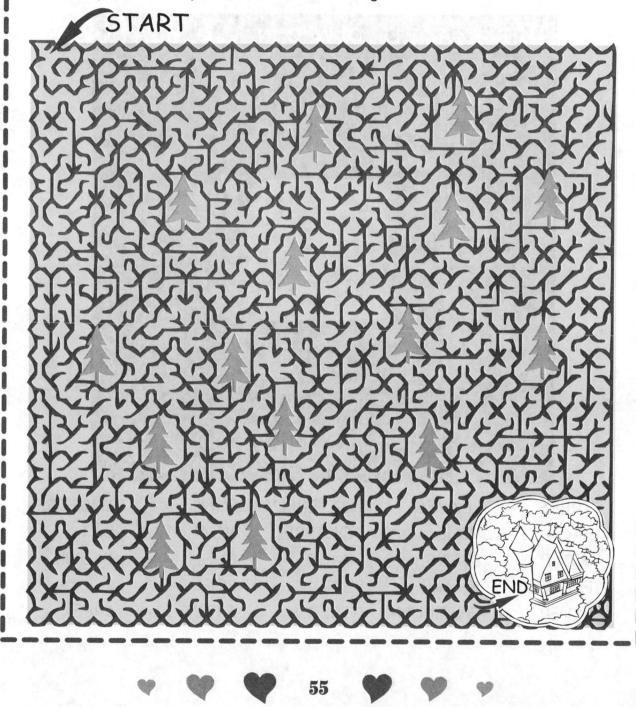

Things in the Forest

Can you find the things Snow White saw in the forest?
Look up, down, across, backward, and diagonally.

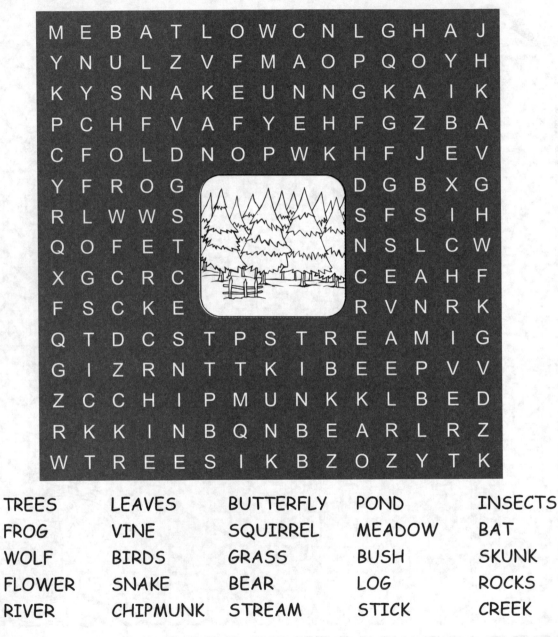

```
M E B A T L O W C N L G H A J
Y N U L Z V F M A O P Q O Y H
K Y S N A K E U N N G K A I K
P C H F V A F Y E H F G Z B A
C F O L D N O P W K H F J E V
Y F R O G       D G B X G
R L W W S       S F S I H
Q O F E T       N S L C W
X G C R C       C E A H F
F S C K E       R V N R K
Q T D C S T P S T R E A M I G
G I Z R N T T K I B E E P V V
Z C C H I P M U N K K L B E D
R K K I N B Q N B E A R L R Z
W T R E E S I K B Z O Z Y T K
```

TREES	LEAVES	BUTTERFLY	POND	INSECTS
FROG	VINE	SQUIRREL	MEADOW	BAT
WOLF	BIRDS	GRASS	BUSH	SKUNK
FLOWER	SNAKE	BEAR	LOG	ROCKS
RIVER	CHIPMUNK	STREAM	STICK	CREEK

Seven of Everything

There are seven of everything in the dwarf's cottage. Find the three items on this page that do not have exactly seven copies.

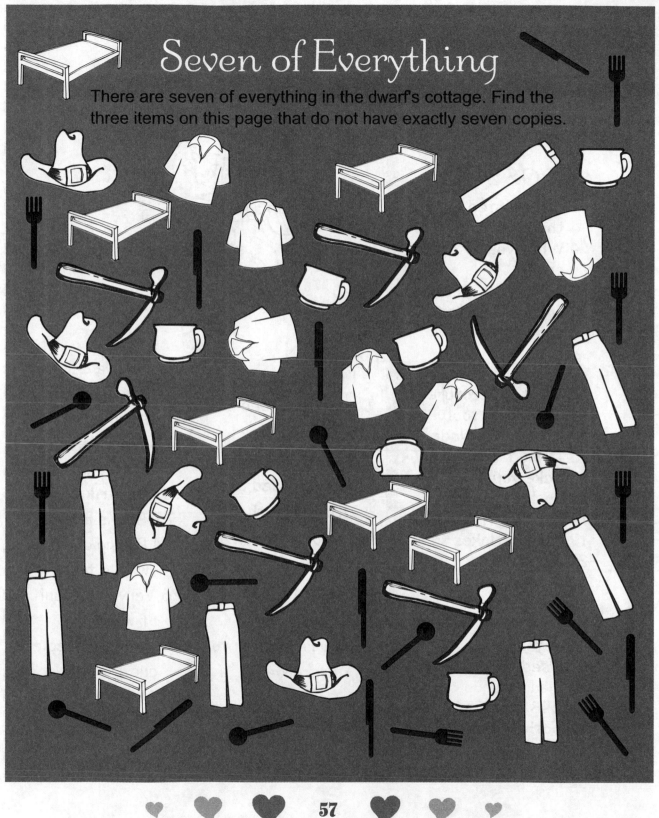

Snow White's Crossword

The dwarfs adored Snow White. They made this crossword puzzle for her with words that use only letters from her name: SNOW WHITE.

ACROSS

2 It's printed in the paper
4 What you do on a chair
6 Smart like an owl
9 Informal letter, maybe passed in class
10 The color of milk
12 Red temperature
14 Gardening tool with a flat blade
15 If loud it can wake you
16 Rock
17 Catches fish
19 Falls in flakes
21 Here is a _____: it starts with the letter H
23 Covered with water
25 Used for smelling
27 Hearty soup
29 548 minus 547
30 Father's boy

DOWN

1 One of two identical babies
3 Annoying cry
4 Worn on the feet
5 210 divided by 21
7 Seen in a theater
8 Short version of hello
11 Truthful, like Abe
12 Carries water to a sprinkler
13 The first even number after one
14 Female chicken
18 Like a city only smaller
20 Direction away from east
21 To strike
22 Bird's home
24 Pulling a car with a truck
26 Very heavy unit of weight
27 To use a needle and thread
28 Make a ____ at the well.

Doesn't Belong

Can you pick out the one equation
for each dwarf that doesn't belong?

A. $5 + 2 =$
B. $11 - 4 =$
C. $3 \times 2 =$
D. $35 \div 5 =$

A. $3 \times 3 \times 8 =$
B. $99 \div 3 =$
C. $59 + 5 + 6 + 2 =$
D. $98 - 26 =$

A. $37 + 6 =$
B. $22 \times 2 =$
C. $62 - 19 =$
D. $86 \div 2 =$

A. $25 \times 2 =$
B. $2 + 1 + 2 =$
C. $55 \div 11 =$
D. $100 - 95 =$

A. $5 \times 5 =$
B. $15 + 10 =$
C. $100 - 75 =$
D. $30 - 3 =$

A. $93 + 3 + 4 =$
B. $500 \div 5 =$
C. $10 \times 10 =$
D. $102 - 3 =$

A. $76 \div 2 =$
B. $21 + 27 =$
C. $19 \times 2 =$
D. $50 - 12 =$

The Poisoned Apple

The evil queen has turned herself into an old woman selling apples. She has a poisoned apple for Snow White. Follow the clues to figure out which apple is poisoned.

1. The poisoned apple is in a row with a turtle.
2. The poisoned apple does not have a heart below it.
3. The poisoned apple is not in the middle column.

Wedding Cake

The prince rescued Snow White and they were married! At the wedding celebration they had a three-layer cake and three tables. Each table had one cake layer to divide however they saw fit. Can you figure out who sat at what table based on the size of their piece of cake?

Table A has 5 seats:

1 _____
2 _____
3 _____
4 _____
5 _____

Diane had 1/8 of a layer.

Emma had 1/3 of a layer.

Shawn had 1/3 of a layer.

Mary had 3/10 of a layer.

Donnie had 1/4 of a layer.

Dave had 2/5 of a layer.

Nick had 1/6 of a layer.

Laura had 1/6 of a layer.

Therese had 1/8 of a layer.

Steve had 1/4 of a layer.

Violet had 3/10 of a layer.

Suzanne had 1/4 of a layer.

Table B has 3 seats:

1 _____
2 _____
3 _____

Table C has 4 seats:

1 _____
2 _____
3 _____
4 _____

Chapter 6

Prince Charmings

Prince Names from A to Z

Add one letter to complete these names. Each letter from A to Z is used only once, so cross them off once you use them:

A B C D E F G H I J K L M
N O P Q R S T U V W X Y Z

___van

___amuel

___ogan

___aul

___uincy

___unter

___enneth

___arlos

___ylan

___scar

___arrett

___annick

___achary

___imothy

___arcus

___oah

___lysses

___an

___ranklin

___aymond

___ason

___ndrew

___illiam

___avier

___ictor

___enjamin

Clueless Princes

Once you figure out all 26 of the names, try and fit them into this clueless crossword puzzle. Each name will be used only once and must fit exactly into the number of boxes. One name has already been entered for you.

Flowers from the Prince

The prince has brought you flowers
every day from Sunday until Saturday!

Every day he brought one of these:

On days starting with the letter T (like
Tuesday) he also brought one of these:

Wednesday through Friday he also brought one of these:

On days with 6 letters (like Sunday)
he also brought one of these:

Each flower lasts only three days and then must be discarded. For example, flowers received on Sunday must be discarded Wednesday. What does the bouquet of flowers look like on Saturday, after receiving and discarding?

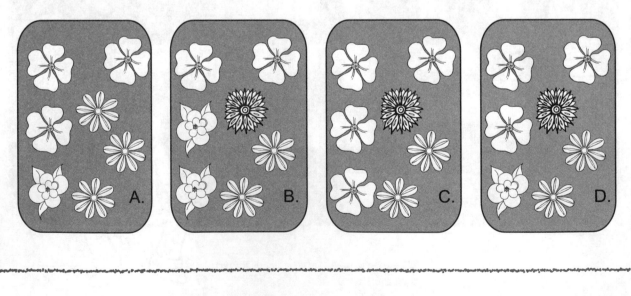

A.   B.   C.   D.

Out of This World

Have a friend or someone in your family help you create this story. Don't show them the story first! Ask them for the kind of word needed for each blank. Write the words in the blanks, then read the story out loud! Tip: Use a pencil so you can do it again with different words.

One day I was listening to _____ in front of my house.
(favorite song)

Suddenly, a large _____ stopped and a young man jumped out
(vehicle)

exclaiming, "My name is Prince _____ and you are listening to my
(boy's name)

favorite song!" The prince had _____ hair and was dressed in
(color)

_____ clothes. His _____ was shaped like a _____. Boy was he
(color)   (body part)   (fruit)

_____! He said that he was from _____. Suddenly, a monster
(adjective)   (planet)

_____ the size of a _____ appeared and threatened us with a
(snack food)   (something big)

_____! "Have no fear," the prince said bravely, "it is lunch time!"
(vegetable)

And he ate the monster in a single bite and drank _____ cups of
(large number)

_____. "Goodbye," he said as he got back into his vehicle, "I am
(beverage)

off to see _____ but I will return on _____."
(name of a friend)   (holiday)

Smarty Prince

A prince must be smart! The king has made this test for the prince. Can you figure out these phrases?

Example:

STAND
I

Answer: I understand, because I is under STAND

poFISHnd

r
o
roads
d
s

long
⎯⎯
do

u
p
s
i
d
e

rest
⎯⎯
your

LO head VE
heels

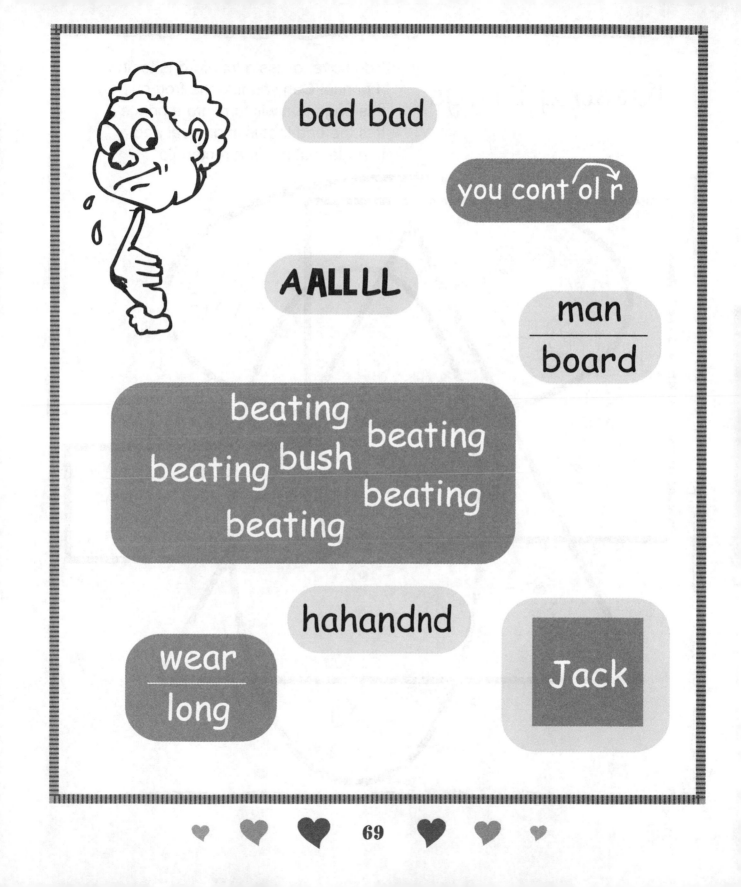

Kissing Frogs

You have to kiss a lot of frogs to find a prince! Can you find the frog on this page that will turn into a prince? It is the one that is in an oval and a triangle, but not in a rectangle.

70

Peculiar Prince Preferences

These girls use rules to pick a prince based on the letters in his name.
For each girl, you are given three examples that illustrate her rule.
Can you figure out which prince each girl likes from the choices?

Jennifer likes Prince Alex but not Prince Adam.
Jennifer likes Prince Max but not Prince Mark.
Jennifer likes Prince Rex but not Prince Andy.

Which Prince does Jennifer like?
A. Prince Randy   B. Prince Waldo   C. Prince Felix   D. Prince Peter

Audrey likes Prince Todd but not Prince Elroy
Audrey likes Prince Eli but not Prince Wesley
Audrey likes Prince Ian but not Prince Seth

Which Prince does Audrey like?
A. Prince Don   B. Prince Daniel   C. Prince Barry   D. Prince Ross

Grace likes Prince Isaac but not Prince Gary
Grace likes Prince Aaron but not Prince Lawrence
Grace likes Prince Coolidge but not Prince Bryan

Which Prince does Grace like?
A. Prince Ivan   B. Prince Lee   C. Prince George   D. Prince Robin

Heather likes Prince Tony but not Prince Robert
Heather likes Prince Timothy but not Prince Carlos
Heather likes Prince Tobias but not Prince Reuben

Which Prince does Heather like?
A. Prince Walter   B. Prince Keith   C. Prince Alfred   D. Prince Titus

A Very Handsome Prince

Copy each of the nine squares from the next page into this grid.
The letters and numbers tell you where each square belongs.

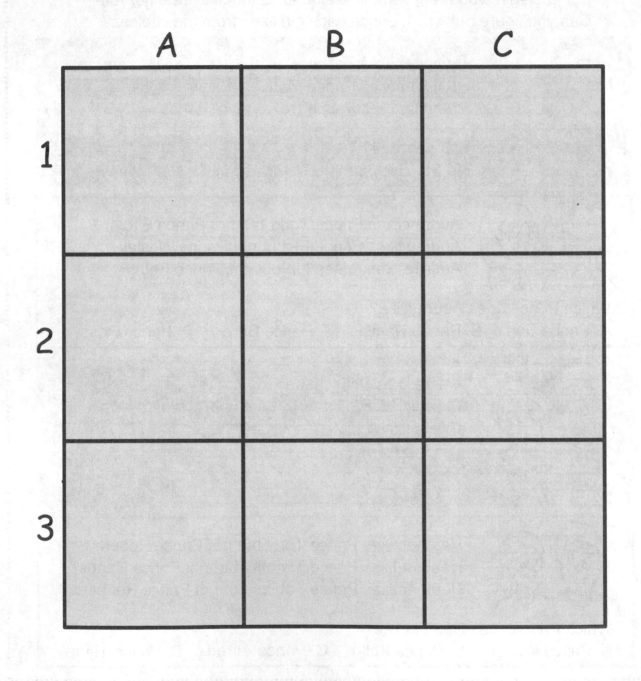

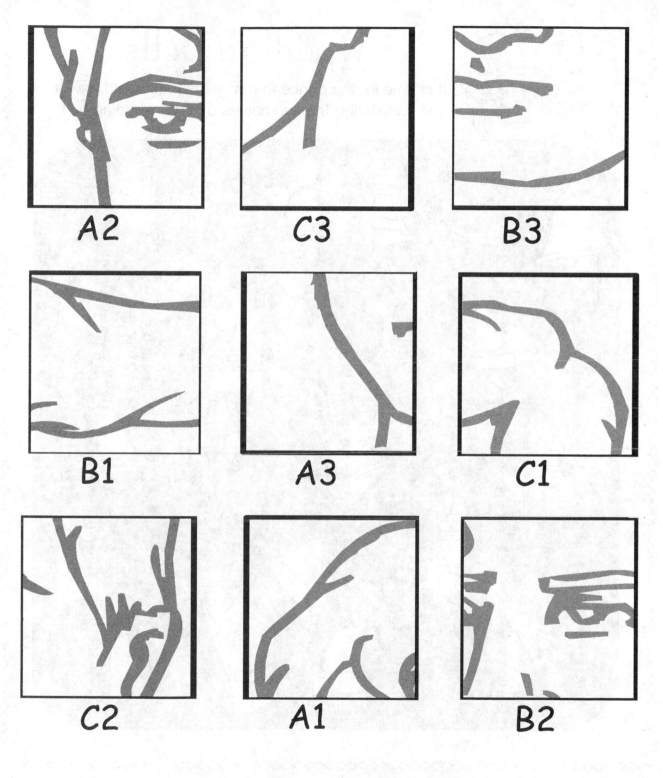

A2　　　C3　　　B3

B1　　　A3　　　C1

C2　　　A1　　　B2

73

Wedding Bells

It is time for the prince to marry the princess! Draw a line connecting the two halves of each wedding bell.

Castles Around the World

Castles are found all over the world and were built to house and protect royal families. Find some of the countries where castles are located by looking up, down, across, backward, and diagonally. Some letters may be used more than once.

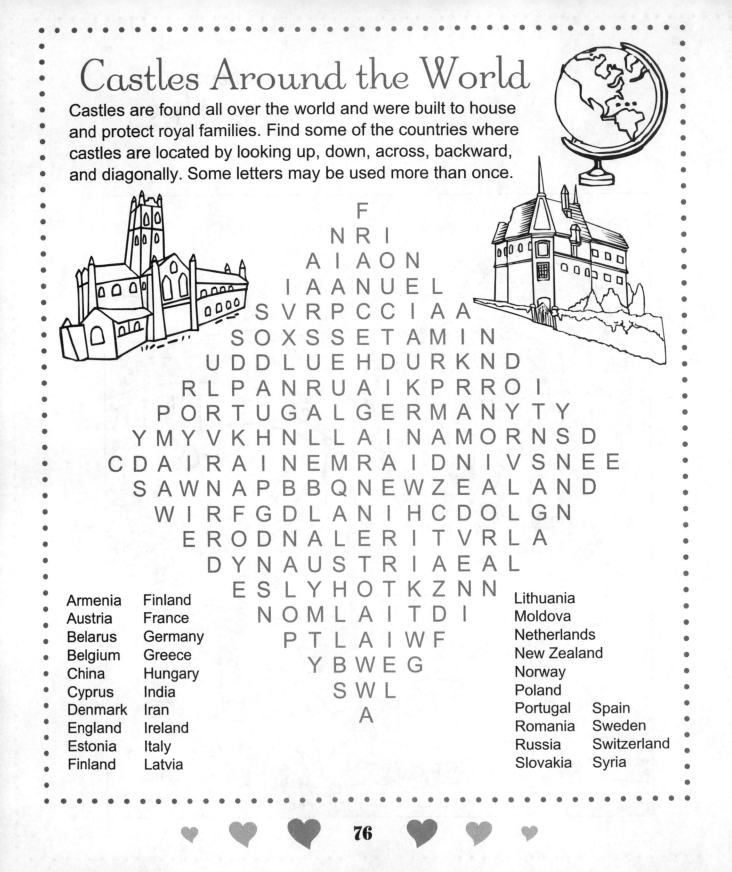

```
                    F
                N  R  I
            A  I  A  O  N
            I  A  A  N  U  E  L
        S  V  R  P  C  C  I  A  A
        S  O  X  S  S  E  T  A  M  I  N
        U  D  D  L  U  E  H  D  U  R  K  N  D
        R  L  P  A  N  R  U  A  I  K  P  R  R  O  I
    P  O  R  T  U  G  A  L  G  E  R  M  A  N  Y  T  Y
    Y  M  Y  V  K  H  N  L  L  A  I  N  A  M  O  R  N  S  D
C  D  A  I  R  A  I  N  E  M  R  A  I  D  N  I  V  S  N  E  E
    S  A  W  N  A  P  B  B  Q  N  E  W  Z  E  A  L  A  N  D
        W  I  R  F  G  D  L  A  N  I  H  C  D  O  L  G  N
        E  R  O  D  N  A  L  E  R  I  T  V  R  L  A
        D  Y  N  A  U  S  T  R  I  A  E  A  L
            E  S  L  Y  H  O  T  K  Z  N  N
            N  O  M  L  A  I  T  D  I
            P  T  L  A  I  W  F
            Y  B  W  E  G
            S  W  L
            A
```

Armenia	Finland	Lithuania
Austria	France	Moldova
Belarus	Germany	Netherlands
Belgium	Greece	New Zealand
China	Hungary	Norway
Cyprus	India	Poland
Denmark	Iran	Portugal Spain
England	Ireland	Romania Sweden
Estonia	Italy	Russia Switzerland
Finland	Latvia	Slovakia Syria

The Castle Flags

Cross out the one flag in each
set that doesn't belong.

Royal Bricklayers

These bricklayers help build castles. Can you help them with these math problems?

Mason Jason needs to build a wall that is 3 bricks thick, 9 bricks high, and 100 bricks long. How many bricks does he need?

Can you help Mason Marvin put numbers on the blank bricks so that all the rows and columns add up to the same total?

3	4		4	2
	3		1	6
2		6		4
1		3	6	3
	4	1	3	5

Mason Mike needs to build a pyramid with eight bricks in the bottom layer. Each layer going up should have one less brick than the previous layer. The top layer should have only one brick. How many bricks does Mason Mike need?

Matching Bricks

This castle has thousands of bricks. Can you find where these four bricks match the samples below?

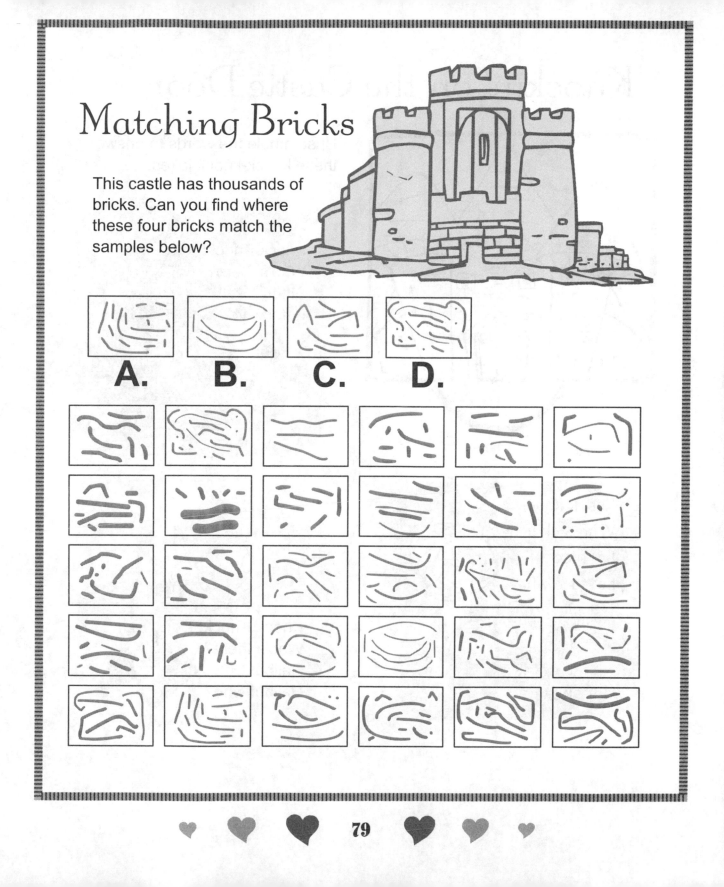

A.   **B.**   **C.**   **D.**

Knockin' on the Castle Door

Unscramble the words to answer these knock-knock jokes.

Knock Knock!
Who's there?
Eiffel.
Eiffel who?

my   down   Eiffel
and   knee   hurt

Knock Knock!
Who's there?
Lettuce.
Lettuce who?

again   lettuce
tomorrow   try

Knock Knock!
Who's there?
Halibut.
Halibut who?

kiss   a
halibut

Knock Knock!
Who's there?
Jewel.
Jewel who?

know | door | Jewel | open | you | if | the

Knock Knock!
Who's there?
Ice cream soda.
Ice cream soda who?

whole world | a | soda | are | cream | will | Ice | know what | nut you

Knock Knock!
Who's there?
Dwayne.
Dwayne who?

bathtub | the | drowning | I'm | Dwayne

Knock Knock!
Who's there?
Island.
Island who?

your | with | roof | my | Island | on | parachute

Knock Knock!
Who's there?
Archibald.
Archibald who?

head | of | on | Archibald | your | top

An aMAZEing Castle

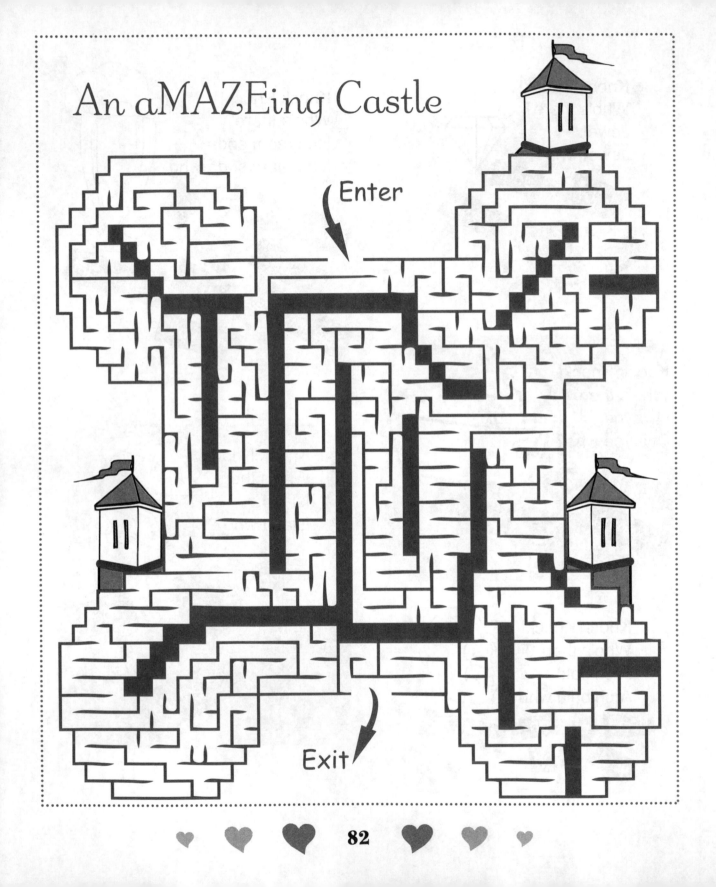

Enter

Exit

In the Kitchen

A Castle's kitchen needs to stock a lot of food to feed the royal family. These bags of grain need to be put into pots. Draw a line from each bag to a pot of the same size.

1 gallon = 4 quarts
1 quart = 2 pints
1 pint = 2 cups

7 pints 1 cup

3 quarts 1 pint

1 gallon

1 gallon 2 quarts

20 cups

3 quarts 2 pints

12 pints

1 quart 10 cups

1 gallon 2 pints

3 quarts 3 cups

Farmer Adam gives Princess Pauline one gallon of apple juice every week. If she drinks one cup every morning and another cup every afternoon, how many cups will she have left at the end of the week?

Missing Pieces

Draw a line from each castle to its missing piece.

A Colorful Moat

Moats are usually filled with water and surround a castle for protection. This moat is filled with colors!

```
Y E A     G
B L U E
O L O W
R A N F
M S G E
W H I T
K P L E
G R A Y
P U J A
L A C K
B R O W
J K E N
G R E T
G O L D
V I V E
S I L R
P I N K
```

You can cross this moat by finding strings of letters that spell the names of colors. Start with a letter on the left side and then move right, up, or down. Some letters may be used more than once. One color crossing has been done for you. Can you find twelve more?

Castle Furniture Store

mirror $8

What set of items can Princess Priscilla buy for exactly $92?

desk $64

What set of items can Princess Angela buy for exactly $162?

couch $128

lamp $1

bed $16

chair $4

rug $2

table $32

There is only one of each item available at this furniture store.

Chapter 8

Crowns and Tiaras

Tiara Maze

Start

Finish

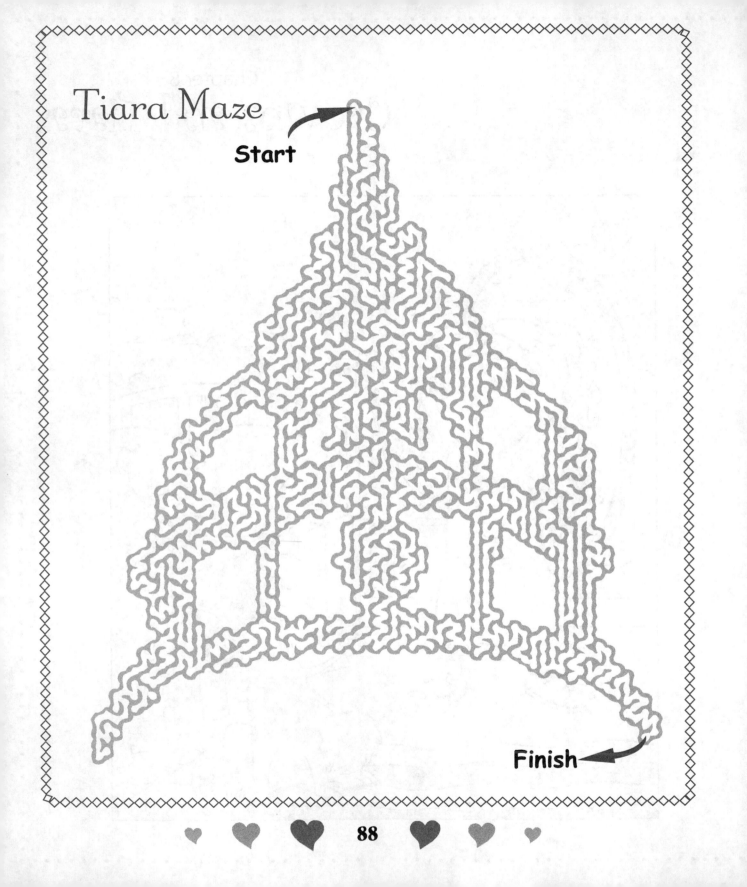

One of a Kind

Can you find the one crown that does not exactly match any other crown on this page?

Is there an **even** or an **odd** number of crowns on this page? Do you have to count them to find out?

Comparing Tiaras

Princess Tiffany

Princess Lilly

Sophie's tiara has 3 more emeralds than Tiffany's. Veronica's tiara has twice as many emeralds as Lilly's, and half as many as Tiffany's. Whose tiara has the most emeralds?

Lilly's tiara has one more ruby than Tiffany's. Veronica's tiara has one more ruby than Sophie's. Tiffany's and Lilly's tiaras together have a total of 9 rubies. All four tiaras together have a total of 24 rubies. How many rubies are there in each tiara?

Princess Sophie

Princess Veronica

Tiffany's tiara has fewer diamonds than Veronica's. Lilly's tiara has more diamonds than Veronica's. Sophie's tiara has the least number of diamonds. Whose tiara has the most diamonds?

Whose Crown?

Can you figure out the names on these well-worn tags?

Portraits With a Crown

Complete these princess portraits:

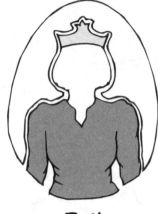

Happy Princess

Sad Princess

Evil Princess

Half and Half

Complete the other half of these crowns:

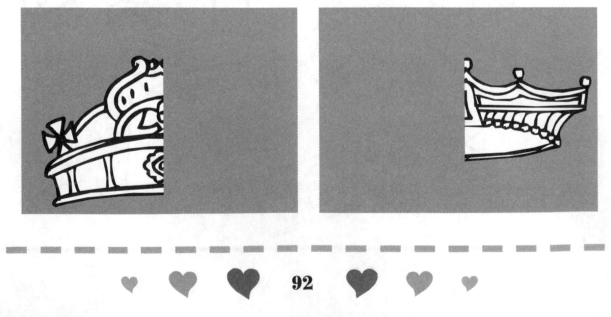

Jim the Gem Appraiser

Can you help Jim figure out the value of the gems on each of these crowns?

Here is a guide to help you determine the values:

Diced Crowns

Drop two letters from CROWN and make a bovine:

___ ___ ___

Change one letter in CROWN and get a joker:

___ ___ ___ ___ ___

Change one letter in CROWN and turn a smile upside down:

___ ___ ___ ___ ___

Drop two letters from CROWN and propel a boat:

___ ___ ___

Drop one letter from CROWN and it can fly:

___ ___ ___ ___

Tiara Jewels

This jeweler makes tiaras. Find the set of jewels below that exactly match these jewels needed for a tiara:

The Next Crown

Can you guess which crown comes after the first two?

1.

2.

3.

4.

5.

6.

OR

Chapter 9

Dresses and Dress Up

Dress Code

Circle the dress that exactly matches this one:

A Well-Worn Crossword Puzzle

Use the pictures as clues to this crossword puzzle.

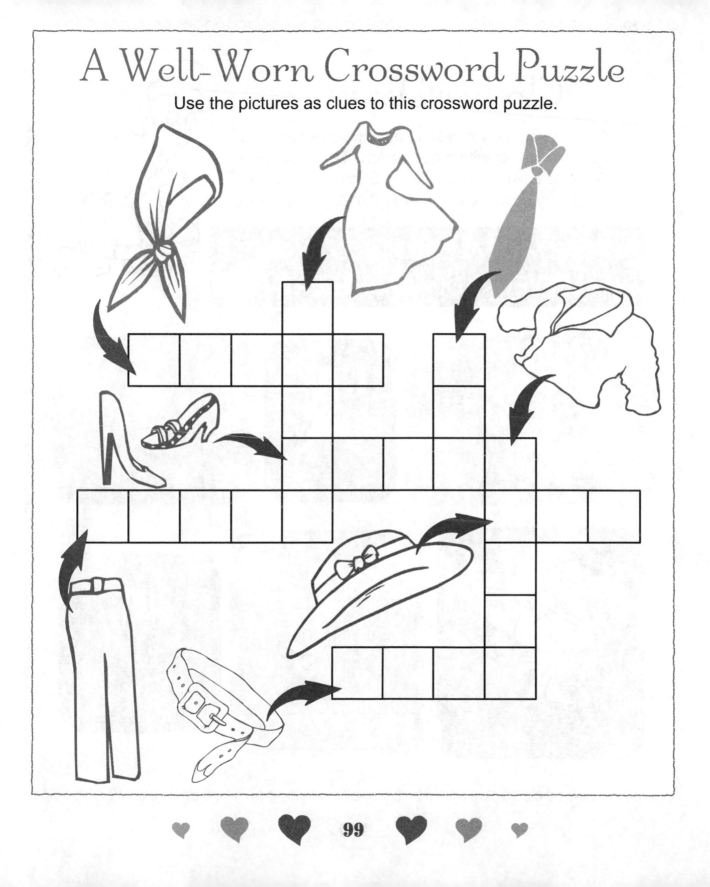

Clothes Detective

Clothes can tell you a lot about a person. Can you fill in the blanks with a description of each person? Below is a list of letters to use. Each letter will be used only once, so cross 'em off after you use 'em.

AEPEMOAOFALERIOTBCLPRYCHESE
RMALERLEURADLABALNELERINFNR

_ _ _ _ _ _ _ _ _ _ _ _

_ _ _ _ _

_ _ _ _ _ _ _ _ _

_ _ _ _ _ _

_ _ _ _ _ _ _ _

_ _ _ _ _ _

Sew What?

These princesses like to sew their own dresses. Can you figure out which dress belongs to which princess? Untangle the thread from each princess to her dress. Write the correct name in each box.

Princess Madison

Princess Makayla

Princess Pauline

Princess Hannah

Dress Colors

Unscramble the colors on this page and see if you can find your favorite color.

EBEIG _ _ _ _ _

BURNGDUY _ _ _ _ _ _ _ _

RGYA _ _ _ _

WNORB _ _ _ _ _

RPEULP _ _ _ _ _ _

AYCN _ _ _ _

LRNVAEED _ _ _ _ _ _ _ _

PKIN _ _ _ _

ATN _ _ _

ILCLA _ _ _ _ _

LVSREI _ _ _ _ _ _

SAIUHCF _ _ _ _ _ _ _

AOMNOR _ _ _ _ _ _

UTQUSEIOR _ _ _ _ _ _ _ _ _

AKKHI _ _ _ _ _

YIOVR _ _ _ _ _

LEOIV _ _ _ _ _

ELOLWY _ _ _ _ _ _

BULE _ _ _ _

NEARGO _ _ _ _ _ _

NTMEAGA _ _ _ _ _ _ _

GLDO _ _ _ _

EDR _ _ _

IELOVT _ _ _ _ _ _

ITEHW _ _ _ _ _

ABKLC _ _ _ _ _

CHEPA _ _ _ _ _

GOIDIN _ _ _ _ _ _

LATE _ _ _ _

NGEER _ _ _ _ _

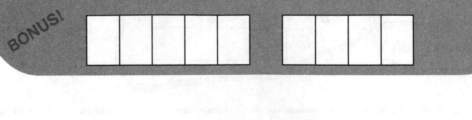

Now unscramble the letters in the boxes to make a spotty pattern:

BONUS!

[_ _ _ _ _] [_ _ _ _]

102

Find all of the unscrambled colors and bonus words by looking up, down, across, backward and diagonally. Some letters may appear in more than one word.

```
F Q T B N
H C A E P P Y
O Y T X S D P
T A N E N O O
U N E U L B O
X R J G K G O L D
S Q R A T I A I O
M U D M T V I V V
O B O I O E I S E F F
D T I N N T S H E O O
S M S D A I P C U I C
O A E I D H I U T G K
Y S R V G L W N F R T Q R
F D O M O N V K E A P H U
B R O W N L A E T G L L O
Y H N E G Q N R R R I U E
G W M Y U R V W O L L E Y
T G H I I K A H K C A L B
S J D H R O P Y I N C Y N
```

Dressed-Up Riddles

Answer the clues below and fill the letters into the grid. Work back and forth between the grid and the clues until you figure it out.

A. It is found between the hand and the arm

___ ___ ___ ___ ___
12 22 26 24 13

B. This can help if you have trouble walking.

___ ___ ___ ___
3   17 27 15

C. A vehicle that goes fast down a snow-covered hill.

___ ___ ___ ___
6   18 23 20

D. Small and round, they can make a necklace.

___ ___ ___ ___ ___
1   7   4   21 25

E. A meat commonly eaten at breakfast.

___ ___ ___ ___ ___ ___ ___
10 19 5   16 11 28 2

F. To strike.

___ ___ ___
14 8   9

Why did the tomato blush?

1D	2E	3B	4D	5E	6C	7D		8F	9F
10E	11E	12A		13A	14F	15B			
16E	17B	18C	19E	20C					
21D	22A	23C	24A	25D	26A	27B	28E		

I'm a fancy dress,
and I start with G;
Wear me to the ball,
where the prince you will see.
What am I?

___ ___ ___ ___ ___

I make a bow on a dress,
if I'm tied in a knot;
I might be seen around a gift,
if they are brought.
What am I?

___ ___ ___ ___ ___ ___

Embroidery

Can you trace the patterns on these dresses with one continuous line? Do not cross over or go back along any line.

What to Wear?

Madeline has 5 pairs of shoes and 7 dresses. How many different combinations of shoes and dresses can Madeline wear? Assume that any of the shoes can be worn with any of the dresses.

Pretty Ugly

Divide the words into two groups by connecting the dots. One group should be "pretty" words and the other group "ugly" words. The puzzle has been started for you:

beautiful   attractive   yucky

lovely   repulsive   disgusting

fetching   charming   foul

cute   homely   beastly

elegant   hideous   frightful

appealing   pleasing   nasty

glamorous   alluring   handsome

Clueless Cloth

Dresses and clothes can be made with many different types of fabric. See if you can fit all of these fabrics into this clueless crossword puzzle. Each word is used only once, so cross it off the list when you've found the spot for it. One of the words is done for you.

3 Letters
FUR

4 Letters
FELT
JUTE
SILK
WOOL

5 Letters
DENIM
GAUZE
LINEN
NYLON
RAYON
SATIN
SUEDE
VINYL

6 Letters
BURLAP
CALICO
COTTON
VELVET

7 Letters
CHIFFON
FLANNEL
GINGHAM
LEATHER
SPANDEX
TAFFETA

8 Letters
CORDUROY

9 Letters
POLYESTER

10 Letters
SEERSUCKER
TERRYCLOTH

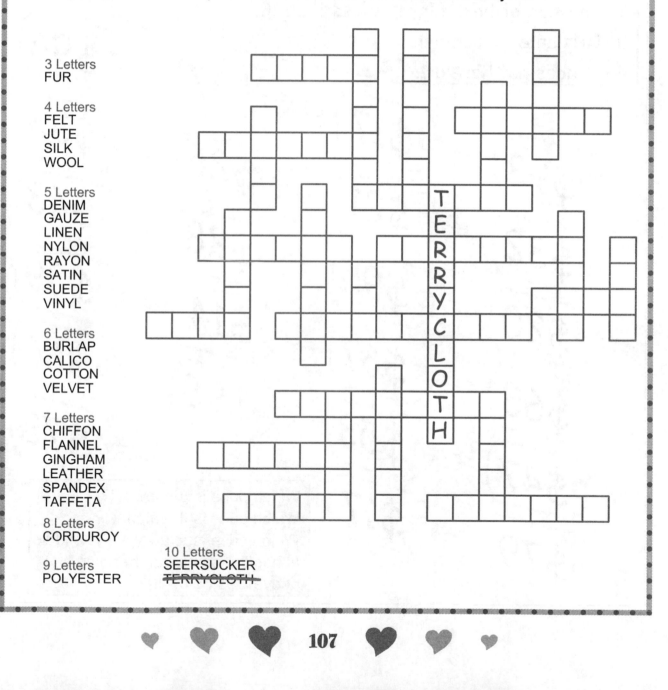

How Much for the Dress?

Can you find the correct price tag for this dress?
It will fit all of these rules:

1. The tens digit is less than the ones digit.
2. The sum of both digits is less than 10.
3. It is an even number.
4. It does not have a 1.

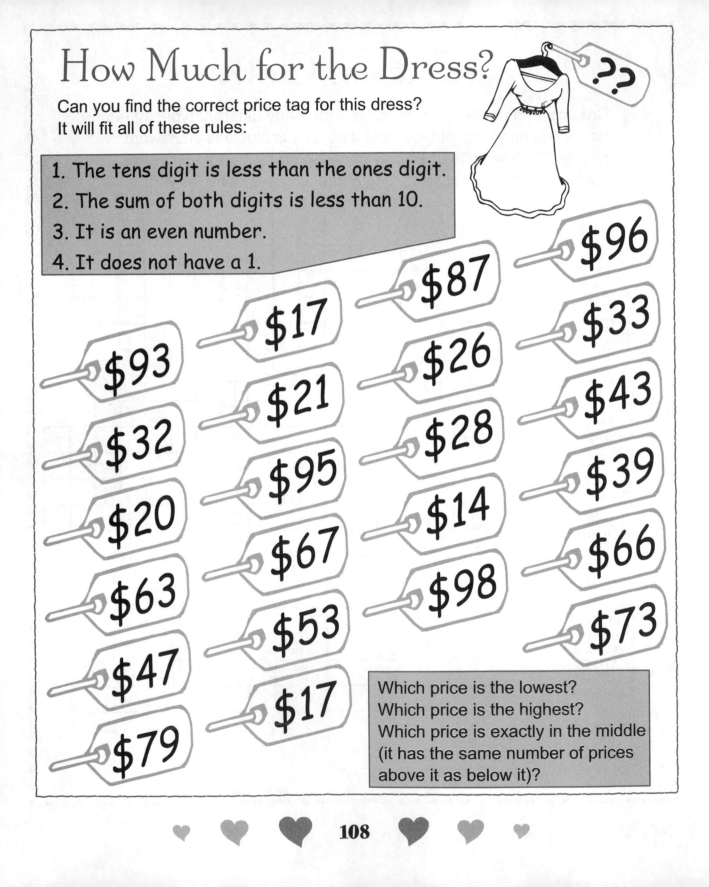

$96

$87

$17

$93

$26

$33

$32

$21

$28

$43

$20

$95

$14

$39

$63

$67

$98

$66

$47

$53

$73

$79

$17

Which price is the lowest?
Which price is the highest?
Which price is exactly in the middle
(it has the same number of prices
above it as below it)?

Puzzle Answers

Chapter 1

page 4 •
Mixed-up Kitchen

1. kettle
2. knife
3. oven
4. stove
5. spoon
6. fork
7. bowl
8. plate
9. pitcher
10. pot
11. cup
12. pan
13. table

page 6 •
The Magic Wand

Drop the first letter from... ...and turn it into drops from the sky. **TRAIN & RAIN**

Drop the last two letters from... ...and turn it into the event where Cinderella and the Prince meet. **BALLET & BALL**

Drop the first two letters from... ...and turn it into gorillas. **GRAPES & APES**

Drop the first letter from this... ...and turn it into something heartfelt. **GLOVE & LOVE**

Drop the first letter from these... and turn it into something cold **DICE & ICE**

Drop the first letter from a... ...and turn it into a garden tool. **SHOE & HOE**

Drop the last letter from... ...and turn it into a drink made with leaves. **TEAR & TEA**

Drop the last letter from this... ...and turn it into a baby bear. **CUBE & CUB**

Drop the first letter from... ...and turn it into what you breathe. **HAIR & AIR**

Drop the first two letters from a... ...and turn it into a creative work. **HEART & ART**

Drop the first letter from these... ...and turn them into noisemakers **THORNS & HORNS**

The crossword grid:

```
            S
      F     T
S P O O N   O V E N
      R   P V
    P K N I F E
    L     I
P A N     C U P
    A     H   O
K E T T L E   T
    B     R
B O W L   E
    E
```

Puzzle Answers

page 8 • **Riding to the Ball**

page 10 • **The Last Dance**

Cinderella must leave after Momma Mambo.

page 11 • **The Confused Prince**

The center dots are the same size. In both cases, the vertical lines are the same size. Don't believe it? Then measure them with a ruler!

page 12 • **If the Shoe Fits, Wear It!**

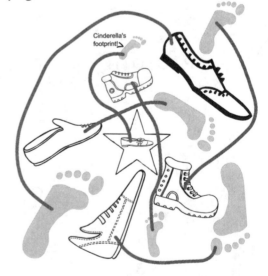

Cinderella's footprint!

page 9 • **Dancing by the Numbers**

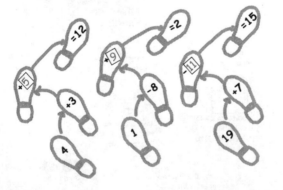

page 13 • **Wedding Seating**

The Marquis of Macadamia   The Countess of Calypso   The Earl of Eaton   The Duchess of Duncan

page 14 • **Wedding Cake**

page 14 • **Cryptic Conclusion**

AND THEY LIVED HAPPILY EVER AFTER...

Puzzle Answers

Chapter 2

page 16 • **My Real Name**

M A T O A K A
1 2 3 4 5 6 7

page 16 • **Where I'm From**

EM**VS**I**M**SE
R**E**MS**GI**M**S**
M**EN**S**MIA**E

VIRGINIA

page 18 • **The Path to Jamestown**

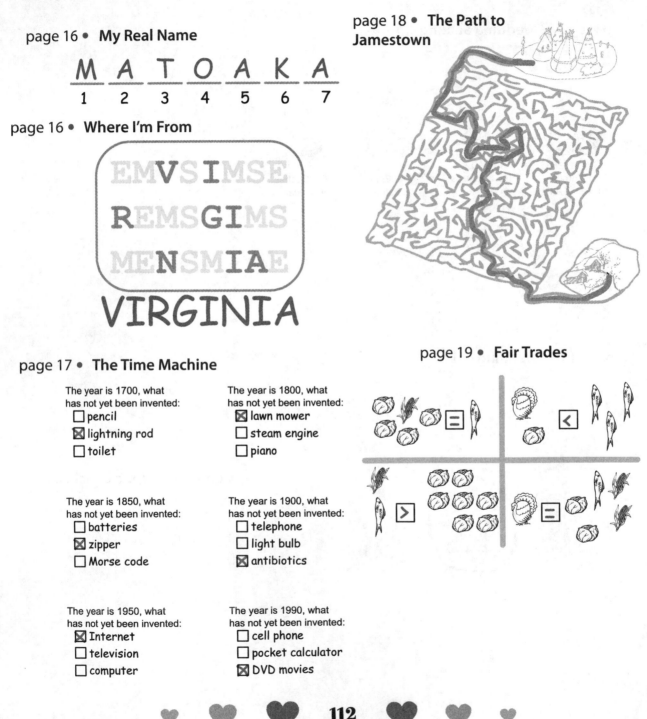

page 17 • **The Time Machine**

The year is 1700, what has not yet been invented:
- ☐ pencil
- ☒ lightning rod
- ☐ toilet

The year is 1800, what has not yet been invented:
- ☒ lawn mower
- ☐ steam engine
- ☐ piano

The year is 1850, what has not yet been invented:
- ☐ batteries
- ☒ zipper
- ☐ Morse code

The year is 1900, what has not yet been invented:
- ☐ telephone
- ☐ light bulb
- ☒ antibiotics

The year is 1950, what has not yet been invented:
- ☒ Internet
- ☐ television
- ☐ computer

The year is 1990, what has not yet been invented:
- ☐ cell phone
- ☐ pocket calculator
- ☒ DVD movies

page 19 • **Fair Trades**

page 20 • John Smith and Pocahontas

A. A large stream of water.

R I V E R
17 22 63 27 6

B. A group of players on the same side.

T E A M
4 24 39 13

C. Title at the top of a newspaper.

H E A D L I N E
11 60 48 43 28 29 42 31

D. What you get when you boil water.

S T E A M
54 21 36 41 23

E. Ten cents.

D I M E
40 51 15 53

F. 12 inches.

F O O T
20 56 16 25

G. Opposite of low.

H I G H
26 62 66 47

H. Bird's home.

N E S T
52 12 55 34

I. Do it at a red light.

S T O P
9 10 32 49

J. To turn over.

F L I P
30 61 64 50

K. Stay out of sight.

H I D E
59 8 37 46

L. Not no.

Y E S
18 38 3

M. Between fourth and sixth.

F I F T H
33 2 57 44 45

N. Capable of burning.

H O T
35 19 58

O. Bees make it.

H O N E Y
1 5 65 14 7

1O	2M	3L	4B	5O	6A	7O		8K	9I		
H	I	S	T	O	R	Y		I	S		
10I	11C	12H		13B	14O	15E	16F	17A	18L		
T	H	E		M	E	M	O	R	Y		
19N	20F		21D	22A	23D	24B		25F	26G	27A	
O	F		T	I	M	E,		T	H	E	
28C	29C	30J	31C		32I	33M		34H	35N	36D	
L	I	F	E		O	F		T	H	E	
37K	38L	39B	40E		41D	42C	43C		44M	45M	46K
D	E	A	D,		A	N	D		T	H	E
47G	48C	49I	50J	51E	52H	53E	54D	55H		56F	57M
H	A	P	P	I	N	E	S	S		O	F
58N	59K	60C		61J	62G	63A	64J	65O	66G		
T	H	E		L	I	V	I	N	G	.	

Pocahontas was 12 years old
when she rescued John Smith.

page 22 • Missing Flowers

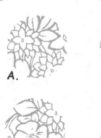

Puzzle Answers

page 23 • **A Vase for Pocahontas**

page 24 • **Mathematical Teepee**

page 25 • A Corny Pyramid

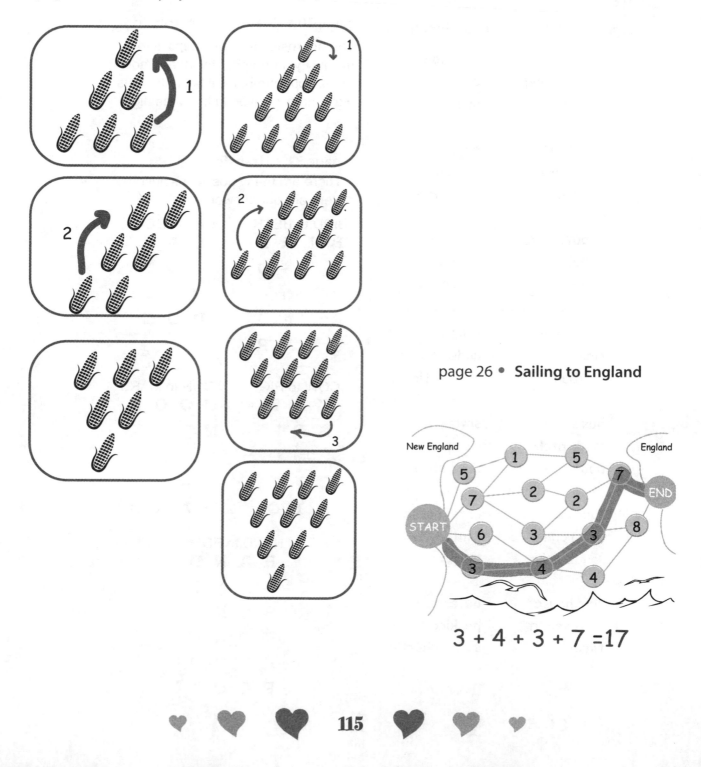

page 26 • Sailing to England

$$3 + 4 + 3 + 7 = 17$$

Chapter 3

page 28 • Interesting Combinations

blast**off**	down**town**
offspring	break**down**
cut**off**	melt**down**

foot**ball**	red *cross*
foot**print**	**cross**word
bare**foot**	**cross**walk

bottle *cap*	**sun**burn
hub**cap**	**sun**flower
ice*cap*	**sun**set

---

kicks**tand**	camp**ground**
sidekick	**under**ground
kick**ball**	ground *floor*

bus *stop*	saw**dust**
stopwatch	dust**pan**
door**stop**	dust *storm*

rail**road**	green**house**
road**runner**	winter**green**
road**block**	ever**green**

light**house**	outer *space*
light**weight**	parking *space*
flashlight	space *shuttle*

page 30 • Mathmagic Mermaid

The net result of all the steps is to multiply your number by 10 and add 7. Thus, your number will be in the tens digit and a 7 will be in the ones digit.

page 31 • Transform

There are many possible solutions. Here are our answers:

BIRD to BEAR

B I R D
B I N D
B E N D
B E A D
B E A R

CAT to DOG

C A T
C O T
D O T
D O G

COW to PIG

C O W
B O W
B O G
B I G
P I G

MOON to MARS

M O O N
M O R N
M O R E
M A R E
M A R S

HAND to FOOT

H A N D
B A N D
B O N D
F O N D
F O O D
F O O T

Puzzle Answers

page 32 • **Fishy Friends**

SHARK
DARTER
GUPPY
BLUEGILL
FLUKE
CRAPPIE
CHUB
GOBY
COD

FLOUNDER
YELLOWTAIL
GOLDFISH
CATFISH
MINNOW
ALBACORE
SOLE
TUNA
CARP
HALIBUT
WALLEYE
HADDOCK
ANCHOVY
SALMON
GUITARFISH
ANGEL

PIKE
MARLIN
GRUNION
GROUPER
HERRING
BASS
PERCH
STURGEON
BARRACUDA
BULLHEAD
TROUT
MACKEREL
SNAPPER
SARDINE
MUSKIE
PARROTFISH

page 34 • **Save the Prince**

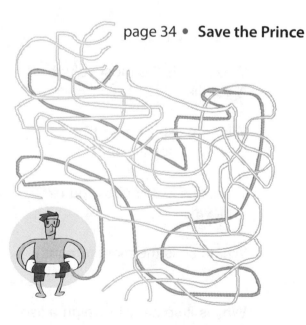

page 35 • Predictions

page 37 • Where is My Prince?

1709 Neptune Lane

page 36 • Mermaid Riddles

What fish is the most valuable?
A goldfish.

Why are fish so smart?
Because they live in schools.

What fish likes bubble gum?
A blowfish.

What fish is the most famous?
A starfish.

Why is it so easy to weigh a fish?
They have their own scales.

page 38 • Treasure Watcher

Chapter 4

page 40 • Good Fairies

page 41 • Fairy Gifts

page 42 • What's in a Name?

Here are some of the words found in SLEEPING BEAUTY:

able ail angel ate base bee belt big blue bus eagle else eye gas get glue guy lab lean lip nail net paint past peanut pet pine plan plus put sang set slant snug spit staple stay suit tail tea tiny tip ugly up yes

There are many more possible words. How many did you find?

page 43 • Spinning Wheel Spell

PRINCESS

BEWARE!

SPINNING

WHEELS ARE

POISONOUS!

119

Puzzle Answers

page 44 • **Dreaming Beauty**

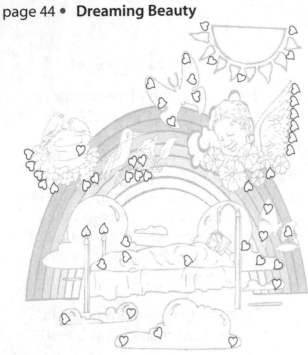

page 45 • **One Hundred Years**

page 46 • **Double E**

BEETLE

NEEDLE

BEE

TREE

WHEEL

QUEEN

DEER

TEETH

SHEEP

SEEDS

CHEESE

GEESE

CHEERLEADER

Puzzle Answers

page 48 • **The Path to Sleeping Beauty**

page 50 • **A Message from the Prince**

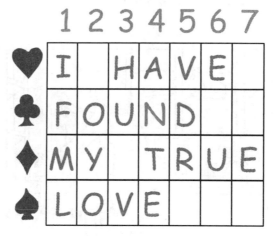

page 49 • **Castle Maze**

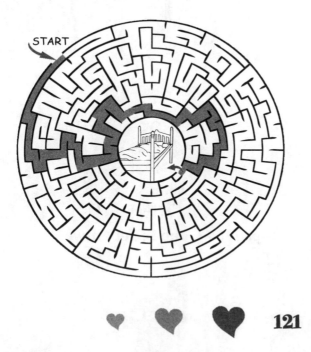

Chapter 5

page 52 • **Mirror, Mirror**

SNOW WHITE
IS A
THOUSAND
TIMES FAIRER
THAN YOU!

page 54 • **The Secret Answer**

Puzzle Answers

page 55 • **Twisty Walk**

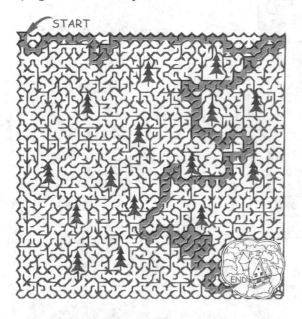

page 56 • **Things in the Forest**

```
M E B A T L O W C N L G H A J
Y N U L Z V F M A O P Q O Y H
K Y S N A K E U N N G K A I K
P C H F V A F Y E H F G Z B A
C F O L D N O P W K H F J E V
Y F R O G       D G B X G
R L W W S       S F S I H
Q O F E T       N S L C W
X G C R C       C E A H F
F S C K E       R V N R K
Q T D C S T P S T R E A M I G
G I Z R N T T K I B E E P V V
Z C C H I P M U N K K L B E D
R K K I N B O N B E A R L R Z
W T R E E S I K B Z O Z Y T K
```

page 57 • **Seven of Everything**

There are only 6 of these:

There are 8 of these:

page 58 • **Snow White's Crossword**

```
T        N E W S    S I T
W I S E      H      H    E
I        H      I      O    N
N        O    H  N O T E
      W H I T E
H O T    O      H O E
O    W  N O I S E
S T O N E      N E T
E      S N O W      O
  H I N T      E      W E T
  I      E  N O S E    N    O
  T      S      T          W
T  S T E W    W
O N E      I
N    W      S O N
      H
```

123

Puzzle Answers

page 60 • **Doesn't Belong**

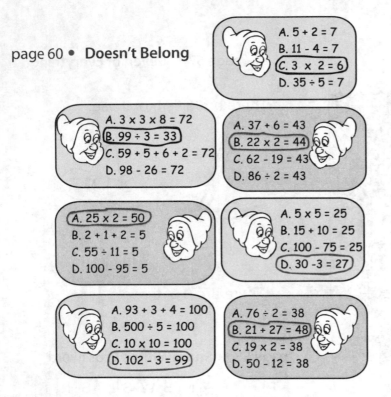

A. 5 + 2 = 7
B. 11 - 4 = 7
C. 3 × 2 = 6
D. 35 ÷ 5 = 7

A. 3 × 3 × 8 = 72
B. 99 ÷ 3 = 33
C. 59 + 5 + 6 + 2 = 72
D. 98 - 26 = 72

A. 37 + 6 = 43
B. 22 × 2 = 44
C. 62 - 19 = 43
D. 86 ÷ 2 = 43

A. 25 × 2 = 50
B. 2 + 1 + 2 = 5
C. 55 ÷ 11 = 5
D. 100 - 95 = 5

A. 5 × 5 = 25
B. 15 + 10 = 25
C. 100 - 75 = 25
D. 30 -3 = 27

A. 93 + 3 + 4 = 100
B. 500 ÷ 5 = 100
C. 10 × 10 = 100
D. 102 - 3 = 99

A. 76 ÷ 2 = 38
B. 21 + 27 = 48
C. 19 × 2 = 38
D. 50 - 12 = 38

page 62 • **Wedding Cake**

Table A:
1. Diane
2. Therese
3. Steve
4. Donnie
5. Suzanne

Table B:
1. Mary
2. Dave
3. Violet

Table C:
1. Emma
2. Shawn
3. Nick
4. Laura

page 61 • **The Poisoned Apple**

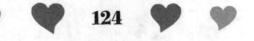

Chapter 6

page 64 • Prince Names from A to Z

Evan	Timothy
Samuel	Marcus
Logan	Noah
Paul	Ulysses
Quincy	Ian
Hunter	Franklin
Kenneth	Raymond
Carlos	Jason
Dylan	Andrew
Oscar	William
Garrett	Xavier
Yannick	Victor
Zachary	Benjamin

page 66 • Flowers from the Prince

page 65 • Clueless Princes

page 67 • Out of This World

Everybody will have a different story. Here's ours:

One day I was listening to **Jingle Bells** (favorite song) in front of my house.

Suddenly, a large **trash truck** (vehicle) stopped and a young man jumped out

exclaiming, "My name is Prince **Billy** (boy's name) and you are listening to my

favorite song!" The prince had **yellow** (color) hair and was dressed in

pink (color) clothes. His **head** (body part) was shaped like a **pear** (fruit). Boy was he

heavy (adjective)! He said that he was from **Pluto** (planet). Suddenly, a monster

cookie (snack food) the size of a **elephant** (something big) appeared and threatened us with a

carrot (vegetable)! "Have no fear," the prince said bravely, "it is lunch time!"

And he ate the monster in a single bite and drank **1,000** (large number) cups of

apple juice (beverage). "Goodbye," he said as he got back into his vehicle, "I am

off to see **Holly** (name of a friend) but I will return on **Halloween** (holiday)."

page 68 • Smarty Prince

a big fish in a little pond

crossroads

long overdue

upside down

you're under arrest

head over heels in love

too bad

you are out of control

all in all

man overboard

beating around the bush

hand in hand

jack-in-the-box

long underwear

page 70 • Kissing Frogs

page 71 • Peculiar Prince Preferences

Jennifer likes C. Prince Felix because his name ends with the letter X.

Audrey likes A. Prince Don because his name has three letters.

Grace likes B. Prince Lee because his name has a double letter.

Heather likes D. Prince Titus because his name starts with the letter T.

page 72 • **A Very Handsome Prince**

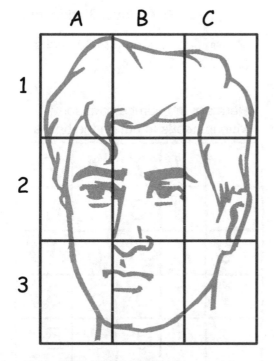

page 74 • **Wedding Bells**

Chapter 7

page 76 • **Castles Around the World**

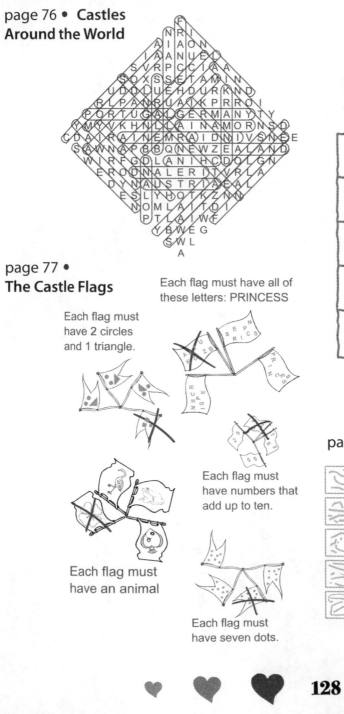

page 77 • **The Castle Flags**

Each flag must have 2 circles and 1 triangle.

Each flag must have all of these letters: PRINCESS

Each flag must have numbers that add up to ten.

Each flag must have an animal

Each flag must have seven dots.

page 78 • **Royal Bricklayers**

Mason Jason needs 2,700 bricks. (9 X 3 X 100)

Here are the numbers Mason Marvin needs to put on the bricks:

3	4	7	4	2
7	3	3	1	6
2	2	6	6	4
1	7	3	6	3
7	4	1	3	5

Mason Mike needs 36 bricks. (8+7+6+5+4+3+2+1)

page 79 • **Matching Bricks**

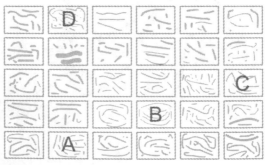

Puzzle Answers

page 80 • **Knockin' on the Castle Door**

Knock Knock!
Who's there?
Lettuce.
Lettuce who?
Lettuce try again
tomorrow!

Knock Knock!
Who's there?
Jewel.
Jewel who?
Jewel know if you
open the door!

Knock Knock!
Who's there?
Dwayne.
Dwayne who?
Dwayne the
bathtub I'm
drowning!

Knock Knock!
Who's there?
Archibald.
Archibald who?
Archibald on top
of your head?

Knock Knock!
Who's there?
Eiffel.
Eiffel who?
Eiffel down and
hurt my knee!

Knock Knock!
Who's there?
Halibut.
Halibut who?
Halibut a kiss!

Knock Knock!
Who's there?
Ice cream soda.
Ice cream soda
who?
Ice cream soda
whole world will
know what a nut
you are!

Knock Knock!
Who's there?
Island.
Island who?
Island on your
roof with my
parachute!

page 82 • **An aMAZEing Castle**

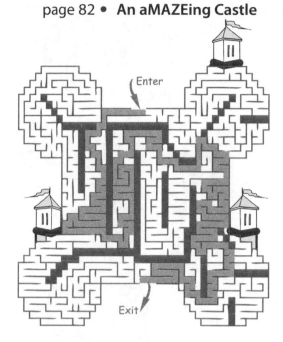

page 83 • **In the Kitchen**

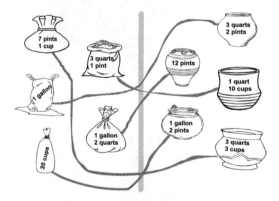

Princess Pauline will have two cups of
apple juice left at the end of the week.

Puzzle Answers

page 84 • **Missing Pieces**

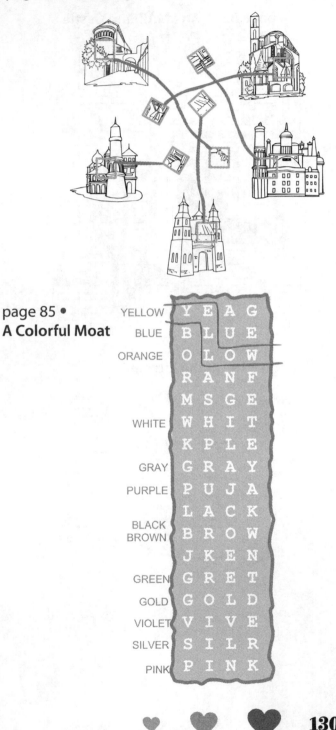

page 85 •
A Colorful Moat

YELLOW
BLUE
ORANGE

WHITE

GRAY
PURPLE

BLACK
BROWN

GREEN
GOLD
VIOLET
SILVER
PINK

page 86 • **Castle Furniture Store**

Princess Priscilla will buy the desk, bed, chair, and mirror.

Princess Angela will buy the couch, table, and rug.

Puzzle Answers

Chapter 8

page 88 • **Tiara Maze**

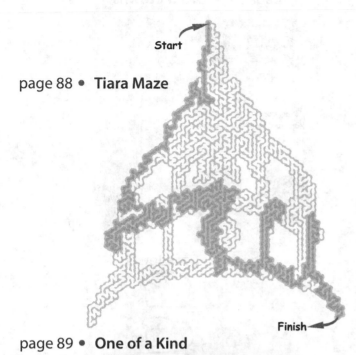

page 89 • **One of a Kind**

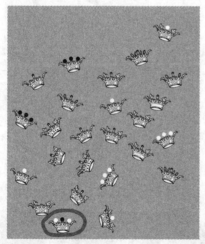

There must be an odd number of crowns because they are all in pairs (an even number) except for one (making the total an odd number).

page 90 • **Comparing Tiaras**

Princess Sophie's tiara has the most emeralds.

Princess Tiffany's tiara has 4 rubies.
Princess Lilly's tiara has 5 rubies.
Princess Veronica's tiara has 8 rubies.
Princess Sophie's tiara has 7 rubies.

Princess Lilly's tiara has the most diamonds.

page 91 • **Whose Crown?**

Puzzle Answers

page 92 • Portraits with a Crown

Happy Princess   Sad Princess   Evil Princess

page 92 • Half and Half

page 93 • Jim the Gem Appraiser

First, determine the value of each gem:

= $120   = $20

= $40   = $180

Then you can determine the values of the gems in each crown:

$120 $840

$280 $460

page 94 • Diced Crowns

Drop two letters from CROWN and make a bovine: COW

Change one letter in CROWN and get a joker: CLOWN

Change one letter in CROWN and turn a smile upside down: FROWN

Drop two letters from CROWN and propel a boat: ROW

Drop one letter from CROWN and it can fly: CROW

page 95 • Tiara Jewels

1.
2.
3.
4.
5.
6.

page 96 • The Next Crown

C.

Puzzle Answers

Chapter 9

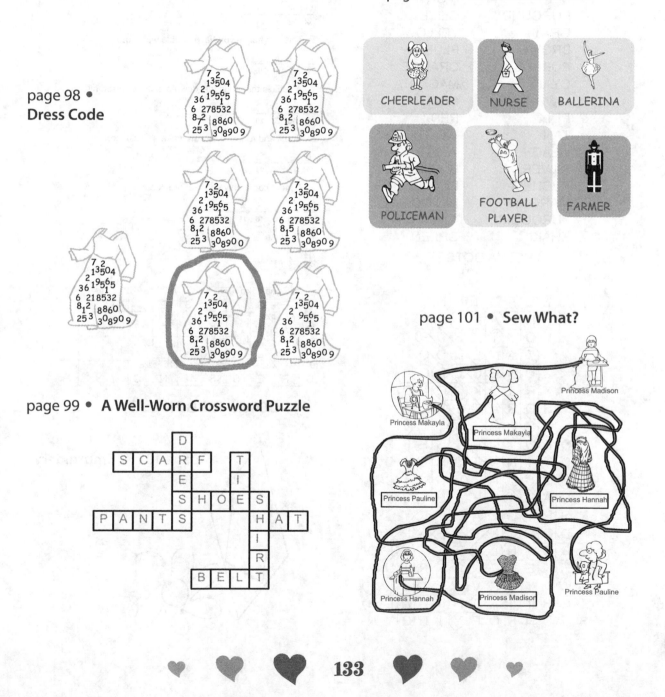

page 98 • **Dress Code**

page 99 • **A Well-Worn Crossword Puzzle**

page 100 • **Clothes Detective**

CHEERLEADER   NURSE   BALLERINA

POLICEMAN   FOOTBALL PLAYER   FARMER

page 101 • **Sew What?**

Princess Makayla
Princess Madison
Princess Makayla
Princess Pauline
Princess Hannah
Princess Hannah
Princess Madison
Princess Pauline

Puzzle Answers

page 102 • Dress Colors

BEIGE	IVORY
BURGUNDY	OLIVE
GRAY	YELLOW
BROWN	BLUE
PURPLE	ORANGE
CYAN	MAGENTA
LAVENDER	GOLD
PINK	RED
TAN	VIOLET
LILAC	WHITE
SILVER	BLACK
FUCHSIA	PEACH
MAROON	INDIGO
TURQUOISE	TEAL
KHAKI	GREEN

POLKA DOTS

page 104 • Dressed-Up Riddles

A. It is found between the hand and the arm

<u>W</u> <u>R</u> <u>I</u> <u>S</u> <u>T</u>
12 22 26 24 13

B. This can help if you have trouble walking.

<u>C</u> <u>A</u> <u>N</u> <u>E</u>
3 17 27 15

C. A vehicle that goes fast down a snow-covered hill.

<u>S</u> <u>L</u> <u>E</u> <u>D</u>
6 18 23 20

D. Small and round, they can make a necklace.

<u>B</u> <u>E</u> <u>A</u> <u>D</u> <u>S</u>
1 7 4 21 25

E. A meat commonly eaten at breakfast.

<u>S</u> <u>A</u> <u>U</u> <u>S</u> <u>A</u> <u>G</u> <u>E</u>
10 19 5 16 11 28 2

F. To strike.

<u>H</u> <u>I</u> <u>T</u>
14 8 9

1D	2E	3B	4D	5E	6C	7D		8F	9F
B	E	C	A	U	S	E		I	T
10E	11E	12A		13A	14F	15B			
S	A	W		T	H	E			
16E	17B	18C	19E	20C					
S	A	L	A	D					
21D	22A	23C	24A	25D	26A	27B	28E		
D	R	E	S	S	I	N	G	.	

GOWN, RIBBON

page 105 • Embroidery

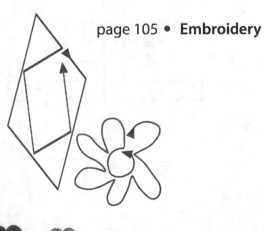

134

Puzzle Answers

page 106 • What to Wear?

Each dress can be worn with 5 possible pairs of shoes. There are 7 dresses. So the answer is 7 X 5, or 35 different combinations.

page 106 • Pretty Ugly

page 108 • How Much for the Dress?

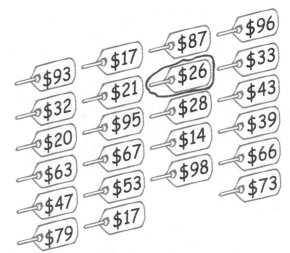

The lowest price is $14
The highest price is $98
The middle price is $47

page 107 • Clueless Cloth

135

PART 2
Fairy Puzzles

Chapter 10

Fairyland

The Path to Fairyland

Can you help this boy find the path
back to his home in fairyland?

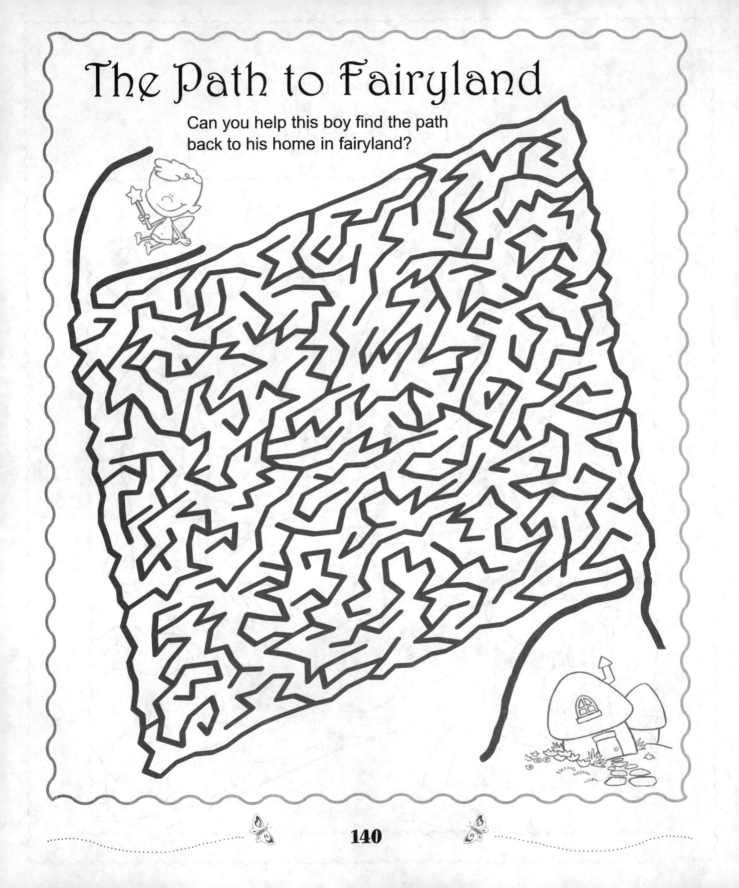

Butterfly Twins

In fairyland, every butterfly has a twin. Circle the butterflies on this page who are missing their twin.

Fairyland Photos

It's not easy to take accurate photos in fairyland! These two photos are supposed to be identical. Can you spot eight differences?

Fairy Foods

Fairies are very picky eaters. Can you find all of these fairy foods in the letters below? Look up, down, sideways, backwards, and diagonally.

BISCUIT
BREAD
CAKE
CANDY
CHEESE

CHOCOLATE
CUSTARD
GUMDROP
HONEY
LICORICE

MILK
NECTAR
NUTMEG
PECANS
PEPPERMINT

PERSIMMON
STRAWBERRY
SUGARPLUM
WHIPPED CREAM
ZUCCHINI

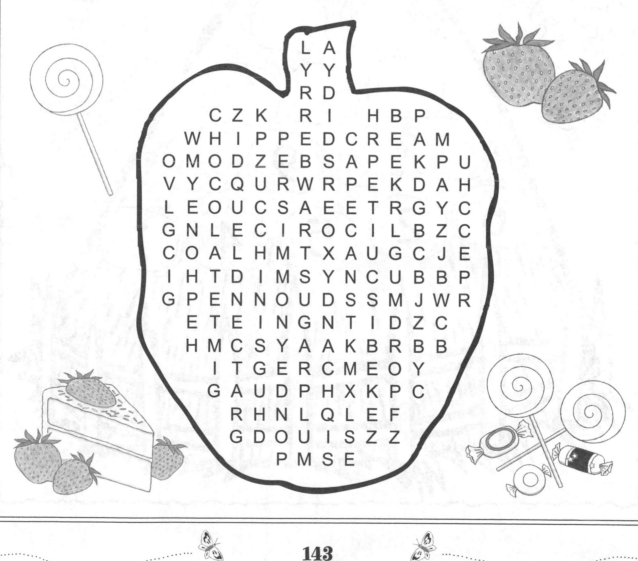

```
        L A
        Y Y
        R D
    C Z K   R I   H B P
   W H I P P E D C R E A M
  O M O D Z E B S A P E K P U
  V Y C Q U R W R P E K D A H
  L E O U C S A E E T R G Y C
  G N L E C I R O C I L B Z C
  C O A L H M T X A U G C J E
  I H T D I M S Y N C U B B P
  G P E N N O U D S S M J W R
  E T E I N G N T I D Z C
  H M C S Y A A K B R B B
    I T G E R C M E O Y
    G A U D P H X K P C
    R H N L Q L E F
    G D O U I S Z Z
      P M S E
```

Fairy Hill

Fairies often live inside hollow hills. They need your help to complete this mathemagical home. For each empty rock below, enter the sum of the two numbers beneath it on either corner. One example is already done (5 + 4 = 9). Complete all of the rocks to the very top.

Fairyland Code

In fairyland, codes are often used to send secret messages. Can you decode the message below using the following key?

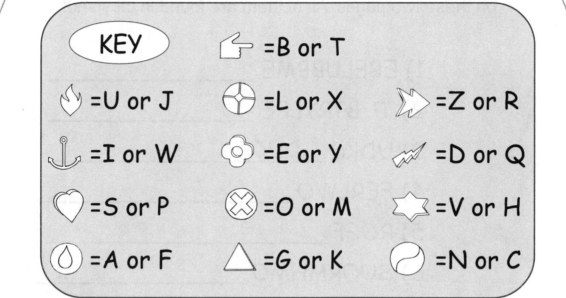

KEY
- 👉 = B or T
- 🔥 = U or J
- 🛟 = L or X
- ➤ = Z or R
- ⚓ = I or W
- 🌸 = E or Y
- ⚡ = D or Q
- 💙 = S or P
- ⊗ = O or M
- ✶ = V or H
- 💧 = A or F
- △ = G or K
- ☯ = N or C

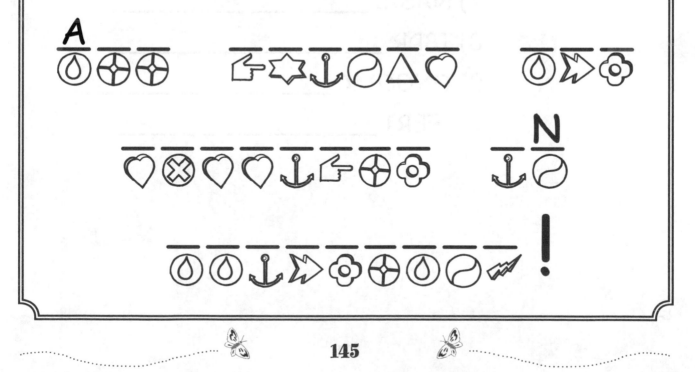

ALL THINGS ARE

POSSIBLE IN

FAIRYLAND!

Fairyland Plants & Animals

Unscramble the letters to name the plants and animals displayed on these two pages. All of them are found in fairyland!

1) EBELUBBME _____

2) TUBTRYLFE _____

3) UDKC __DUCK_____

4) FERLWO _____

5) ROGF _____

6) SUORMHMO _____

7) NASIL _____

8) IBDR _____

9) ONOCRAC _____

10) EERT _____

Fit all of the unscrambled plant and animal names into this clueless crossword puzzle. Each word is used only once, and must fit exactly into the number of boxes.

The Language of Fairyland

Fairies love to make rhymes! Use the given
clues to determine pairs of words that rhyme.

For example:

A playground for a
toothy ocean animal is a:

_ _ _ _ _ _ _ _ _ _

A gorilla garment is an:

APE CAPE

A rodent abode is a:

_ _ _ _ _ _ _ _ _ _

A birthday treat for
a scaly friend is a:

_ _ _ _ _ _ _ _ _

A utensil to eat a
dried plum is a:

_ _ _ _ _ _ _ _ _ _

148

Triangle Mushrooms

Fairyland is filled with mushrooms. Can you help this fairy find these mushrooms on this page?

1. The mushroom with an even number of triangles
2. The mushroom with the least number of triangles
3. The mushroom with exactly seven triangles
4. The mushroom with the most number of triangles

Fairyland Riddles

I'm found in the fairy forest
and I end with an E;
I provide plenty of shade,
and you can climb on me.
Draw a picture of what I am:

I'm red and I'm tasty
and I start with an A;
fairyland teachers love me,
and I keep the doctor away.
Draw a picture of what I am:

Flowers & Mushrooms

Draw two flowers and three mushrooms in the boxes below.
No flower should be next to another flower.
No mushroom should be next to another mushroom.

Chapter 11

Fairy Godmothers

Directions Home

In many stories, fairy godmothers give advice and direction. Can you pick the one set of directions that will lead the beetle home through this flower maze?

U=move up   D=move down   L=move left   R=move right

A) U, R, R, D, R, U, U, U, U, L, L, U   C) U, R, R, D, R, R, U, U, U, L, U, U

B) U, R, R, D, R, R, U, U, U, D, L, U   D) U, R, R, D, R, R, U, U, U, L, L, U

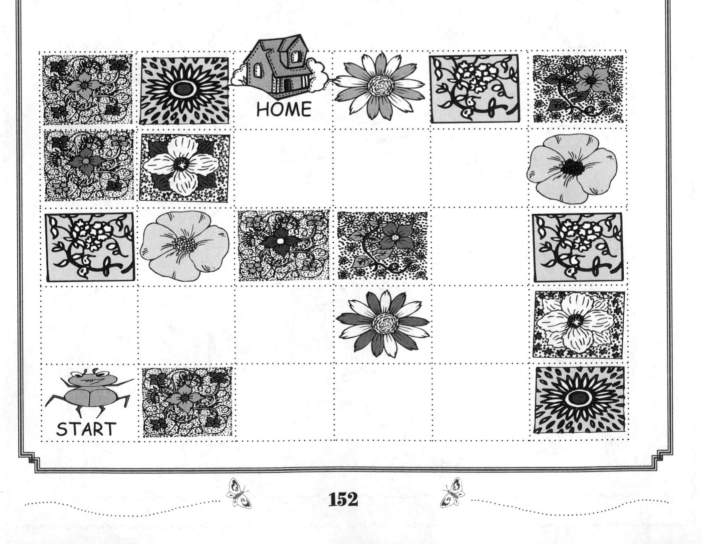

HOME

START

Fairy Dust Letters

Help fairy godmother sprinkle these letters to form animal names. Each group of letters will be used only once to complete the name of an animal.

MST
IG
RB
CU
LP
NOC
RA
YO
BR
RS
PA
PM
ABB
ETA
CCO
EPH
M
GEH
GU
POP

POR_____PINE

LEO_____RD

HO_____E

RHI_____EROS

RA_____ON

ZE_____A

R_____IT

EL_____ANT

GI_____FFE

CA_____EL

GE_____IL

CHE_____H

CHI_____UNK

JA_____AR

HED_____OG

HA_____ER

HIP_____OTAMUS

T_____ER

DO_____HIN

CO_____TE

Magical Changes

Fairy godmothers know how to magically change things.
Change these words into other words by rearranging the letters.

For example:
Rearrange the letters in the
word **gum** and make this:

M U G

Rearrange the letters in the
word **art** and make this:

_ _ _

Rearrange the letters in the
word **disk** and make these:

_ _ _ _

Rearrange the letters in the
word **flea** and make this:

_ _ _ _

Rearrange the letters in the word **fowl** and make this:

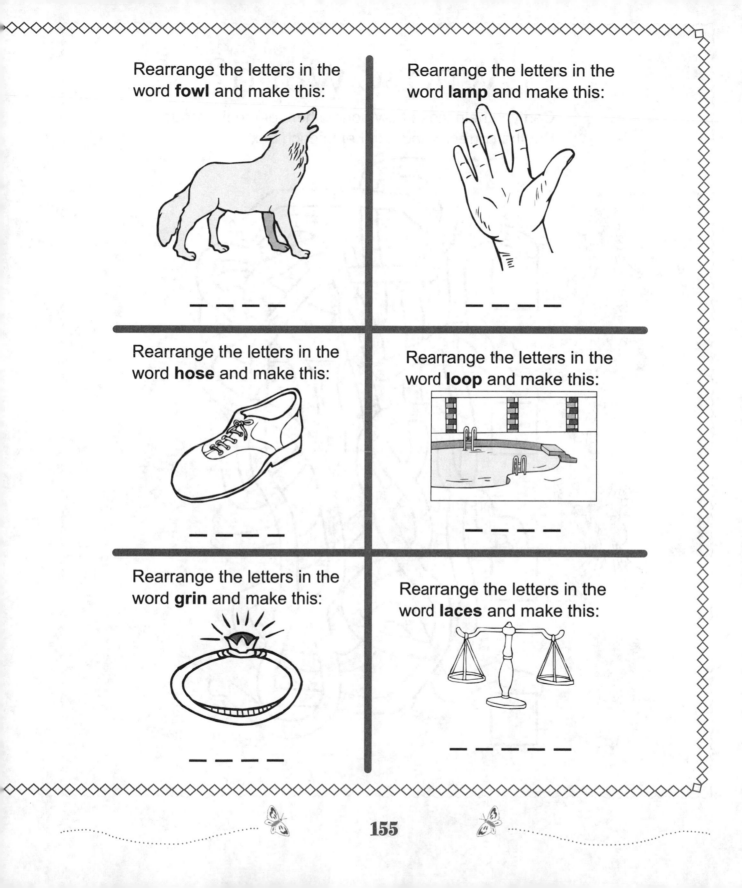

_ _ _ _

Rearrange the letters in the word **lamp** and make this:

_ _ _ _

Rearrange the letters in the word **hose** and make this:

_ _ _ _

Rearrange the letters in the word **loop** and make this:

_ _ _ _

Rearrange the letters in the word **grin** and make this:

_ _ _ _

Rearrange the letters in the word **laces** and make this:

_ _ _ _ _

Whose Wand?

Can you help these fairy godmothers get their wands?
Put the correct wand number in each box.

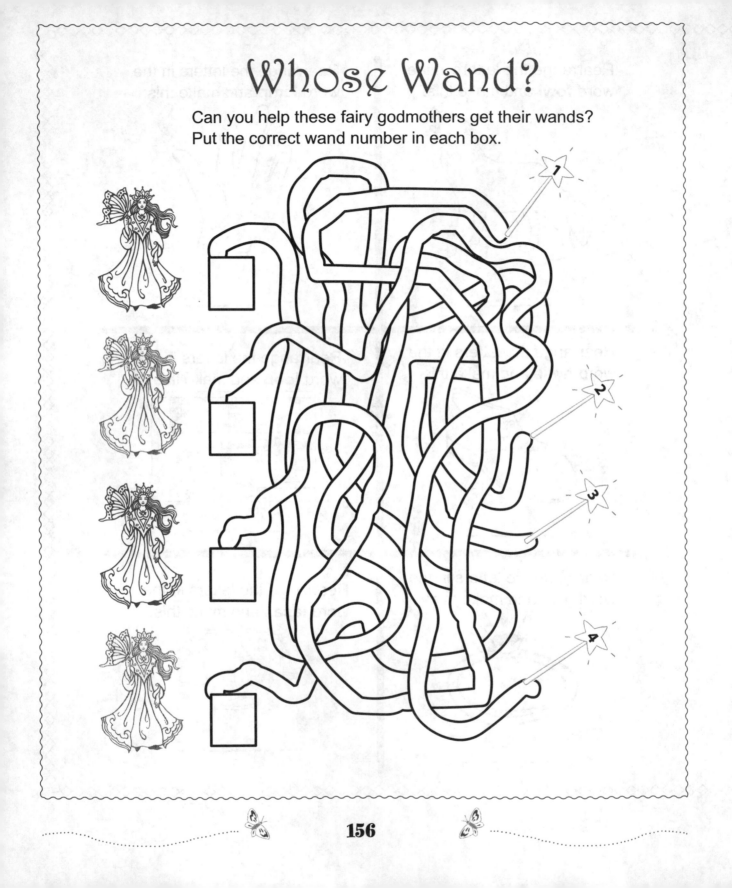

Break the Spell

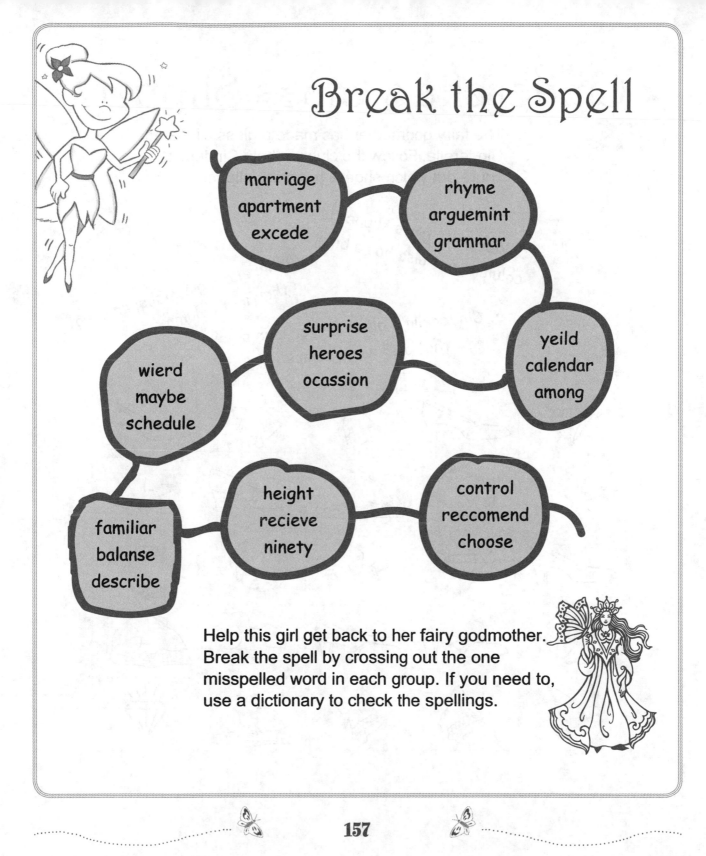

marriage
apartment
excede

rhyme
arguemint
grammar

surprise
heroes
ocassion

yeild
calendar
among

wierd
maybe
schedule

height
recieve
ninety

control
reccomend
choose

familiar
balanse
describe

Help this girl get back to her fairy godmother. Break the spell by crossing out the one misspelled word in each group. If you need to, use a dictionary to check the spellings.

Cinderella's Glass Slipper

The fairy godmother has made a glass slipper for Cinderella. Follow the clues to help Cinderella figure out which shoe is her glass slipper.

Cinderella's glass slipper is in a column that also has a bird.

Cinderella's glass slipper is not in the first column.

Cinderella's glass slipper is in a row that also has a pumpkin.

Cinderella's Magic Time

The fairy godmother's magic spell ends at midnight! Rank each clock by the amount of time it shows remaining until midnight. Start by putting a 1 next to the clock with the most time remaining.

Riddles

Just for fun, your fairy godmother has prepared these riddles for you! Translate the answers using this code: 1 = A, 2 = B, 3 = C, etc.

Why is six afraid of seven?

_ _ _ _ _ _ _   _ _ _ _ _
2 5 3 1 21 19 5   19 5 22 5 14

_ _ _ _ _   _ _ _ _ !
5 9 7 8 20   14 9 14 5 !

What clothing does a house wear?

_ _ _ _ _ _ _ !
1 4 4 18 5 19 19 !

What is in the middle of Paris?

$\overline{20}\ \overline{8}\ \overline{5}$ $\overline{12}\ \overline{5}\ \overline{20}\ \overline{20}\ \overline{5}\ \overline{18}$ $\overline{18}$!

What happens when an egg laughs?

$\overline{9}\ \overline{20}$ $\overline{3}\ \overline{18}\ \overline{1}\ \overline{3}\ \overline{11}\ \overline{19}$ $\overline{21}\ \overline{16}$!

What month has 28 days?

$\overline{1}\ \overline{12}\ \overline{12}$ $\overline{15}\ \overline{6}$ $\overline{20}\ \overline{8}\ \overline{5}\ \overline{13}$!

What has four legs but only one foot?

$\overline{1}$ $\overline{2}\ \overline{5}\ \overline{4}$!

What's Next?

Fairy godmothers can often predict the future. Can you predict the next number in these sequences? Hint: look for a pattern.

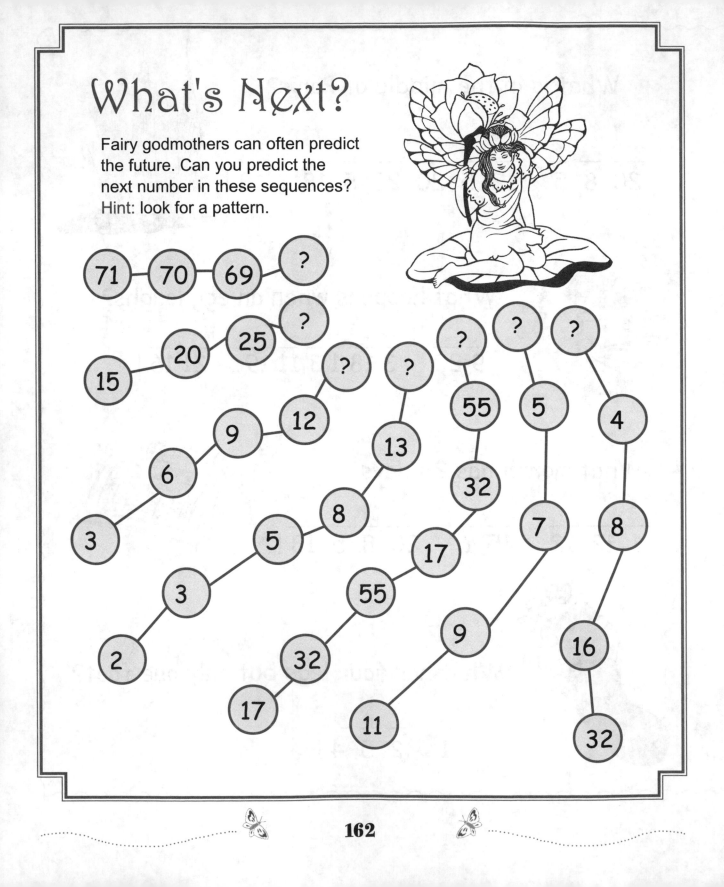

71 — 70 — 69 — ?

15 — 20 — 25 — ?

3 — 6 — 9 — 12 — ?

2 — 3 — 5 — 8 — 13 — ?

17 — 32 — 55 — 17 — 13 — ?

11 — 9 — 55 — 32 — 55 — ?

32 — 16 — 8 — 7 — 5 — ?

32 — 16 — 8 — 4 — ?

Chapter 12

Flower Fairies

Flower Maze

Can you help the flower fairy
find a path through this flower?

START

FINISH

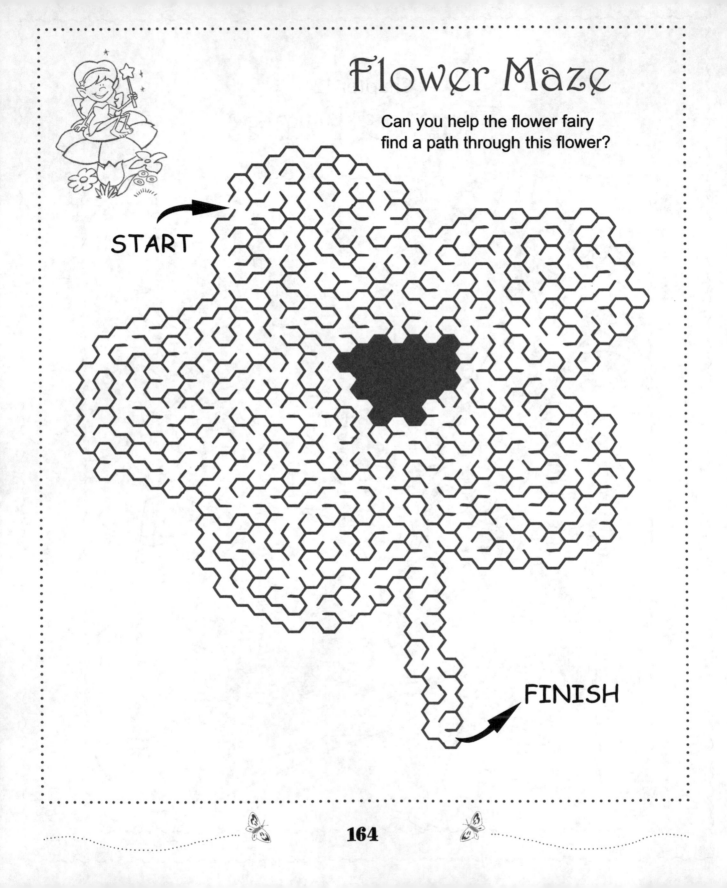

A Flower Fairy Christmas

The flower fairy has a Christmas present for you! To find out what it is, cross out all of these letters from the grid: U V W X Y Z

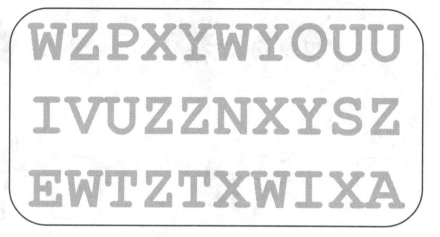

WZPXYWYOUU
IVUZZNXYSZ
EWTZTXWIXA

Flowery Dividers

Draw three straight lines that will separate each flower into its own section. Hint: think triangle.

Flower Values

Help the fairies determine the values of these sets of flowers. Rank them from 1 to 4, from most to least valuable.

Here is a guide to help you determine the relative values:

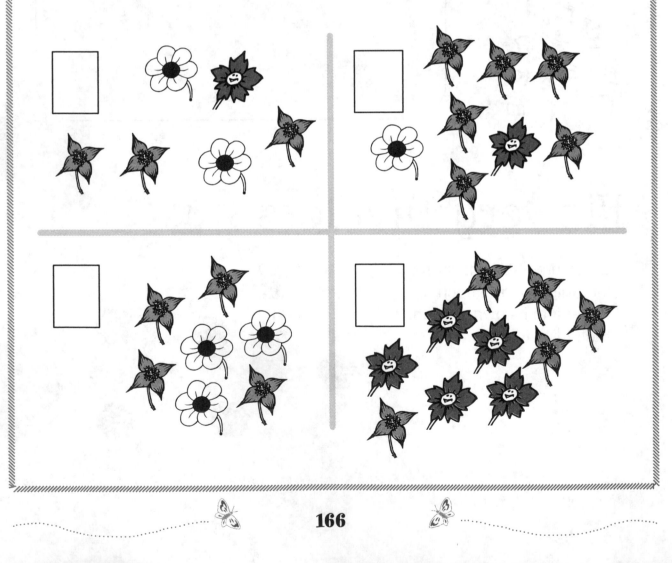

The Flower Fairy Garden

Change one letter in each capitalized word so that the sentences will make sense.

1. LATER makes the garden grow. _____

2. Besides flowers, the fairies also grow HORN. _____

3. The fairies use a HOG to help plant their garden. _____

4. The HUGS were asked to please not eat the flowers! _____

5. In the spring, the fairies plant SLEDS in the garden. _____

6. The TOPSAIL is just right to grow flowers. _____

7. Use your NOTE to smell the fragrant flowers. _____

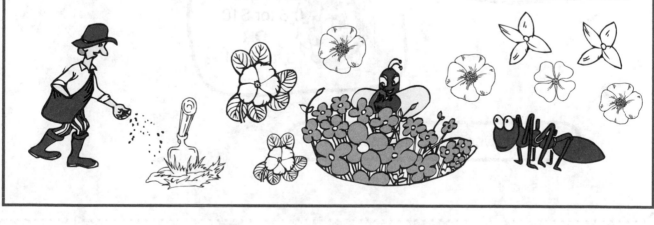

Smart Shopper

Help the flower fairy figure out which price is the best buy for each flower.

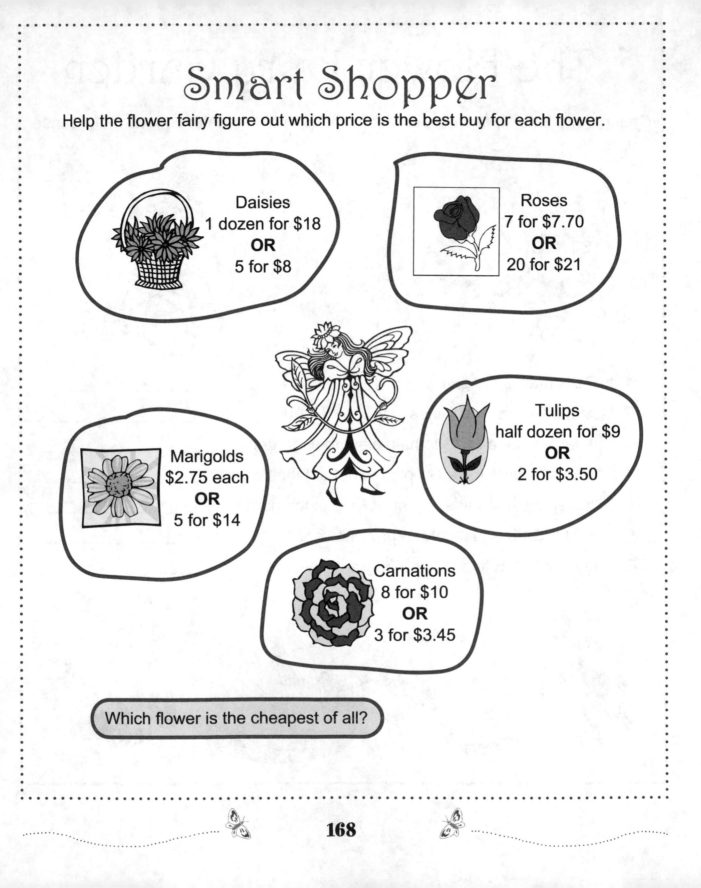

Daisies
1 dozen for $18
OR
5 for $8

Roses
7 for $7.70
OR
20 for $21

Marigolds
$2.75 each
OR
5 for $14

Tulips
half dozen for $9
OR
2 for $3.50

Carnations
8 for $10
OR
3 for $3.45

Which flower is the cheapest of all?

OWER Words

The word *flower* ends with the letters OWER. Fill in the blanks to make more words that end with OWER.

_ O W E R

_ _ _ _ _ _ _ O W E R

_ _ O W E R

_ _ _ O W E R

_ _ _ _ _ O W E R

Flower Riddles

Answer the clues below and fill the letters into the grid. Work back and forth between the grid and the clues until you figure it out.

Why couldn't the flower ride its bike?

1D	2C	3C	4D	5E	6E	7D		8E	9B
10D	11C	12C	13D		14B	15E	16B		
17A	18A	19C	20A	21C	22E	!			

C. A place for coats.

___ ___ ___ ___ ___ ___
3 21 11 12 2 19

A. Vegetable found in a pod.

___ ___ ___
17 18 20

D. Something with four legs.

___ ___ ___ ___ ___
13 4 1 10 7

B. What do you do on a chair?

___ ___ ___
16 14 9

E. Clubs, diamonds, hearts, and spades.

___ ___ ___ ___ ___
6 5 8 15 22

If April showers bring May flowers,
what do May flowers bring?

170

Flower Equations

Can you help the flower fairy figure out what numbers should go in the boxes to complete these equations?

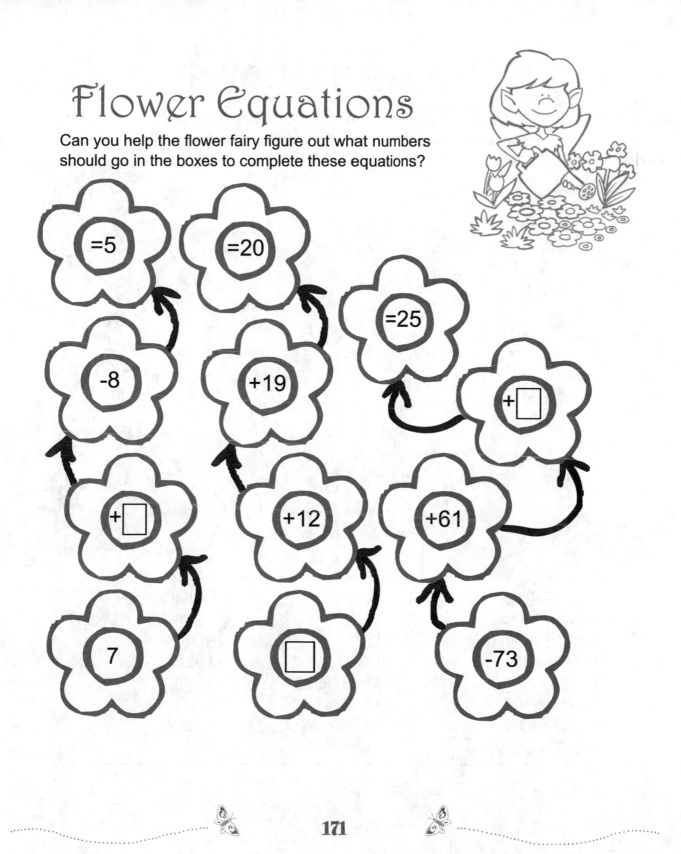

=5

=20

=25

-8

+19

+☐

+☐

+12

+61

7

☐

-73

Flowery Search

Can you find all of the flowers in the letters below?
Look up, down, sideways, backwards, and diagonally.

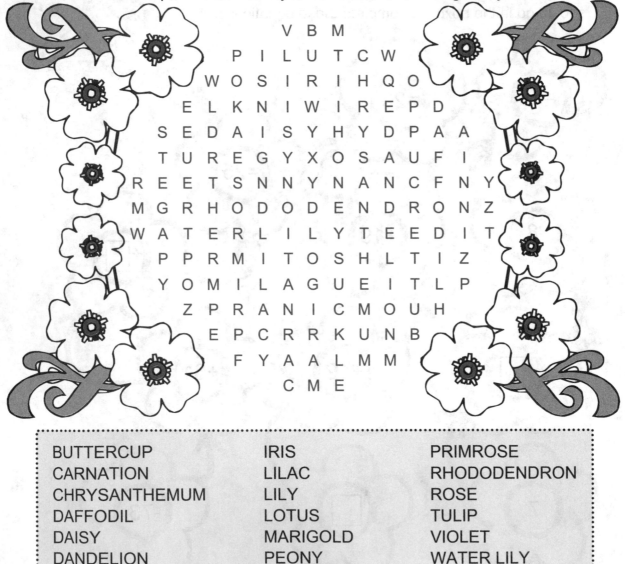

```
          V  B  M
       P  I  L  U  T  C  W
    W  O  S  I  R  I  H  Q  O
    E  L  K  N  I  W  I  R  E  P  D
    S  E  D  A  I  S  Y  H  Y  D  P  A  A
    T  U  R  E  G  Y  X  O  S  A  U  F  I
    R  E  E  T  S  N  N  Y  N  A  N  C  F  N  Y
    M  G  R  H  O  D  O  D  E  N  D  R  O  N  Z
    W  A  T  E  R  L  I  L  Y  T  E  E  D  I  T
    P  P  R  M  I  T  O  S  H  L  T  I  Z
    Y  O  M  I  L  A  G  U  E  I  T  L  P
    Z  P  R  A  N  I  C  M  O  U  H
    E  P  C  R  R  K  U  N  B
       F  Y  A  A  L  M  M
          C  M  E
```

BUTTERCUP	IRIS	PRIMROSE
CARNATION	LILAC	RHODODENDRON
CHRYSANTHEMUM	LILY	ROSE
DAFFODIL	LOTUS	TULIP
DAISY	MARIGOLD	VIOLET
DANDELION	PEONY	WATER LILY
GERANIUM	PERIWINKLE	ZINNIA
HONEYSUCKLE	POPPY	

Flower Fairy Delivery

The flower fairy brings you one of these flowers every day except Wednesday:

The flower fairy brings you one of these flowers on days that start with the letter T (like Tuesday):

The flower fairy brings you one of these flowers on days that have six letters (like Monday):

What flowers will you have from the Monday through Friday deliveries?

A.   B.   C.

Fractured Flowers

Help the fairy put these flowers together again by drawing a line connecting the two halves of each flower.

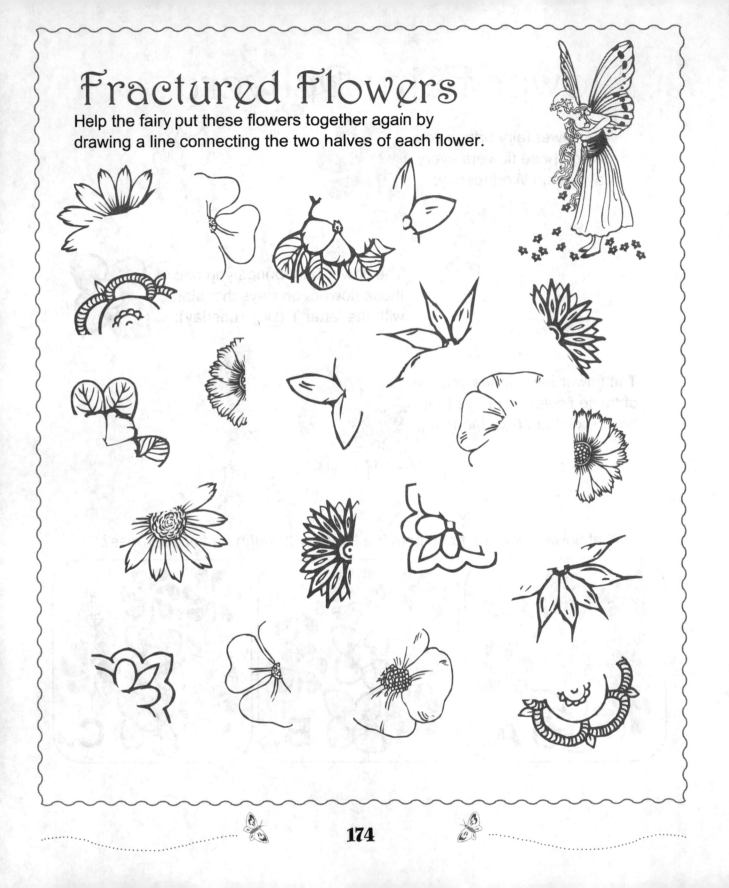

Chapter 13

Fairy Tales

Antique Books

Most fairy tales are very old and have been told for generations. These antique books are well-worn. Fill in the missing letters and reveal the fairy tale titles.

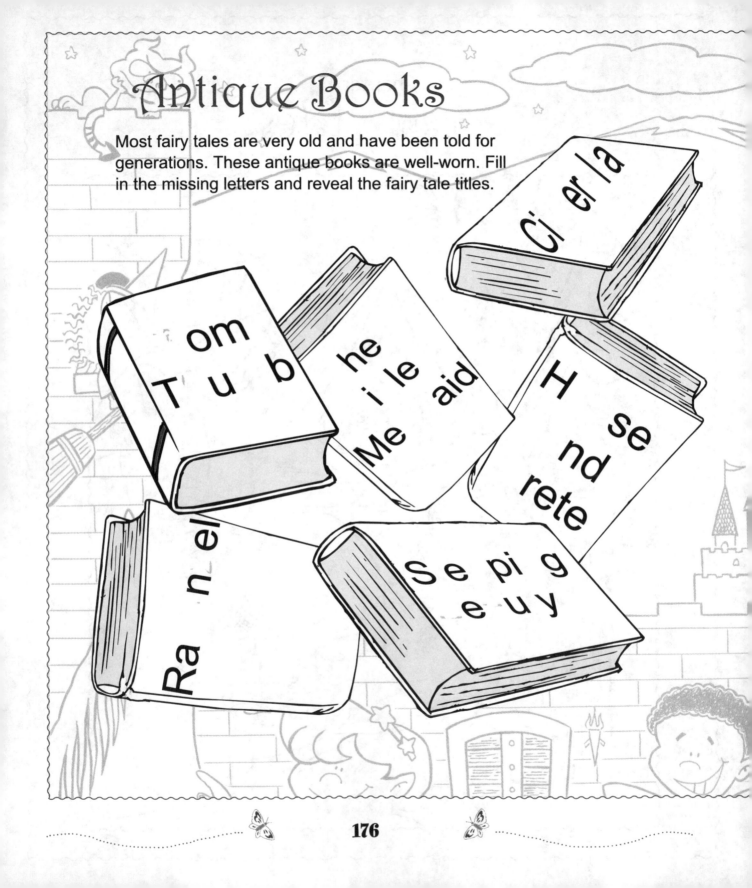

C   er la

T om
 u b

he
 i le
Me   aid

H   se
 nd
rete

Ra   n el

Se pi g
  e u y

177

Three Bears' Bingo

In this version of the fairy tale, Goldilocks finds bingo cards for the three bears. Solve the equations and cross out the answers on the cards. The winner is the card with four answers in a row across, down, or diagonally. Which bear wins?

17 + 3 = _____

11 + 11 = _____

11 + 17 + 8 = _____

9 + 8 + 7 = _____

33 + 28 + 33 = _____

82 - 4 = _____

93 - 9 = _____

78 - 11 = _____

56 ÷ 8 = _____

10 X 5 = _____

5 X 9 = _____

34 ÷ 2 = _____

26 ÷ 13 = _____

4 X 11 = _____

90 ÷ 9 = _____

27 - 8 = _____

10 + 20 + 7 = _____

25 ÷ 5 = _____

37 - 26 = _____

2 X 7 = _____

Papa Bear

69	27	2	51
50	7	24	91
13	74	5	96
62	32	39	17

Mama Bear

19	68	99	77
98	57	60	33
11	84	45	36
67	65	56	10

Baby Bear

20	53	81	22
42	94	78	44
80	58	14	82
38	54	37	97

Rapunzel's Hair Connection

The Prince needs to know which strand of hair belongs to Rapunzel.
In each box, write the name of the person connected to it by their hair.

Ursula Rapunzel Trixy Glenda

Mother Goose Words

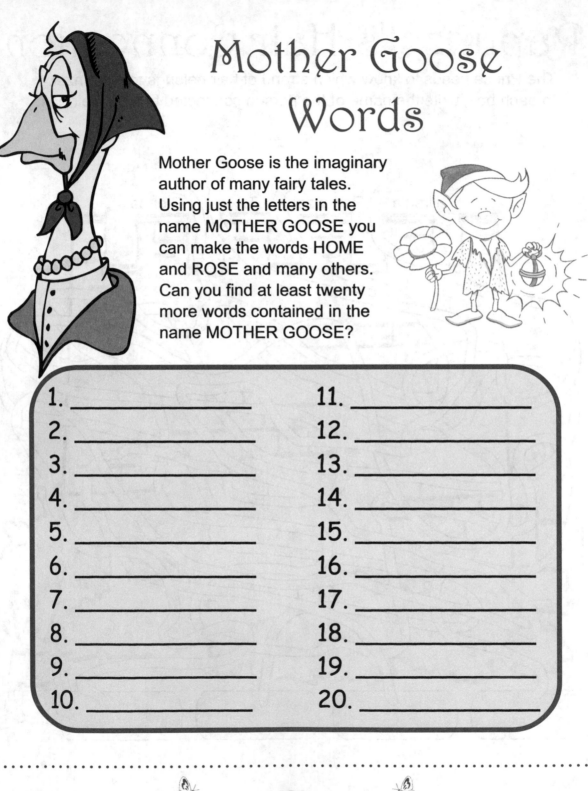

Mother Goose is the imaginary author of many fairy tales. Using just the letters in the name MOTHER GOOSE you can make the words HOME and ROSE and many others. Can you find at least twenty more words contained in the name MOTHER GOOSE?

1. _____
2. _____
3. _____
4. _____
5. _____
6. _____
7. _____
8. _____
9. _____
10. _____
11. _____
12. _____
13. _____
14. _____
15. _____
16. _____
17. _____
18. _____
19. _____
20. _____

The Prince's Real Clothes

The emperor needs your help to find his real clothes.
Circle the suit with these characteristics:

1. Buttons on the jacket.
2. No stripes on the tie.
2. Stars on the jacket.
3. No flower.

Hansel & Gretel

Can you help Hansel and Gretel find the gingerbread house? They dropped three of each of these charms on the only safe path:

The Gingerbread House

Hansel and Gretel are looking for candy! Find three groups of candy on the roof that look like these:

The Three Little Pigs

Straw

Reassemble these pieces of a sign to find out the address of the little piggy who built his house out of straw.

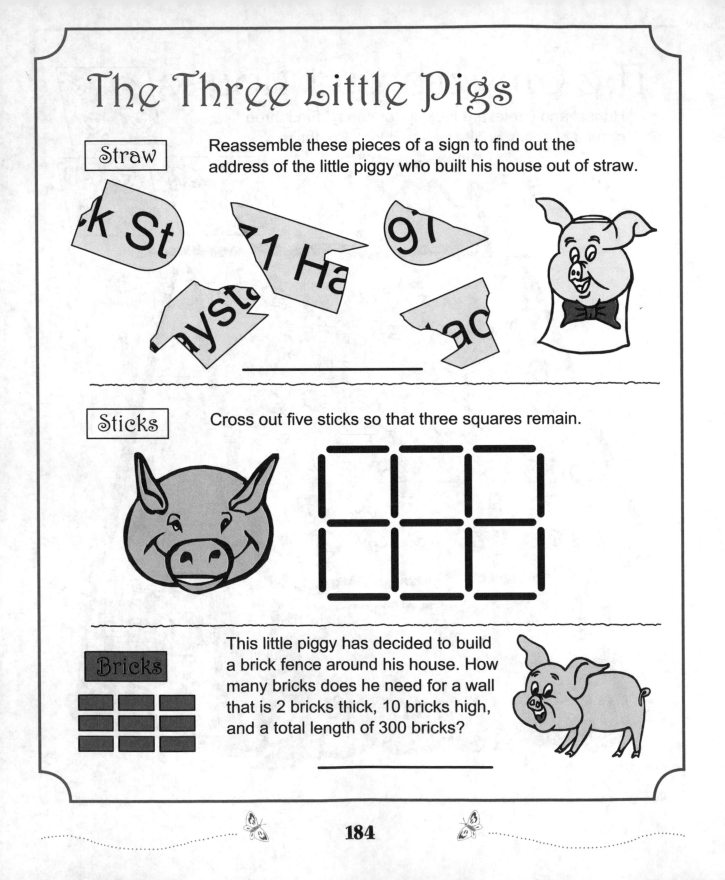

_____

Sticks

Cross out five sticks so that three squares remain.

Bricks

This little piggy has decided to build a brick fence around his house. How many bricks does he need for a wall that is 2 bricks thick, 10 bricks high, and a total length of 300 bricks?

_____

The Princess and the Pea

The Princess and the Pea is a Danish fairy tale by Hans Christian Andersen. All of the answers to this puzzle should contain these letters together: **PEA**. Fill in the blanks to name each picture.

For example:

SPEAKER

_ _ _ _ _

_ _ _ _ _ _

_ _ _ _ _ _ _

_ _ _ _

_ _ _ _ _

_ _ _ _ _

_ _ _ _ _

185

Wedding Bells

Often a fairy tale will end with a wedding. Circle the three fragments below that can be put together to make these wedding bells:

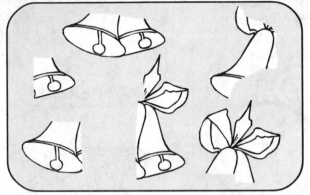

The End...

Figure out where to put each of the scrambled letters. They all fit in the spaces directly underneath. When you have filled in the grid correctly, you will see the line that ends many fairy tales.

	N	A		R								
A	F	T	P	R	H	L	Y		E	V	R	
A	H	D	E	T	I	E	Y		L	I	E	E	D
											V	
				P								
A												

Chapter 14

Unicorns

Latin Unicorn

In Latin, *UNI* means one and *CORN* means horn.
Put them together and you get a word that means one horn.

Figure out these words that also start with *UNI*:

one wheel:
U N I _ _ _ _ _ _

one outfit:
U N I _ _ _ _

together as one:
U N I _ _ _

one sound:
U N I _ _ _

Unscramble these letters, add them to CORN, and make a type of horn. If you need to, use a dictionary to help figure this one out:

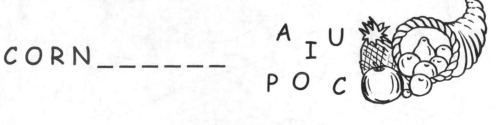

C O R N _ _ _ _ _ _

A I U
P O C

Secret Message

Decode this message to find out what the unicorn said to Alice in the story *Through the Looking-Glass* by Lewis Carroll. Every letter is coded as the next letter in the alphabet. For example, HELLO is coded as IFMMP.

JG ZPV'MM CFMJFWF JO NF, J'MM CFMJFWF JO ZPV.

Unicorn Healers

Unicorns are known for their mystical healing abilities. Separate the "sick" words from the "well" words by drawing one horizontal line and one vertical line.

hardy

bright-eyed

vigorous

chipper

queasy

frail

feeble

flourishing

wholesome

bushy-tailed

bedridden

nauseated

strong

weak

lousy

ill

feverish

ailing

impaired

hospitalized

rotten

robust

fit

Horse Barn

Unicorns are pretend creatures with the body of a horse and a head with a horn. Can you find all of these real horse breeds in the letters below? Look up, down, sideways, backward, and diagonally.

Appaloosa
Arabian
Ardennes
Azteca
Bashkir
Clydesdale
Fleuve
Holsteiner
Konik
Lokai
Morgan
Mustang
Noriker
Palomino
Percheron
Salerno
Sardinian
Thoroughbred
Tinker
Walkaloosa

```
S A R D I N I A N I U T D X G
R R R E R E K I R O N H E U U I
B E S E N N E D R A R L S N F
C K O N I K B S E B C A X G Q
P N A I B A R A H A A D W B Q
A I I S S D M G C L C S R B M
A T A H O L U W R A W E M B O
D S K S R O V O E Y N D T O R
T I O A R Z L V P I L Y D Z G
R I L O L Q U A E E C L B S A
Y W H F L E R T K H C C B I N
I T E E L A S S A L E R N O W
M W U F K L P A G N A T S U M
S N P Q O X Q P W L C W A T K
F G P H L V O P A L O M I N O
```

Hidden Horns

In each sentence, read between the words to find an animal that has horns. For example, this sentence has a yak hidden in it: *Surprisingly, Akron was a great place for the alligator to live.*

Rather than have a big wedding, the elephant eloped with his bride.

The melodic owl played trumpet in the band.

The monkey ate a mango atop the house.

Suzy has been a film buff a long time and loves romantic comedies.

Be a Deer

Fill in the blanks: A deer's horns are called _____. They are made of _____ and are shed and regrown each _____.

Ullric **Ulysses** **Umberto**

The Unicorn Trio

At 3:33 the princess called the unicorn trio and told them to come at once!
What time will each unicorn arrive?

⬚ : ⬚   ← Ullric is 12 miles away and will travel 24 miles per hour.

⬚ : ⬚   ← Ulysses is 30 miles away and will travel 60 miles per hour for 15 minutes, then 30 miles per hour for the rest of the way.

⬚ : ⬚   ← Umberto is 15 miles away and will travel at 20 miles per hour after he spends five minutes eating an apple.

The unicorn with three repeated letters in his name will deliver a letter for the princess. Who is it? _____	The unicorn whose name has all the letters in the word **TURBO** will pull the princess's carriage. Who is it? _____	An even number of letters is in the name of the unicorn who will find a lost lamb for the princess. Who is it? _____

Lunch Time!

Ullric has an apple in his lunch box.
Ulysses has three different items in his lunch box.
Umberto does not have corn in his lunch box.
Label each lunch box with the name of the unicorn:

_____ _____ _____

Better Barns

Umberto's barn has a star on it.
Ulysses' barn has a heart on it.
Ullric's barn is not next to Umberto's barn.
Label each barn with the name of the unicorn:

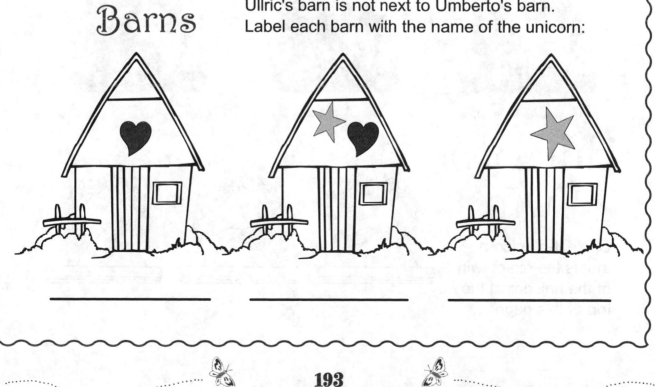

_____ _____ _____

Shadow of a Unicorn

Circle the shadow that exactly matches this unicorn.

Unicorn Twin

Circle the unicorn that is the exact twin of the unicorn at the top of this page.

194

Maiden's Song

Help the unicorn find the path to the maiden.

Portrait of a Unicorn

Copy each of the nine squares from the next page into this grid.
The letters and numbers tell you where each square belongs.
Complete the portrait by coloring the picture.

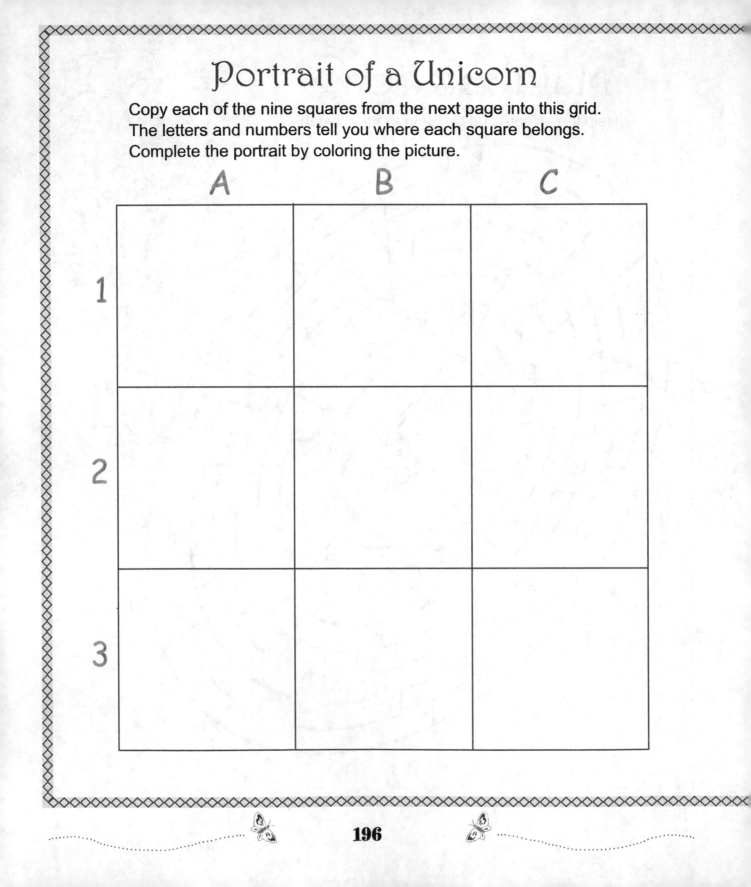

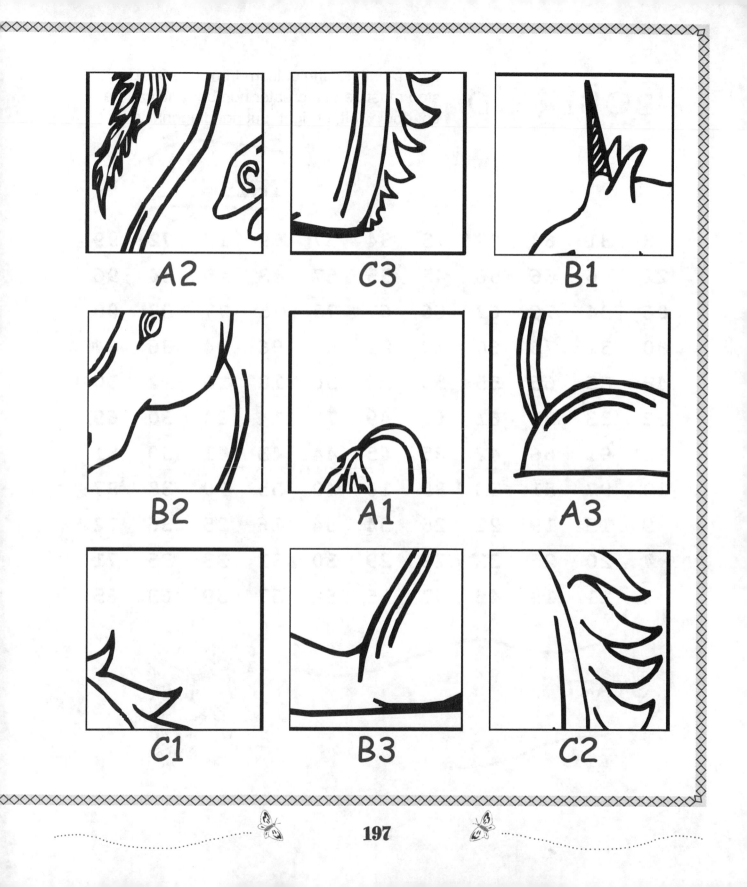

A2

C3

B1

B2

A1

A3

C1

B3

C2

Going Up

Find a path for the unicorn from 1 to 99. Each step must be to a greater number and can be up, down, left, or right, but not diagonally.

FINISH

2	31	64	79	75	94	37	69	19	72	99
22	6	66	56	45	55	67	43	45	54	96
86	34	76	62	66	67	73	75	77	87	90
80	31	75	60	19	81	59	96	94	86	84
48	35	65	55	53	50	36	18	10	92	50
22	33	31	61	60	49	71	14	84	30	69
11	91	66	42	85	45	44	43	41	39	81
10	97	51	33	85	10	40	55	70	38	87
9	15	19	22	25	54	54	16	25	36	72
7	20	25	33	28	29	30	31	33	35	71
1	21	19	45	47	55	56	57	59	63	65

START

Chapter 15

The Tooth Fairy

Tooth Fairy Animal

Solve this puzzle to find out what animal takes the place of the tooth fairy in some countries.

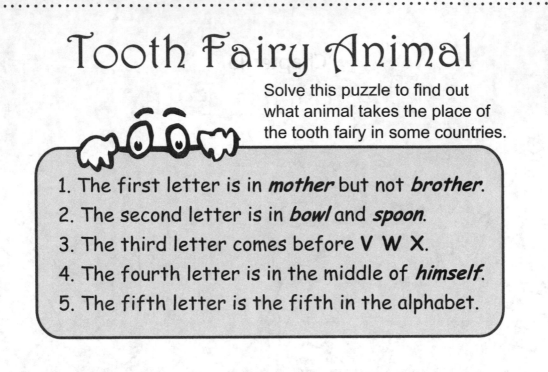

1. The first letter is in *mother* but not *brother*.
2. The second letter is in *bowl* and *spoon*.
3. The third letter comes before **V W X**.
4. The fourth letter is in the middle of *himself*.
5. The fifth letter is the fifth in the alphabet.

_____ _____ _____ _____ _____
  1   2   3   4   5

Baby Teeth

Solve this crazy formula to determine the total number of baby teeth for each person.

number of colors in the U.S. flag

- number of cups in a pint

+ number of seconds in a minute

- even number between 2 and 5

- number of cents in a quarter

- number of inches in a foot

―――――――――――――

= total number of baby teeth

A Healthy Smile

Can you find all of these dental words in the letters below?
Look up, down, sideways, backwards, and diagonally.

floss	dentist	smile	enamel	chew	lip
toothpaste	molar	jaw	incisor	cuspid	gums
brush	decay	bite	cavity	checkup	mouth

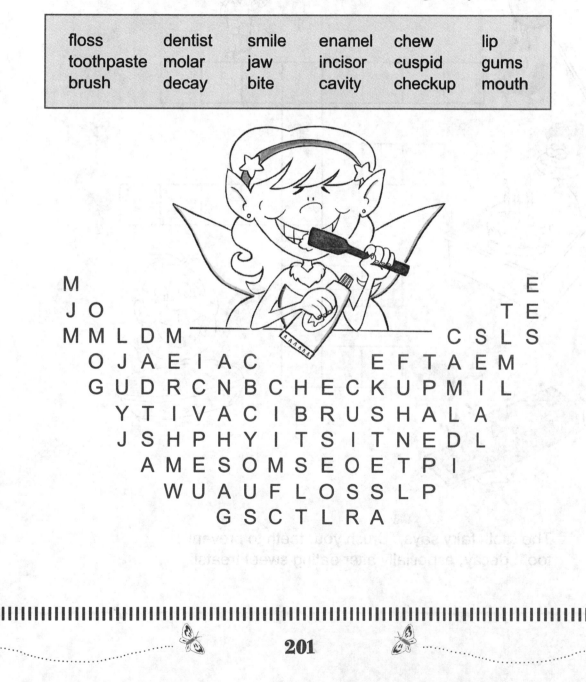

```
M                                                    E
J O                                              T E
M M L D M                                  C S L S
  O J A E I A C                  E F T A E M
  G U D R C N B C H E C K U P M I L
  Y T I V A C I B R U S H A L A
  J S H P H Y I T S I T N E D L
  A M E S O M S E O E T P I
  W U A U F L O S S L P
  G S C T L R A
```

Sweet Tooth

Complete this crossword puzzle using the pictures as clues.

The tooth fairy says, "Brush your teeth to prevent tooth decay, especially after eating sweet treats!"

A Good Deal

The tooth fairy has offered George a choice of two deals for his eight remaining baby teeth:

> **25 cents for each tooth**

> **OR**

> 1 cent for the first tooth
> 2 cents for the second tooth
> 4 cents for the third tooth
> and so on, with the payment doubling for each new tooth

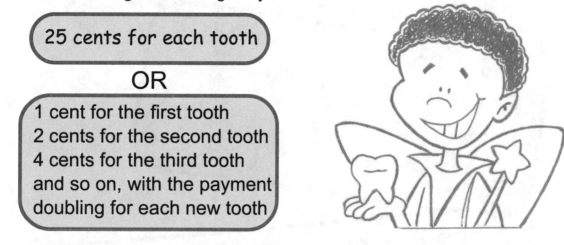

Which deal will give George the most money for his eight teeth? _____
How much money will George receive? _____

Fast Fairy

It takes the tooth fairy 7 minutes for each tooth collected. The tooth fairy starts at 11:24 p.m. and has 19 teeth to collect. At what time will the tooth fairy be done?

_____

🦷 Step by Step 🦷

Follow these steps to convert *tooth* into *coin*.

Step 1. Drop a letter from TOOTH and get the sound of a horn:

___ ___ ___ ___

Step 2. Take the answer from Step 1, change one of the letters to an R, and get a tooth's anchor:

___ ___ ___ ___

Step 3. Take the answer from Step 2, remove two letters, add an A, and get a rodent:

___ ___ ___ ___

Step 4. Take the answer from Step 3, change one of the letters to a C, and get something that chases the answer to Step 3:

___ ___ ___

Step 5. Take the answer from Step 4, insert the letter O, and get something to wear in the cold:

___ ___ ___ ___

Step 6. Take the answer from Step 5, change one of the letters to an L, and get a young horse:

___ ___ ___ ___ ___

Step 7. Take the answer from Step 6, change one letter to an N, change another letter to an I, and get a *COIN!*

Chewed Up Words

Find the letters asked for and place them in order on the teeth. You will spell out three types of teeth. The first one has been done for you.

The first 75% of *inch*
The middle 3 letters of *bison*
the last 2/5 of *alarm*
The first third of *olives*
the middle 3 letters of *march*
The last half of *plus*
The last 60% of *rapid*

Row 1: I N C __ __ __ __

Row 2: __ __ __ __ __

Row 3: __ __ __ __ __ __

Pillow Search

There are teeth under some of these pillows. Can you help the tooth fairy find the matching pillow for each kid?

Jamie   Bob   Emma   Olivia   Ryan

Pulling Teeth

Untangle the string from each person's tooth and write the correct name in the connected boxes.

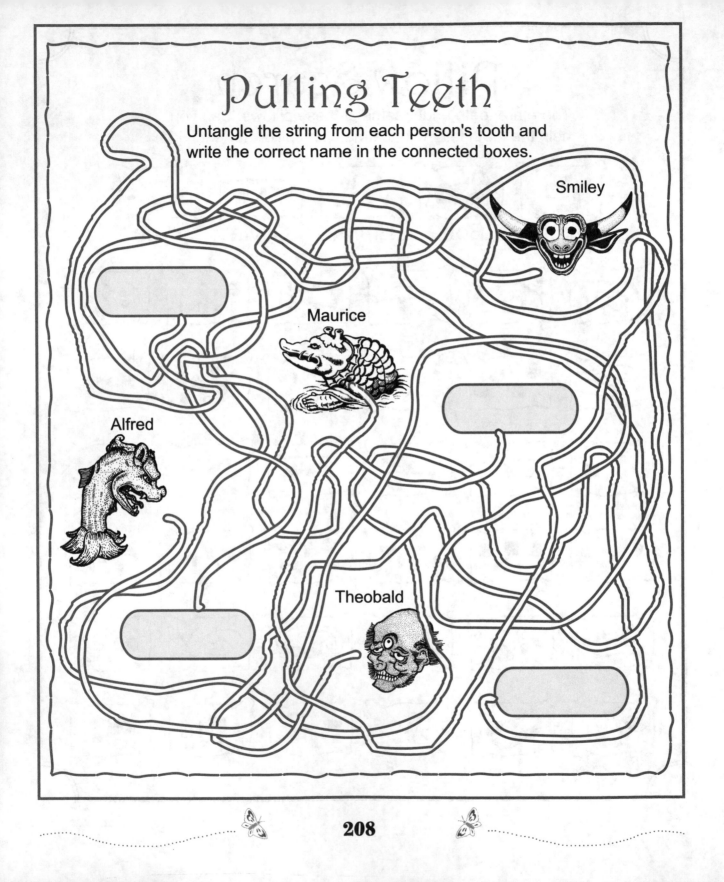

Smiley

Maurice

Alfred

Theobald

Smart Riddle

Answer the clues below and fill the letters into the grid. Work back and forth between the grid and the clues until you figure it out.

A. Horse feet

$\overline{4}$ $\overline{9}$ $\overline{17}$ $\overline{12}$ $\overline{6}$

B. It gets wetter the more it dries

$\overline{19}$ $\overline{11}$ $\overline{13}$ $\overline{20}$ $\overline{8}$

C. Found under a tree on a sunny day

$\overline{15}$ $\overline{23}$ $\overline{7}$ $\overline{16}$ $\overline{21}$

D. A drink made with leaves

$\overline{22}$ $\overline{3}$ $\overline{5}$

E. Black____: one who works with a hammer and anvil

$\overline{1}$ $\overline{18}$ $\overline{14}$ $\overline{10}$ $\overline{2}$

Why is the tooth fairy so smart?

1E	2E	3D	■	4A	5D	6A	■
7C	■	8B	9A	10E	■	11B	12A
13B	14E	15C	16C	17A	18E	■	■
19B	20B	21C	22D	23C	■	■	■

Baby teeth are also known as:
___ ___ ___ ___ teeth

Hint: think drink

209

Chapter 16
Fairy Friends

Fairy Friend Names

Using the clues below, put the correct name under each fairy friend.

1. Dante is between Boris and Kirby.
2. Fred is directly below Boris.
3. Alex is in the lower-left corner.
4. Edgar and Dante are in the same column.

Goblin Numbers

Cross out the one entry in each set that was added by this mischievous goblin.

Set 1:
5   30   10   17   15   20   25

Set 2:
$\frac{9}{12}$ .75 $\frac{5}{8}$ $\frac{3}{4}$ $\frac{75}{100}$ 75%

Set 3:
5+4   4+3   2+7   8+1   3+6   7+1+1

Set 4:
2-2   0+0   15-12-1   12-4-8   99-99   14+1-15

Set 5:
9-6   5-2   4-1   10-7   7-5   6-3

Set 6:
4 X 6   3 X 4 X 2   8 X 3   2 X 12   5 X 7   6 X 2 X 2

Set 7:
$\frac{3}{15}$ $\frac{25}{100}$ $\frac{1}{5}$?   20% $\frac{5}{25}$

Gremlin's Half Spell

This gremlin accidentally cast a spell that removed half of each of these things. Can you draw the missing halves?

Dwarf Shoppers

Dwarfs are expert miners and very wealthy. Can you figure out what the dwarfs are going to buy with their jewels? Draw a line between each set of jewels and the item with the same value. Here is a guide to the value of each jewel:

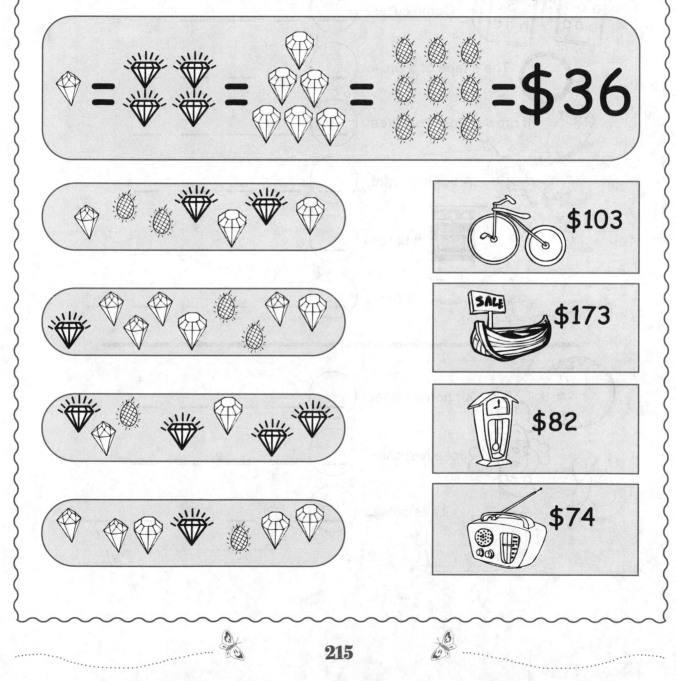

Creature Acrostics

Use the clues and pictures to fill in the blanks. The circled
letters will spell the names of creatures that are fairy friends.

Game cubes: ◯ __ __ __ __

The shape of a circle: ◯ __ __ __ __

It grows into an oak tree: ◯ __ __ __ __

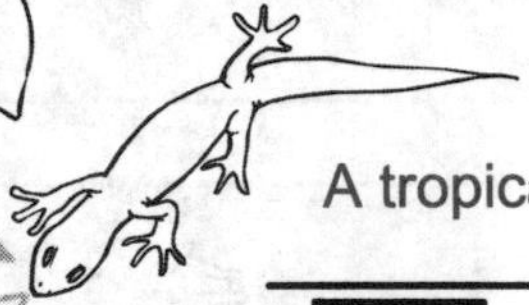

A tropical lizard: ◯ __ __ __ __

It bakes: ◯ __ __ __ __

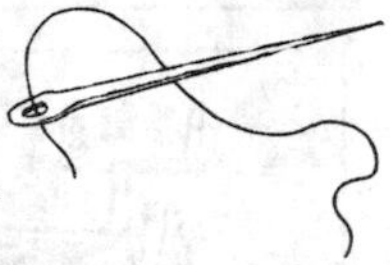

It sews: ◯ __ __ __ __ __

Our home planet: ◯ __ __ __ __

Joke response: ◯ __ __ __ __

It has petals: ◯ __ __ __ __ __ __

You can eat lunch on it: ◯ __ __ __ __

Water falling: ◯ __ __ __ __

Atlantic or Pacific: ◯ __ __ __ __

Found on a tree: ◯ __ __ __ __

It opens with the right key: ◯ __ __ __ __

It fits your hand: ◯ __ __ __ __ __

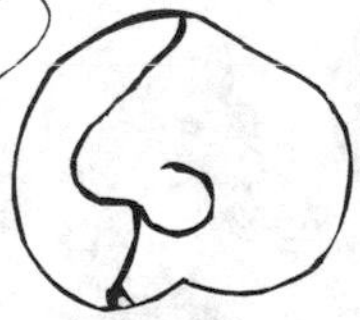

It smells: ◯ __ __ __ __

20-19

Twenty minus nineteen: ◯ __ __ __

Worn on halloween: ◯ __ __ __ __

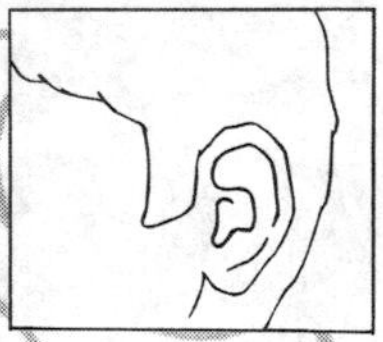

It hears: ◯ __ __ __

Lucky Four-Leaf Clovers

Leprechauns know that four-leaf clovers are lucky! Can you circle all of the four-leaf clovers on this page? There are twenty of them that look like this:

Elf Cards

Use the clues to determine the correct order for the three Elf cards.

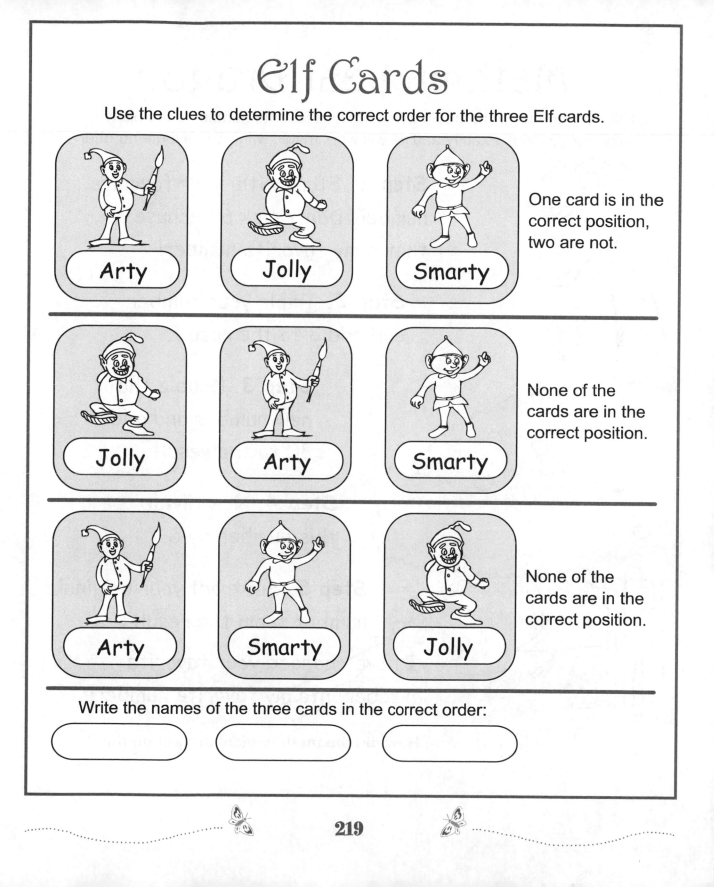

Arty   Jolly   Smarty

One card is in the correct position, two are not.

Jolly   Arty   Smarty

None of the cards are in the correct position.

Arty   Smarty   Jolly

None of the cards are in the correct position.

Write the names of the three cards in the correct order:

Mathmagical Dragon

This dragon can work magic with math. His favorite number is 6. Follow these instructions exactly and he will work magic with your favorite number.

Step 1. Start with your favorite number. Don't pick 6 because that's my favorite number!

Step 2. Triple your number and add 3 to the result.

Step 3. Double that new number and add 30 to the result.

Step 4. Now divide this number by 6.

Step 5. Subtract your original number from the result.

I have changed your favorite number into my favorite number!

How did the mathmagical dragon do this?

Fairy People

Some fairies look just like people. Can you find the fairies on this page? First, draw a line between each description and a person. Then circle the people without a description, they are the fairies!

Graduate   **Pilgrim**   **Chauffeur**

Fireman   **Janitor**

Musician

Doctor

Announcer   **Blacksmith**

Photographer

Logical Leprechaun

Can you circle the shamrock that comes after the first two?

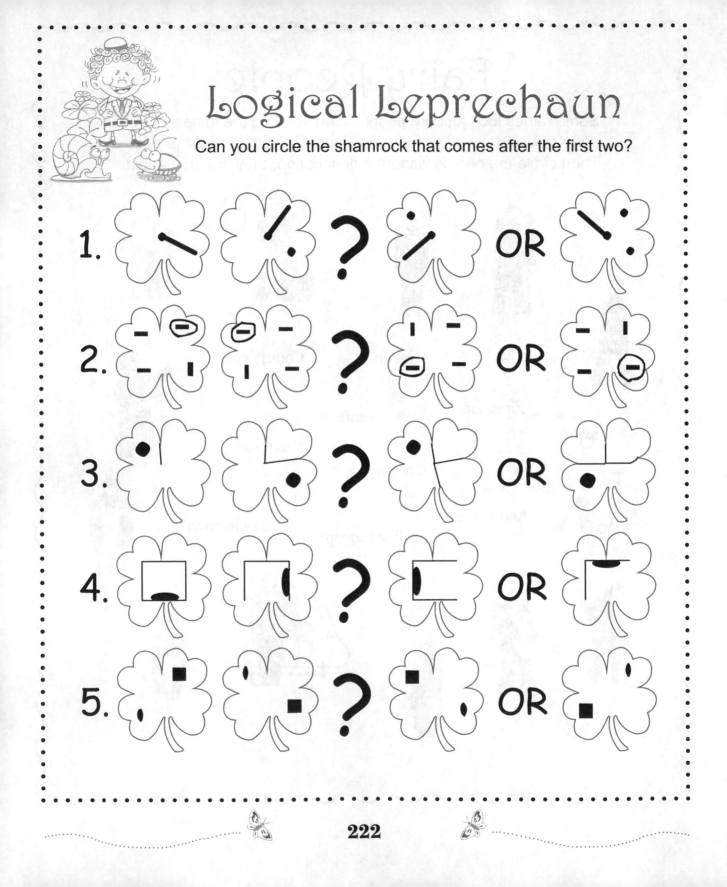

1.

2.

3.

4.

5.

OR

Chapter 17

The Blue Fairy (from "Pinocchio")

Making Pinocchio

The woodcarver Geppetto has 2 hats, 5 shirts, and 3 pants that can fit Pinocchio. How many different combinations of hats, shirts, and pants can Pinocchio wear?

Geppetto's sock drawer is all mixed up! There are 10 black socks, 20 blue socks, and 3 red socks. Without looking at them first, how many socks must Gepetto take out to guarantee that he has a matching pair for Pinocchio?

Help make Pinocchio by drawing his face.

A Heart from the Blue Fairy

Find the heart below that exactly matches the space above for Pinocchio's heart.

Pinocchio's Journey

Help Pinocchio find a path through the woods to the Blue Fairy's castle.

Animal Alphabet

Pinocchio sold his school book so that he could buy a ticket to the puppet show! The Blue Fairy needs your help to teach the alphabet to Pinocchio. Write the name of an animal that begins with each letter below. Some of the letters already have animals.

A _____

B _____

C _____

D _____

E _____

F _____

G _____

H _____

I _____

J _____

K _____

L _____

M _____

Newt _____

O _____

P _____

Q _____

R _____

S _____

T _____

Urchin _____

Vulture _____

W _____

Xenops _____

Yak _____

Z _____

Puppet Shows

Pinocchio saw his brothers and sisters on the stage.
Can you find ten differences between these two shows?

Candy Counter

Pinocchio went to the land of toys where boys play all day and eat only candy. Use the clues to figure out how many pieces of candy each boy has.

Steve has fewer pieces than Pinocchio, but more pieces than Frank.

Frank has as many pieces as Justin and Ray combined.

Justin has twice the number of pieces as Ray.

The Blue Fairy says that Pinocchio has 5 pieces of candy.

Pinocchio has 3 more pieces than Justin.

Fill in the blanks:

Ray has ____ pieces of candy.

Frank has ____ pieces of candy.

Steve has ____ pieces of candy.

Justin has ____ pieces of candy.

Magic Squares

The Blue Fairy is using magic squares to teach Pinocchio about math. Here is an example of a magic square:

2	9	4
7	5	3
6	1	8

A 3x3 magic square has these properties:
1. Each number from 1 to 9 is used once.
2. The sum of each row, column, and diagonal is the same.

Complete these magic squares by putting numbers into the empty boxes:

4	3	8
	5	
2		6

	1	6
	5	7
4		

6		2
		9
	3	

6		
	5	
		4

Can you complete these 4x4 magic squares? They are just like 3x3 magic squares, except the numbers 1 to 16 are used.

16	3		13
5		11	8
9	6	7	12
	15	14	

4		9	
	10		3
	11	7	
1	8	12	13

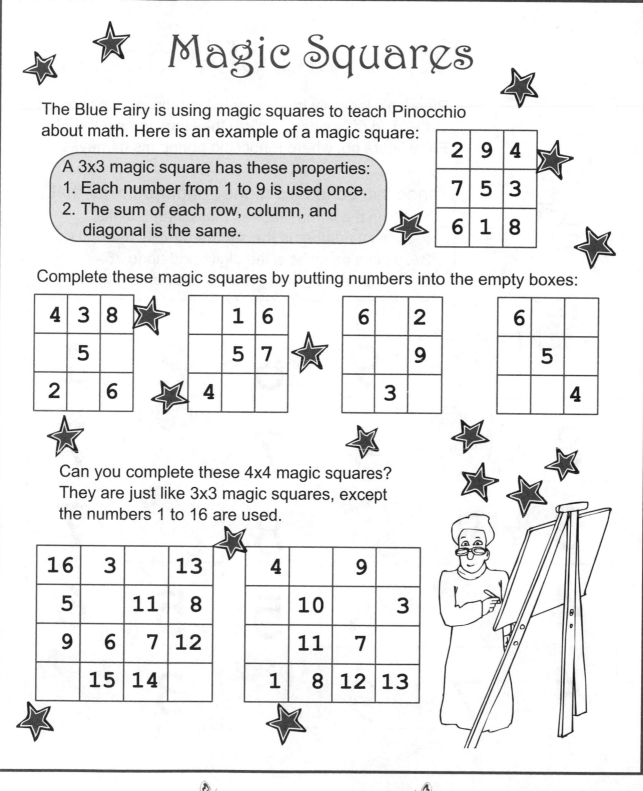

The Field of Wonders

Pinocchio foolishly tried to grow his money by planting it in the field of wonders. Follow the clues to help the Blue Fairy figure out where Pinocchio buried his money.

Pinocchio buried his money under a flower that...
1. ...is in a column that has more than 2 digits.
2. ...has a number in the square directly below it.
3. ...is in a row where the digits add up to 26.
4. ...is not in a column that has a repeated digit.

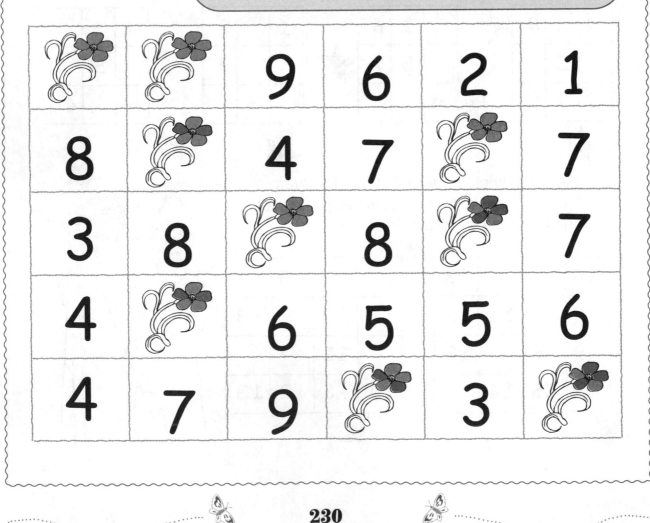

Tell the Truth

Pinocchio's nose grew when he lied to the Blue Fairy about what happened to his money. Circle the kids on this page who are telling the truth.

Andrew has 38¢
"The boys have more money than the girls."

Olivia has 76¢
"All of the kids together have a total of $3.36"

Matthew has 62¢
"Emma has more money than Andrew and Jacob combined."

Samantha has 25¢
"The kids with 6 letters in their names have a total of $1.14"

Jacob has 47¢
"All combined, the girls have an even number of cents."

Emma has 88¢
"The person with the least amount of money is a boy."

How much does a school lunch cost if Emma has exactly enough money to buy one every day from Tuesday through Friday?

Fishing for Father

Pinocchio is looking for his father who is inside a fish sitting at a table with a candle! Find the fish that has all of the letters in these words: GEPPETTO, TABLE, CHAIR, CANDLE.

Back to the Blue Fairy

After rescuing his father from the fish, Pinocchio must swim back to the Blue Fairy. A shark gives him these directions: *"Swim 1 mile north, 2 miles east, 3 miles south, 2 miles west and you will find land."* **Can you find a shorter route?**

Changes

The Blue Fairy helped Pinocchio change from a puppet into a real boy. Can you change one word into another word in these puzzles? Each step must be a real word and differ from the previous word by only one letter. There are many possible solutions, but try to use only the given number of steps.

Example:
CAT to BOY

C A T
B A T
B A Y
B O Y

WIRE to FISH

W I R E
_ _ _ _
_ _ _ _
F I S H

TOE to DOG

T O E
_ _ _
_ _ _
D O G

BALL to COWS

B A L L
_ _ _ _
_ _ _ _
C O W S

HORSE to GOOSE

H O R S E
_ _ _ _ _
_ _ _ _ _
G O O S E

PAPER to TIGER

P A P E R
_ _ _ _ _
_ _ _ _ _
T I G E R

RICE to MULE

R I C E
_ _ _ _
_ _ _ _
M U L E

Geppetto's New Coat

With the help of the Blue Fairy, Pinocchio has earned enough money to buy Geppetto a new coat. Exact change must be used to buy the coats on this page. Circle the coats that Pinocchio can buy.

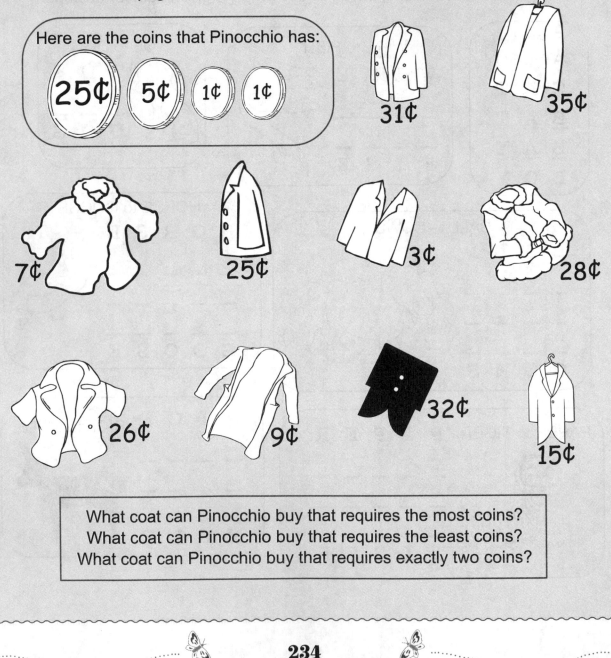

Here are the coins that Pinocchio has:

25¢   5¢   1¢   1¢

31¢

35¢

7¢

25¢

3¢

28¢

26¢

9¢

32¢

15¢

What coat can Pinocchio buy that requires the most coins?
What coat can Pinocchio buy that requires the least coins?
What coat can Pinocchio buy that requires exactly two coins?

Chapter 18

Thumbelina

Magic Seeds

Thumbelina grew like magic from a seed! Draw magic seeds into the empty squares to complete the four garden plots. There are four magic seeds:

heart   diamond   triangle   square

Within every plot, each seed should appear only once in each row, column, and 2x2 box.

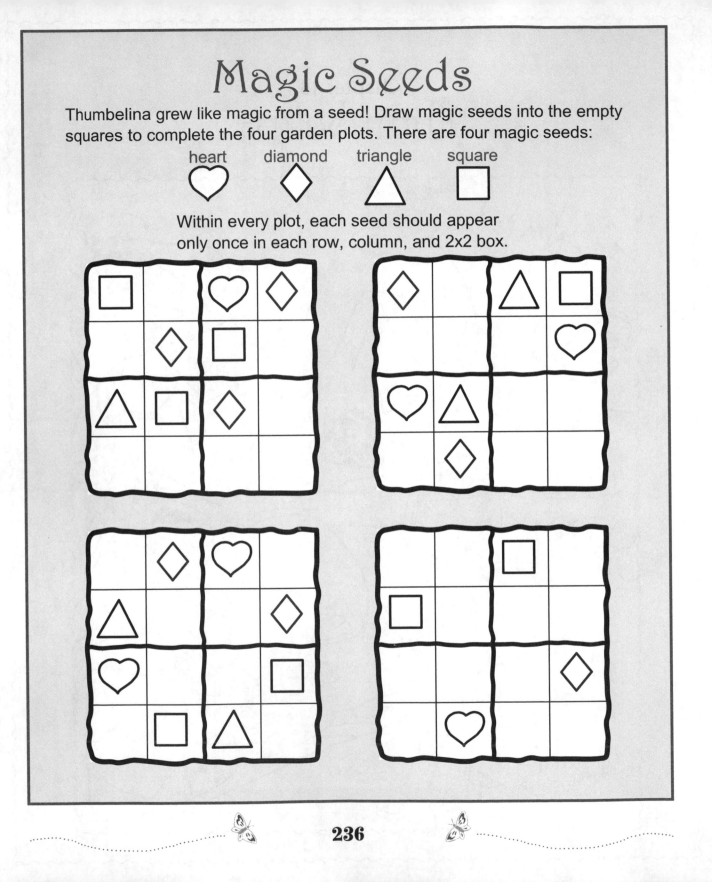

Thumbelina's Country

To find out the country where *Thumbelina* was written, first put a letter in each box that corresponds to the starting letter of the pictures. Then, unscramble the letters to form the name of a country.

‒ ‒ ‒ ‒ ‒ ‒ ‒

Memories

Try to remember all of the details of things you see on this page. Then turn to the next page and see if you can answer some true-false questions from memory.

Don't read this until you have looked at the previous page!

STOP

Memories

After carefully studying the previous page, see if you can answer each of these questions either TRUE or FALSE. No peeking!

_____ There is a paddle with the kayak.

_____ The egg is decorated.

_____ There is an earring on the ear.

_____ There is a ribbon through a nine.

_____ The rug is laid out completely flat.

_____ The dog is standing on one leg.

_____ The arrow is pointing up.

_____ There is a key.

_____ The apple does not have a stem.

_____ There is a horse with a saddle.

_____ The nuts have a shell.

_____ The rope is in a loop.

_____ There are eight groups of pictures.

_____ The needle is threaded.

_____ The magnet has a triangle shape.

Author

Decode the numbers below to find out the author of *Thumbelina*. 1=A, 2=B, 3=C, etc.

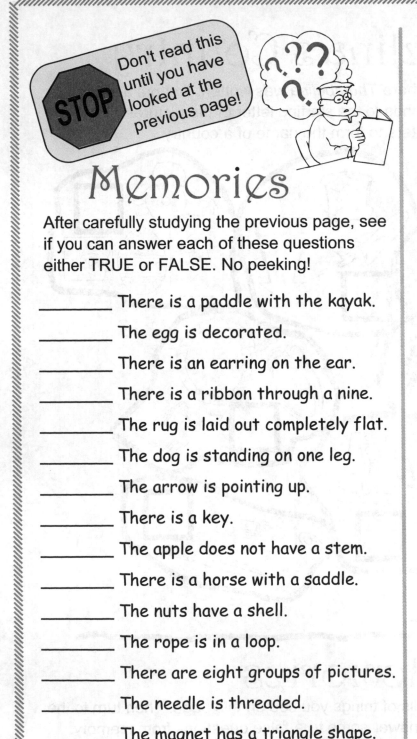

8___
1___
14___
19___
3___
8___
18___
9___
19___
20___
9___
1___
14___

1___
14___
4___
5___
18___
19___
5___
14___

238

Butterfly Friends

Thumbelina was helped by a butterfly who pulled her to safety. Help these butterflies find their way home by drawing a line from each butterfly to a corresponding flower. Can you figure out the pattern that connects each butterfly to a flower? One pair has already been matched.

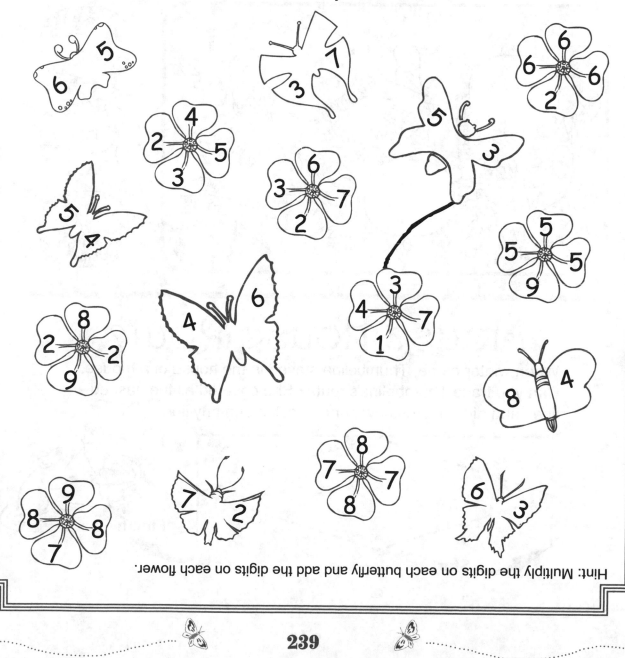

Hint: Multiply the digits on each butterfly and add the digits on each flower.

Falling Leaves

All summer long, Thumbelina lived happily in the forest.
When Fall came, the weather grew cold and the leaves fell.
Draw a line from each piece to its place in the picture.

Mouse House Route

When winter came, Thumbelina stayed in the house of a mouse.
Can you trace Thumbelina's route? She covered all the dashed
lines and did not cross over or go back along any line.

Start

Finish

Escape from Mr. Mole

Help Thumbelina find a path from Mr. Mole to the bird.
The bird will help Thumbelina escape.

241

Carrots and Apples

Thumbelina started her journey to fairyland with no food in her bag! She made four stops along the way...

1 Thumbelina stopped at a lake and found three carrots. She ate one of the carrots and took the rest in her bag to the next stop...

2 Thumbelina stopped at a tree house and found five apples. She ate two of them and took the rest in her bag to the next stop...

3 Thumbelina stopped at a farm and found four more carrots and three more apples. She ate three carrots and one apple and took the rest in her bag to the next stop...

4 Thumbelina stopped at a castle and ate two carrots and two apples from her bag and took the rest to fairyland.

How many carrots and apples did Thumbelina have in her bag after each stop?

	Carrots	Apples
Lake		
Tree House		
Farm		
Castle		

Many Emotions

Thumbelina has all kinds of experiences.
Draw her face to express these emotions...

Surprised when she was kidnapped by the frogs.

Sad when she almost had to marry Mr. Mole.

Happy when she marries the fairy prince.

Dress Up

Thumbelina loves to dress up her friends in fairyland.
Color these friends so they each have a unique dress...

Thumbelina's Crossword

In honor of Thumbelina's arrival in fairyland, the fairy prince made this crossword puzzle. The words use only letters from her name: THUMBELINA.

ACROSS

4 You have a first, middle, and last one
5 Opposite of fat
6 To search for prey
9 A being from outer space
11 Scientists' workplace
12 Green citrus fruit
13 Clue for the stumped
14 A sad color
17 Hamburger bread
18 There are 60 in an hour
19 Part of a dog that wags
20 Mary had a little one
22 Connects two points
24 Furnace output
26 After dinner candy and toothpaste flavor
28 Breakfast, lunch, or dinner
30 Fish that comes in a can
31 Between nine and eleven

DOWN

1 The science of numbers and their operations
2 Not nice
3 A female adult chicken
5 A blue-green color
7 Furniture piece with legs
8 Balloon gas
10 Read when seated at a restaurant
15 Opposite of early
16 Your mother's sister
17 It holds pants up.
21 Delivered daily to your box
22 A fib
23 It is hit with a hammer
25 What you do at a restaurant
27 Clean and tidy
29 Worn on the head
32 Acorn and almond, for example

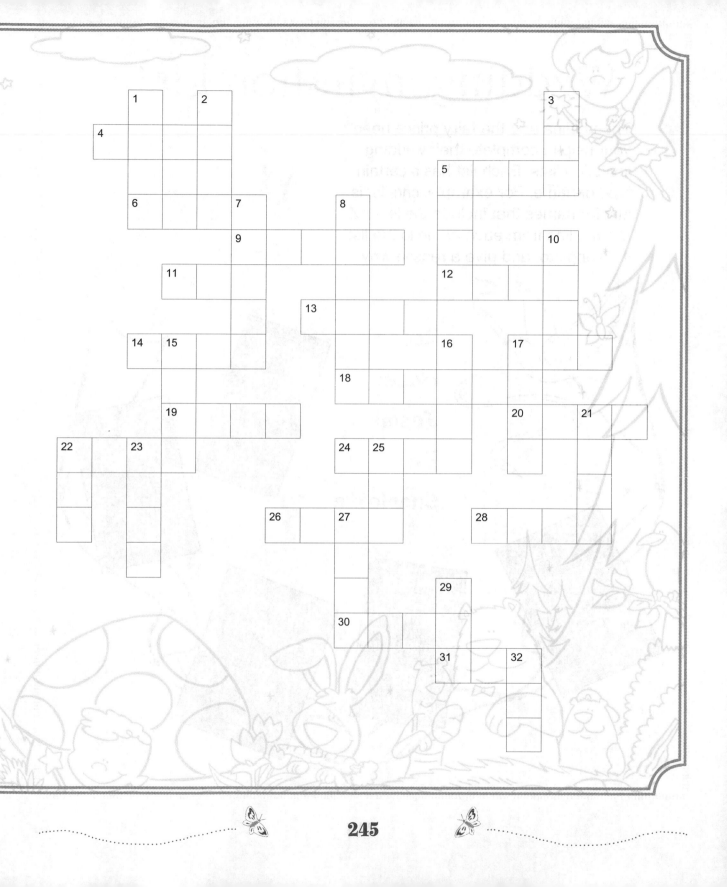

Wedding Invitation Lists

Thumbelina and the fairy prince need your help to complete their wedding invitation lists. Each list has a certain type of name. For example, one list is just for names that include the letter Z. Draw a line from each name to the list it belongs to, and give a reason why.

Reese

Hazel

Jason

Eve

Charlotte

Brook
Isaac
Aaron
Kaylee
Ashlee

Ava
Hannah
Bob
Harrah
Okonoko

Matthew
Garrett
Scott
Brittany
Juliette

Madison
Sonia
Carson
Sonny
Garrison

Elizabeth
Zachary
ZhiRong
Mackenzie
Zane

Puzzle Answers

Page 140 • **The Path to Fairyland**

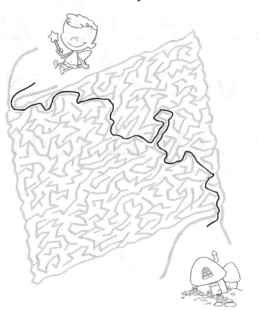

Page 141 • **Butterfly Twins**

Page 142 • **Fairyland Photos**

Page 143 • Fairy Foods

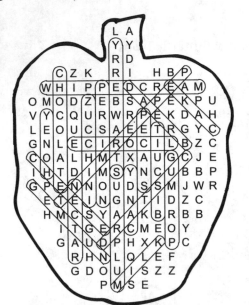

Page 145 • Fairyland Code

ALL THINGS ARE
POSSIBLE IN
FAIRYLAND!

Page 144 • Fairy Hill

Page 146 • Fairyland Plants & Animals

1) BUMBLEBEE
2) BUTTERFLY
3) DUCK
4) FLOWER
5) FROG
6) MUSHROOM
7) SNAIL
8) BIRD
9) RACCOON
10) TREE

Puzzle Answers

Page 147 • **Fairyland Plants & Animals**

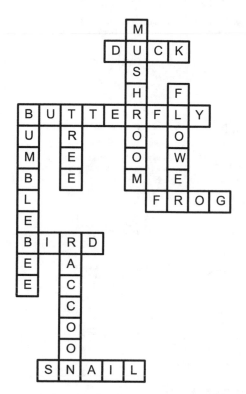

Page 149 • **Triangle Mushrooms**

least

even

seven

most

Page 148 • **The Language of Fairyland**

A playground for a toothy ocean animal is a:
SHARK PARK

A rodent abode is a:
MOUSE HOUSE

A birthday treat for a scaly friend is a:
SNAKE CAKE

A utensil to eat a dried plum is a:
PRUNE SPOON

Page 150 • **Fairyland Riddles**

Tree

Apple

Page 152 • **Directions Home**

D) U, R, R, D, R, R, U, U, U, L, L, U

Page 153 • **Fairy Dust Letters**

PORCUPINE
LEOPARD
HORSE
RHINOCEROS
RACCOON
ZEBRA
RABBIT
ELEPHANT
GIRAFFE
CAMEL

GERBIL
CHEETAH
CHIPMUNK
JAGUAR
HEDGEHOG
HAMSTER
HIPPOPOTAMUS
TIGER
DOLPHIN
COYOTE

Page 154 • **Magical Changes**

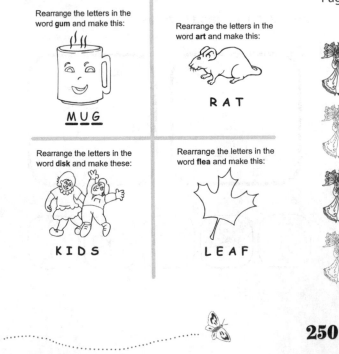

Rearrange the letters in the word **gum** and make this: MUG

Rearrange the letters in the word **art** and make this: RAT

Rearrange the letters in the word **disk** and make these: KIDS

Rearrange the letters in the word **flea** and make this: LEAF

Page 155 • **Magical Changes**

Rearrange the letters in the word **fowl** and make this: WOLF

Rearrange the letters in the word **lamp** and make this: PALM

Rearrange the letters in the word **hose** and make this: SHOE

Rearrange the letters in the word **loop** and make this: POOL

Rearrange the letters in the word **grin** and make this: RING

Rearrange the letters in the word **laces** and make this: SCALE

Page 156 • **Whose Wand?**

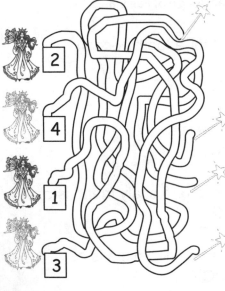

Page 157 • **Break the Spell**

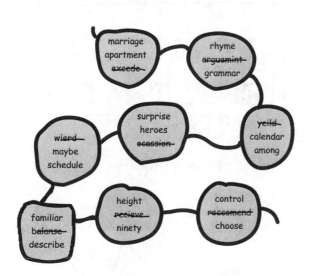

Page 159 • **Cinderella's Magic Time**

Page 158 • **Cinderella's Glass Slipper**

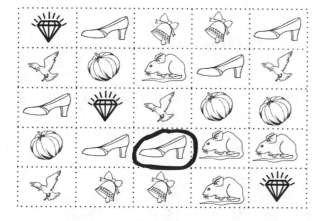

Page 160 • **Riddles**

Why is six afraid of seven?
Because seven eight nine!

What clothing does a house wear?
Address!

What is in the middle of Paris?
The letter R!

What happens when an egg laughs?
It cracks up!

What month has 28 days?
All of them!

What has four legs but only one foot?
A bed!

Page 162 • What's Next?

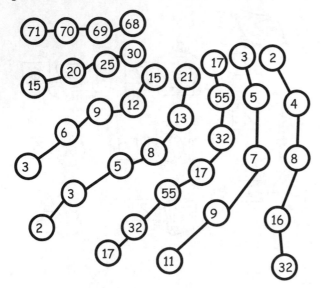

Page 165 • A Flower Fairy Christmas

POINSETTIA

Page 165 • Flowery Dividers

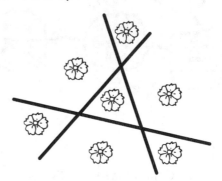

Page 164 • Flower Maze

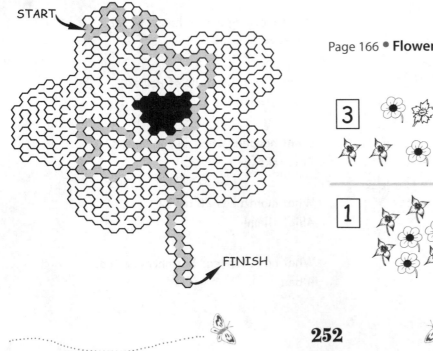

Page 166 • Flower Values

Puzzle Answers

Page 167 • The Flower Fairy Garden

1. WATER
2. CORN
3. HOE
4. BUGS
5. SEEDS
6. TOPSOIL
7. NOSE

Page 168 • Smart Shopper

Daisies
1 dozen for $18 ($1.50 each, **best buy!**)
5 for $8 ($1.60 each)

Marigolds
$2.75 each (**best buy!**)
OR
5 for $14 ($2.80 each)

Roses
7 for $7.70 ($1.10 each)
OR
20 for $21 ($1.05 each, **best buy!**)

Tulips
half dozen for $9 ($1.50 each, **best buy!**)
OR
2 for $3.50 ($1.75 each)

Carnations
8 for $10 ($1.25 each)
OR
3 for $3.45 ($1.15 each, **best buy!**)

The **roses** are the cheapest flower of all.

Page 169 • Ower Words

ROWER
SNOW BLOWER
TOWER
SHOWER
LAWN MOWER

Page 170 • Flower Riddles

A. Vegetable found in a pod.
P E A
17 18 20

B. What do you do on a chair?
S I T
16 14 9

C. A place for coats.
C L O S E T
3 21 11 12 2 19

D. Something with four legs.
T A B L E
13 4 1 10 7

E. Clubs, diamonds, hearts, and spades.
S U I T S
6 5 8 15 22

1D	2C	3C	4D	5E	6E	7D		8E	9B
B	E	C	A	U	S	E		I	T
10D	11C	12C	13D		14B	15E	16B		
L	O	S	T		I	T	S		
17A	18A	19C	20A	21C	22E				
P	E	T	A	L	S	!			

If April showers bring May flowers, what do May flowers bring? **Pilgrims**

253

Puzzle Answers

Page 171 • Flower Equations

Page 173 • Flower Fairy Delivery

Page 172 • Flowery Search

Page 174 • Fractured Flowers

254

Pages 176-177 • Antique Books

Page 178 • Three Bears' Bingo

17 + 3 = 20
11 + 11 = 22
11 + 17 + 8 = 36
9 + 8 + 7 = 24
33 + 28 + 33 = 94
82 - 4 = 78
93 - 9 = 84
78 - 11 = 67
56 ÷ 8 = 7
10 X 5 = 50
5 X 9 = 45
34 ÷ 2 = 17
26 ÷ 13 = 2
4 X 11 = 44
90 ÷ 9 = 10
27 - 8 = 19
10 + 20 + 7 = 37
25 ÷ 5 = 5
37 - 26 = 11
2 X 7 = 14

Mama Bear wins!

Page 179 • Rapunzel's Hair Connection

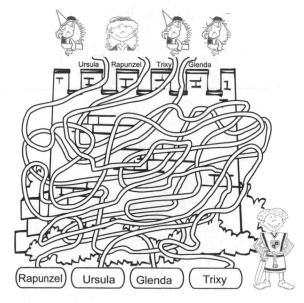

Puzzle Answers

Page 180 • **Mother Goose Words**

Here are some of the words that can be made with the letters in MOTHER GOOSE:

gee, gem, germ, get, ghost, go, gore, gosh, got, greet, groom, he, her, here, hero, hoe, hog, horse, hose, host, hot, me, meet, mere, mesh, met, meter, moose, more, most, moth, motor, oh, or, ore, other, remote, reset, rest, room, roost, root, rot, see, seem, set, she, sheet, shoe, shoot, shore, short, shot, smooth, so, some, sore, sort, steer, stem, store, storm, tee, teem, term, the, them, theme, there, these, those, three, to, toe, too, tore, tree

You might have found others. More words can be made by adding letters to these words.

Page 181 • **The Prince's Real Clothes**

Page 182 • **Hansel & Gretel**

Page 183 • **The Gingerbread House**

Page 184 • **The Three Little Pigs**

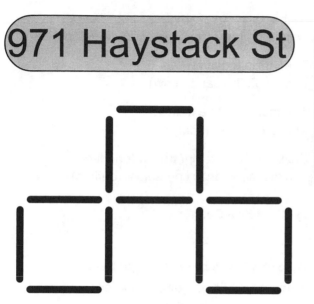

971 Haystack St

6,000 bricks are needed.
(2 X 10 X 300 = 6,000)

Page 186 • **Wedding Bells**

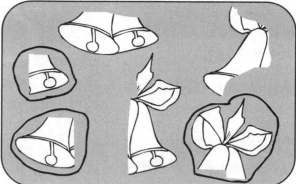

Page 185 • **The Princess and the Pea**

Page 186 • **The End. . .**

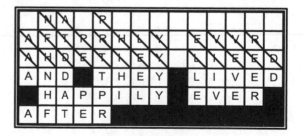

Puzzle Answers

Page 188 • **Latin Unicorn**

one wheel: UNICYCLE
one outfit: UNIFORM
together as one: UNITED
one sound: UNISON

a type of horn: CORNUCOPIA

Page 189 • **Secret Message**

If you'll believe in me, I'll believe in you.

Page 189 • **Unicorn Healers**

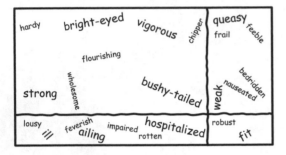

Page 190 • **Horse Barn**

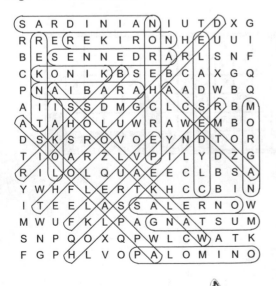

Page 191 • **Hidden Horns**

Rather than have a big wedding, the eleph**ant elope**d with his bride. (antelope)

The melodi**c ow**l played trumpet in the band. (cow)

The monkey ate a man**go at**op the house. (goat)

Suzy has been a film **buff a lo**ng time and loves romantic comedies. (buffalo)

Page 191 • **Be a Deer**

A deer's horns are called _**antlers**_. They are made of _**bone**_ and are shed and regrown each _**year**_.

Pages 192 • **The Unicorn Trio**

Ullric

4:03

Ulysses

4:18

Umberto

4:23

The unicorn with three repeated letters in his name will deliver a letter for the princess. Who is it?

Ulysses

The unicorn whose name has all the letters in the word **TURBO** will pull the princess's carriage. Who is it?

Umberto

An even number of letters is in the name of the unicorn who will find a lost lamb for the princess. Who is it?

Ullric

Page 193 • **Lunch Time!**

<u>**Ullric**</u>   **Umberto**   **Ulysses**

Page 193 • **Better Barns**

<u>**Ullric**</u>   **Umberto**   **Ulysses**

Page 194 • **Shadow of a Unicorn**

Page 194 • **Unicorn Twin**

Page 195 • **Maiden's Song**

Page 196 •Portrait of a Unicorn

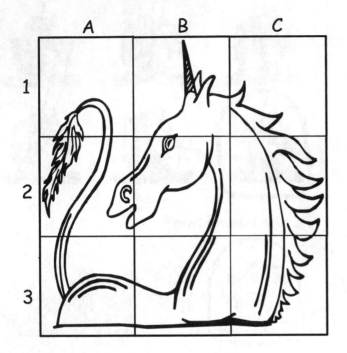

	A	B	C
1			
2			
3			

Page 198 •Going Up

2	31	64	79	75	94	37	69	19	72	99
22	6	66	56	45	55	67	43	45	54	96
86	34	76	62	66	67	73	75	77	87	90
80	31	75	60	19	81	59	96	94	86	84
48	35	65	55	53	50	36	18	10	92	50
22	33	31	61	60	49	71	14	84	30	69
11	91	66	42	85	45	44	43	41	39	81
10	97	51	33	85	10	40	55	70	38	87
9	15	19	22	25	54	54	16	25	36	72
7	20	25	33	28	29	30	31	33	35	71
1	21	19	45	47	55	56	57	59	63	65

Page 200 • **Tooth Fairy Animal**

$$\underline{\text{M}}_{1} \quad \underline{\text{O}}_{2} \quad \underline{\text{U}}_{3} \quad \underline{\text{S}}_{4} \quad \underline{\text{E}}_{5}$$

Page 200 • **Baby Teeth**

```
   3 number of colors in the U.S. flag
-  2 number of cups in a pint
+ 60 number of seconds in a minute
-  4 even number between 2 and 5
- 25 number of cents in a quarter
- 12 number of inches in a foot
```
= 20 total number of baby teeth

Page 201 • **A Healthy Smile**

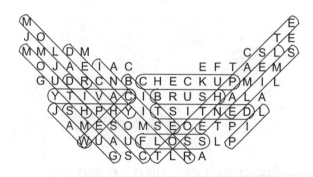

Page 202 • **Sweet Tooth**

Page 203 • **A Good Deal**

25 cents X 8 teeth = $2.00

$.01 + $.02 + $.04 + $.08 + $.16 + $.32
+ $.64 + $1.28 = **$2.55, the best deal!**

Page 203 • **Fast Fairy**

7 minutes X 19 teeth = 133 minutes
133 minutes = 2 hours 13 minutes
11:24 p.m. + 2 hours 13 minutes =
1:37 a.m.

Page 204 • **Step by Step**

Step 1: TOOT
Step 2: ROOT
Step 3: RAT
Step 4: CAT
Step 5: COAT
Step 6: COLT
Step 7: COIN

Page 206 • **Chewed Up Words**

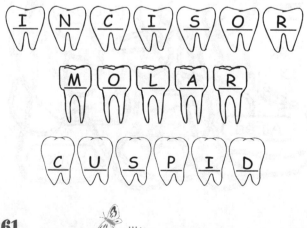

Puzzle Answers

Page 207 • Pillow Search

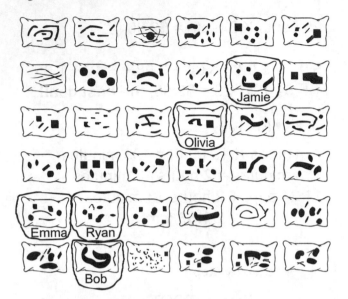

Page 208 • Pulling Teeth

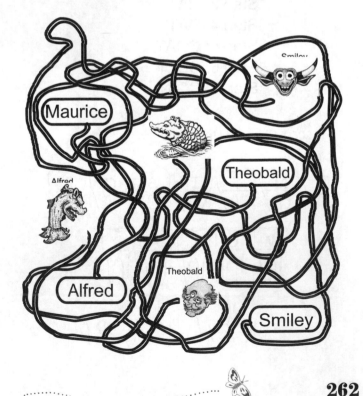

Page 209 • Smart Riddle

A. Horse feet

H O O F S
4 9 17 12 6

B. It gets wetter the more it dries

T O W E L
19 11 13 20 8

C. Found under a tree on a sunny day

S H A D E
15 23 7 16 21

D. A drink made with leaves

T E A
22 3 5

E. Black____: one who works with a hammer and anvil

S M I T H
1 18 14 10 2

1E S	2E H	3D E		4A H	5D A	6A S	
7C A		8B L	9A O	10E T		11B O	12A F
13B W	14E I	15C S	16C D	17A O	18E M		
19B T	20B E	21C E	22D T	23C H			

Baby teeth are also known as:
MILK teeth

262

Page 212 • **Fairy Friend**

Page 213 • **Goblin Numbers**

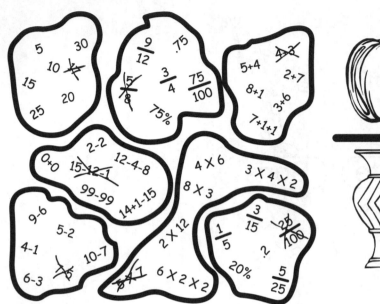

Page 214 • **Gremlin's Half Spell**

Page 215 • **Dwarf Shoppers**

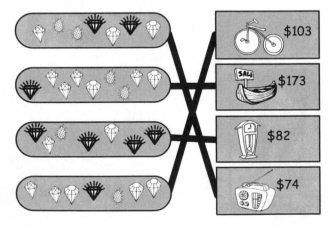

Page 216 • Creature Acrostics

(D) I C E
(R) O U N D
(A) C O R N
(G) E C K O
(O) V E N
(N) E E D L E

(E) A R T H
(L) A U G H
(F) L O W E R

(T) A B L E
(R) A I N
(O) C E A N
(L) E A F
(L) O C K

(G) L O V E
(N) O S E
(O) N E
(M) A S K
(E) A R

Page 218 • Lucky Four-Leaf Clovers

Page 219 • Elf Cards

Smarty   Jolly   Arty

Page 220 • Mathmagical Dragon

This explanation uses algebra:
Step 1. n = your number
Step 2. 3n + 3
Step 3. 2(3n + 3) + 30 = 6n + 36
Step 4. (6n + 36)/6 = n + 6
Step 5. n + 6 — n = 6

Page 221 • **Fairy People**

Page 222 • **Logical Leprechaun**

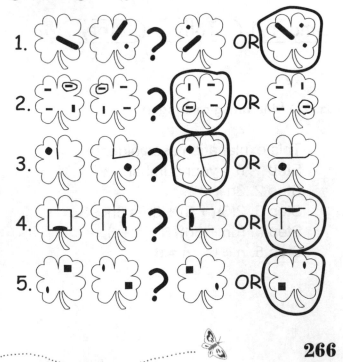

Page 224 • **Making Pinochio**

2 hats X 5 shirts X 3 pants = **30** combinations of hats, shirts, and pants.

Gepetto must take out **4** socks from the drawer to guarantee that at least two of them match.

Page 224 • **A Heart from the Blue Fairy**

Page 225 • **Pinochio's Journey**

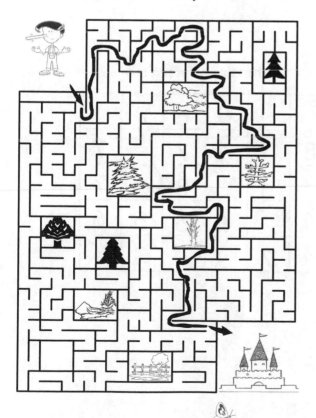

Page 226 • **Animal Alphabet**

Here are some answers for this puzzle. You may have found others.

A Animals: Aardvark Alligator Ape
B Animals: Baboon Bat Bear Beaver Bird Bunny
C Animals: Camel Cat Chameleon Cheetah Chicken Cow Coyote Crab Crocodile
D Animals: Deer Dog Dolphin Donkey Duck
E Animals: Eagle Eel Elephant
F Animals: Falcon Fish Flamingo Fox Frog
G Animals: Gazelle Gecko Giraffe Goat Goose Gorilla Groundhog Guinea Pig
H Animals: Hen Hippopotamus Horse
I Animals: Iguana
J Animals: Jackal Jaguar Jellyfish
K Animals: Kangaroo Kiwi Koala Bear Kookaburra
L Animals: Lamb Leopard Lion Lizard Llama Lobster
M Animals: Monkey Moose Mouse
O Animals: Octopus Orangutan Ostrich Owl Ox
P Animals: Panda Panther Parrot Penguin Pig
Q Animals: Quail
R Animals: Rabbit Raccoon Rattlesnake Rhinoceros
S Animals: Seal Shark Sheep Skunk Snake Squirrel
T Animals: Tiger Tortoise Turkey Turtle
W Animals: Walrus Weasel Whale Wolf
Z Animals: Zebra

Puzzle Answers

Page 227 • Puppet Shows

Page 228 • Candy Counter

Ray has __1__ pieces of candy.

Frank has __3__ pieces of candy.

Steve has __4__ pieces of candy.

Justin has __2__ pieces of candy.

Page 229 • Magic Squares

4	3	8
9	5	1
2	7	6

8	1	6
3	5	7
4	9	2

6	7	2
1	5	9
8	3	4

6	1	8
7	5	3
2	9	4

16	3	2	13
5	10	11	8
9	6	7	12
4	15	14	1

4	5	9	16
15	10	6	3
14	11	7	2
1	8	12	13

Page 230 • The Field of Wonders

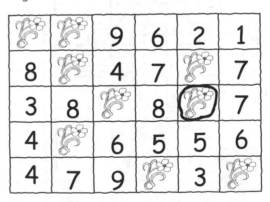

Page 231 • Tell the Truth

Andrew has 38¢
"The boys have more money than the girls."

Olivia has 76¢
"All of the kids together have a total of $3.36"

Matthew has 62¢
"Emma has more money than Andrew and Jacob combined."

Samantha has 25¢
"The kids with 6 letters in their names have a total of $1.14"

Jacob has 47¢
"All combined, the girls have an even number of cents."

Emma has 88¢
"The person with the least amount of money is a boy."

A school lunch costs 22¢

Page 232 • Fishing for Father

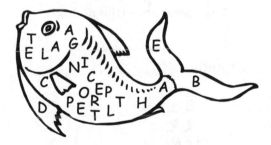

Page 232 • Back to the Blue Fairy

Pinocchio just needs to swim 2 miles south to find land.

Page 233 • Changes

There are many possible solutions. Here are our answers:

WIRE	TOE
WISE	DOE
WISH	DOG
FISH	
	HORSE
BALL	HOUSE
BAWL	MOUSE
BOWL	MOOSE
BOWS	GOOSE
COWS	
	RICE
PAPER	RIDE
TAPER	RUDE
TAMER	RULE
TIMER	MULE
TIGER	

Page 234 • Geppetto's New Coat

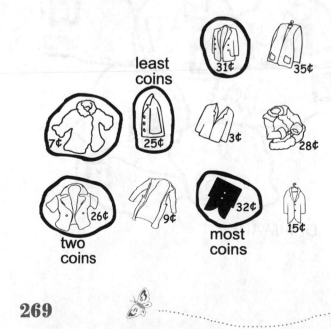

least coins

31¢

35¢

7¢

25¢

3¢

28¢

26¢

two coins

9¢

32¢

most coins

15¢

Page 236 • Magic Seeds

Page 237 • Thumbelina's Country

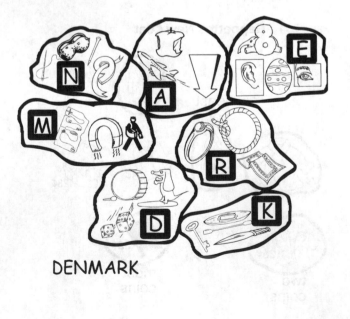

DENMARK

Page 238 • Memories

__TRUE__ There is a paddle with the kayak.

__TRUE__ The egg is decorated.

__FALSE__ There is an earring on the ear.

__TRUE__ There is a ribbon through a nine.

__FALSE__ The rug is laid out completely flat.

__FALSE__ The dog is standing on one leg.

__FALSE__ The arrow is pointing up.

__TRUE__ There is a key.

__FALSE__ The apple does not have a stem.

__FALSE__ There is a horse with a saddle.

__TRUE__ The nuts have a shell.

__TRUE__ The rope is in a loop.

__FALSE__ There are eight groups of pictures.

__TRUE__ The needle is threaded.

__FALSE__ The magnet has a triangle shape.

Page 238 • Author

8 __H__
1 __A__
14 __N__
19 __S__

3 __C__
8 __H__
18 __R__
9 __I__
19 __S__
20 __T__
9 __I__
1 __A__
14 __N__

1 __A__
14 __N__
4 __D__
5 __E__
18 __R__
19 __S__
5 __E__
14 __N__

Page 239 • **Butterfly Friends**

The digits on a butterfly
multiplied should equal the
sum of the digits on a flower.

Page 240 • **Falling Leaves**

Page 240 • **Mouse House Route**

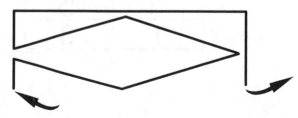

Page 241 • **Escape from Mr. Mole**

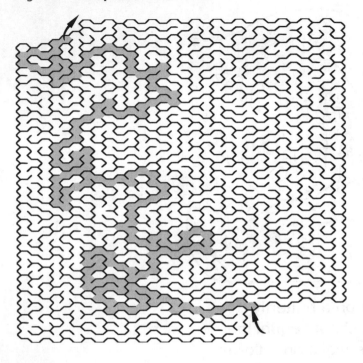

Page 242 • **Carrots and Apples**

	Carrots	Apples
Lake	2	0
Tree House	2	3
Farm	3	5
Castle	1	3

Page 244 • Thumbelina's Crossword

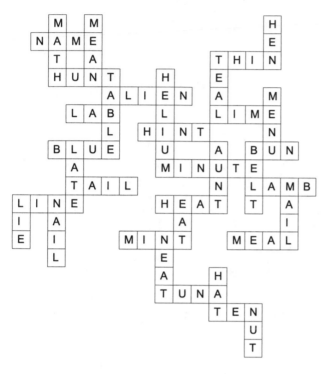

Page 246 • Wedding Invitation Lists

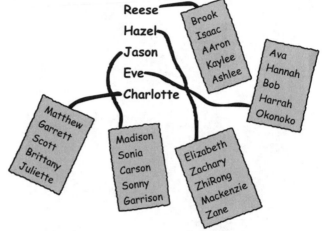

Matthew, Garrett, Scott, Brittany, Juliette, Charlotte: all have TT.

Madison, Sonia, Carson, Sonny, Garrison, Jason: all have SON.

Elizabeth, Zachary, ZhiRong, Mackenzie, Zane, Hazel: all have a Z.

Ava, Hannah, Bob, Harrah, Okonoko, Eve: all are palindromes—they read the same backward or forward.

Brook, Isaac, Aaron, Kaylee, Ashlee, Reese: all have a repeated vowel.

PART 3
The World of Horses

Chapter 19
Horses from the Past

Words to Know

Ancestor

Your *ancestors* are the people who came before you in your family, like your parents, grandparents, and great grandparents. A horse's ancestor is the *Eohippus*.

First Horses

When you see a horse on television stand on its back legs and paw the air with its hooves, would you believe that the horse's ancestors had paws like a dog? If you had been here around 50 million years ago, you could have seen this animal that looked a lot like a dog, was the size of a spaniel and was known as Eohippus. Over time, the horse left those early forests and its paws turned into little hooves that could move easily over grasslands and hard rocks. Many more changes occurred as over time it changed into the horse that scientists today call Equus caballus.

Do you ever look at your cousins and think that they don't look like you at all? One of the horse's relatives is a manatee, an animal that looks like a walrus and lives in the ocean! A rhinoceros is more like a horse than the hippopotamus, whose name means "water horse." Can you think of other animals that aren't what they seem to be? Even though a panda looks like one, it is not a bear, and many people don't believe a

Switch the vowels around to read the end of this silly riddle!

Show me Sir Lancelot's horse...

...und E'll shiw yio u kneght mura!

penguin is a bird! Have you ever seen a picture of a platypus? It has a bill like a duck, a tail like a paddle, and webbed feet with claws on them. It lays eggs and nurses its young like a mother horse does!

Following the Trail

Many people believe the first horses horse originated in the Rocky Mountains of the United States. Many ancient horse fossils (animal bones that have turned into stone) have been found from Florida to California and also in other parts of the world. Almost 8,000 years ago, horses disappeared in North America and were not seen again until explorers from Europe brought them back to their original home on their journeys. Some scientists believe glaciers moving down from the North Pole forced the horses to look for better places to live.

Some of the horses traveled by land down into South America while others trotted over the land bridge that linked North America to Asia. These horses spread all over Europe, Africa, and Asia and became the ancestors of the wild horses that roamed these continents.

For fun, you and a few of your friends can try to find your way around to several flags hidden in your yard by using clues. You will want to have an adult make up four clues for each team and hide four flags (one color for each team) in the four places. Then each team gets the four clues in a mixed up order and the first team to return with all four flags of their team's color wins.

Try This

Mixing it up on the Trail

You can make trail mix using one cup of each of the following things: raisins, peanuts, coated candies, and marshmallows. Or you can mix it up a little by adding things like granola, chocolate chips, popcorn, cereal, butterscotch chips, and candy corn. Then, all that is left to do is place it in a plastic bag or container.

Words to Know

Eohippus

Eohippus was believed to be the first real horse. Fossils from this very small skeleton were found over a hundred years ago and are believed to be around 50 million years old.

Horses in Caves

Imagine you are exploring a cave in Europe and when you look up you see the walls are covered with paintings of horses. Once one cave filled with paintings of horses was found, cave paintings of other horses were discovered. People living in the caves made these paintings, which didn't look anything like stick horses. The horses in their art closely resembled the types of horses that still roam the countryside today. Scientists had known there were many types of wild horses living in different parts of Europe thousands of years ago from the fossils they had found, but now because of the cave paintings, they had even more proof the horses had existed. Scientists are uncertain if the pictures were painted to show the caveman's admiration for the horse's beauty or to record how successful their hunting had been that day.

You can try your hand at painting or drawing horses and see if they if they resemble the paintings in the caves. There are several books that show what kinds of horses there are. Then, ask an adult if you can use poster paint or chalk to draw on the sidewalk. If you make a picture that you really like, see if you can paint a second copy of it on paper or have someone take a picture of it and then hang it in your room. Be daring! Your paintings don't have to look like actual horses. Maybe you can develop a new kind of horse. Try mixing stripes with polka dots or make a horse with a tail like a bunny or even a horse with horns!

What am I?

You might expect me to wear stars and stripes or maybe hold a cone. My milky white color might give me away. **What am I?**

American Cream Draft

Famous Horses

Have you ever heard of a nebula? It's a group of stars in the sky and one of them is called the Horsehead nebula because of its unusual shape! You might be wondering, "How do ordinary horses become famous?" They can win horse races or have children that do and then their name is listed in racing books forever or they might have someone make a movie about them like *Seabiscuit*. Pegasus is a winged horse from Greek mythology that has a horse-shaped constellation named after him. A horse can become famous by being the star in a movie like *My Friend Flicka* or become a star's best friend like Gene Autry's horse, Champion. Maybe you have seen the Crazy Horse Monument in South Dakota. This statue, made out of a mountaintop, is really named after its rider more than the horse!

Sometimes horses are famous just because they survived: Comanche is well-known because he was the only animal that was found alive after Custer's Last Stand (which was also known as the Battle of Little Big Horn). Famous horses have also appeared in comic books, coloring books, and cartoons.

If you like collecting things you could start a collection box of horse items like coloring books, souvenirs of famous horses, or places you visit.

Storybook Horses

Can you imagine the handsome prince being able to charm Sleeping Beauty if he hadn't come to the castle on a beautiful horse? Would Cinderella have won the prince's heart if mice instead of horses had been pulling her coach? King Arthur and the Knights of the Round Table may not have won battles if they weren't all riding horses.

If you would like to see how everything looked at the time of fairy tales, you could see if someone will take you to a Renaissance Fair. At some of these fairs they have a miniature knight area where you can practice riding horses and slaying dragons.

Try This

A Game of Horse

You will need two people, a basketball, chalk, and a hoop. First write the letter H seven feet out from the left of the hoop. The O, R, S, and E follow, with the R straight out from the middle and the E to the right of the hoop. Who can make the shots from all five letters first?

⊔ ⊔ ⊔ ⊔   ⊔ ⊔ ⊔ ⊔

What am I?

You may need a magnifying glass to find me if you believe my name. Many of my breed are closer to the size of a dog than a horse.

What am I?

Miniature Horse

Try This

Make a Motion Picture

Take about ten index cards and glue on each one a picture of a horse standing or moving in a different way. Staple the cards together on the left side and flip them really fast. Watch the horse pictures while you are doing this. Does it look like the horse is moving?

Maybe you would like to have your own fair and invite all your friends. You could ride stick ponies, joust a piñata, have an archery contest with suction cup arrows and apples, do face painting, and make paper crowns.

If you don't want to hold a fair, you can still test your skill at jousting by seeing if you can knock a watermelon or basketball off a bucket with a water noodle while riding your bike. The Knights knew the importance of armor while riding, so remember to put on your helmet and knee pads before going out to battle the watermelon.

Let's Go to the Movies

Horses are so important that many plays, books, and movies have been written about them. You may have read a few of these stories like *Black Beauty* and *National Velvet*, or seen the movie versions of these stories.

The very first motion pictures were made in the 1870s and they showed a running horse! The first movies that told a story were developed in the early 1900s; they were only in black and white and had no sound, so they needed lots of action. Some of them were called Westerns or "horse operas" because they featured horses.

Horses were an important part of everyone's lives and people liked to watch them run, so there were lot of chase scenes. Just like in the moving pictures of today, there was usually a pretty girl, a hero, and a bad guy. There was no doubt who the bad guy was because he always rode a black horse. You probably have seen some of these old movies on your television.

Many of the horses in these movies are more famous than their riders! Have you heard of The Lone Ranger, Tonto,

Movie Madness

Can you put these frames from an old Western movie in order? The result is a very silly scene!

Gene Autry, and Roy Rogers? Probably not. You probably have heard of Roy's famous horse, Trigger, or the riders talking or singing to their horses: "Hi-Yo, Silver," "Get 'em up, Scout," "Happy Trails to You," or "I'm Back in the Saddle Again."

Many horses that were in old Western movies were trained to do special tricks to make the audience think that the horses were much smarter than they really were. A good way to see some of these horses in action is to rent some tapes or DVDs from your library or video store. Why not make some popcorn and watch, pretending you are back in time, when horses and their owners ruled the West?

Words to Know

Saddle

A *saddle* is a special seat designed to allow a rider to sit on the back of a horse. Saddles are made of leather and use cinches or girths to keep them from coming off the horse.

The Old West

Have you ever taken a hike in a state park or followed a path that deer made as they searched the woods for food? You might find it difficult to walk through the woods. When the frontier was just a little ways past Pennsylvania, horses and their riders were responsible for widening those natural trails to open up the new land. Before long, they were leading pack mules to carry food and other things to the settlers.

If you ever get the chance to travel to the Grand Canyon, you can ride a mule, just like the ones the settlers used, all the way down the canyon trails to the river. The gold miners in 1849 rode donkeys and led pack mules. If you were going to look for gold today, what do you think you would need to take along? You might want to pack a canteen, some dried foods, and a few candy bars. Prospectors today still look for treasure, but they often use metal detectors and jeeps rather than horses. Why don't you ask your family if they will draw a map and bury some toys and sealed containers of food, so you can ask your friends to go on a treasure hunt with you?

Famous Riders

Have you ever heard the poem, "The Midnight Ride of Paul Revere"? Paul and his faithful horse warned the soldiers in the first colonies to take up arms against their enemies. Other famous riders were the first mail delivery people known as the Pony Express riders. There were close to a hundred of these mail carriers on horseback and they brought letters across the country through the rain, the snow, and the dark of night. Would you like to deliver mail using a horse?

Pony Express

START with this letter in Missouri and see how quickly you can deliver it to the END in California!

START

Missouri

END

California

What am I?

The first part of my name might be right on the tip of your tongue or the outside of your mouth. I love to travel all over the world showing off my skills as a jumper and performer. Like a chameleon, I change color over time. **What am I?**

Lipizzaner

Try This

Travel Bingo

If you want to keep track of the animals you see on a trip, you can make your own wildlife bingo cards before you start on your way. You might want to add other things like a train, tunnels, and state capitals.

Riding to Win

When you first learned how to ride a bike, what did you think about? Probably, you concentrated on just being able to stay on your bike so it wouldn't throw you to the ground. Then you possibly thought about how much farther you could go on your bike rather than walking. The first horse riders had those same feelings.

Many years ago, a king's battles were fought by foot soldiers, but they could travel only a few miles. After people had tamed the horse and mastered riding it, they felt they could conquer the world! The movie *Ben-Hur* shows the Romans using horse-drawn chariots to fight their battles. Genghis Khan, Alexander the Great, Napoleon, and many other rulers rode their famous horses, which allowed them to control countries and continents that they never could have reached before.

The Wild West

People used to call the West wild back in the days when millions of buffalo and herds of horses used to roam it. Some say the earth shook when the buffalo started to stampede! Today a few of the parks in the West still raise buffalo herds and the park staff will sometimes let visitors watch them being round up in the fall the same way they do with cattle. If you are able to take a vacation to a park, you might be lucky enough to see a buffalo, an elk, a moose, a horse, or other wild animals.

A man called Buffalo Bill Cody used to shoot the buffalo for food for the men who were building the railroad. Eventually, he bought a ranch and developed a Wild West show that traveled all over North America and parts of Europe. The show even included outlaws on horses, which were part of what made the West so wild! These outlaws were known for riding horses while they were holding up trains, stagecoaches, and banks. Some of these horses could be ridden for a hundred miles in a day, which made it easy for the outlaws to make their escape. The performers in the show had to practice shooting all of the time. If you want to do a little Wild West shooting practice of your own, how about shooting a few empty soda cans or paper cups off of a fence with a water pistol?

Fun Fact

The Life of A Horse
Do you know the average life span of a horse? Most of them live to be around twenty to twenty-five years old, while some horses can live over half of a century.

Generally Speaking

All over the world you will find horse statues; most towns or parks have at least one. When you travel you can look for these statues and have your friends do the same thing. See if you and your friends can mark where you found these statues on a map of the country. Each of you should put the first letter of your name by each town. Once the summer is over, total up the number of each person's letters. The winner should get a prize!

Famous generals often have famous horses. One of the most famous horses in the civil war was Traveller, who was a gray horse ridden by General Robert E. Lee. Have your parents ever taken you to see the battle sites in Gettysburg, Pennsylvania? There are statues of generals on their horses everywhere. Some people believe that however many hooves the horse's statue has on the ground tells whether the general who was riding the horse was hurt or killed in the battle. Many times, a horse with an empty saddle will be used in a funeral parade for a general or president to indicate that the leader is gone.

From a Pony to a Horse

If you wanted to buy an animal to ride, would you be better off buying a pony or a horse? Some people say that the main difference is their size: A horse is around 14.2 hands high, while a pony is less than that. Did you know that it is common to measure a horse's height using the width of a man's hand? They measure from the top of a horse's withers, or top of its back, down to the ground. Checking the height of a person in the same way that we check a horse's height would mean that you would only measure from the person's shoulders to the floor. Most grownups would be more than fourteen hands, so you could say they were as tall as a horse!

Not all horses are bigger than ponies, though. Falabella horses are miniature horses that are usually less than thirty inches tall, so although they look like regular horses, they would only be a few hands high. Shetland breeds are what people normally picture when they think of ponies. These ponies look short and stout and tough.

Words to Know

Foal

A *foal* is another name for a baby horse. A foal can be a male or a female, but this name only applies as long as the horse is less than one year old.

Giddy Up

Ahead of the Game

As with anything else you ride, it is always important to look ahead of you any time your horse is moving. Looking away, even for a moment, may cause you to overlook a possible problem. If you do need to check on something, it is always best to stop your horse temporarily.

Island Ponies

Have you read the book called *Misty of Chincoteague?* It is the story of two children and their love for a foal and her mother. Every year a roundup is held on Assateague Island, where ponies, like the ones in this story, live. Some people believe that the horses on this island ended up there from a shipwreck. These ponies are herded through the water to nearby Chincoteague Island and sold at auction. Would you like to buy your own island pony? Some people adopt one by sending money to help care for the ponies. When they adopt it they receive information and pictures of their horse!

Shetland ponies get their names from the islands where they were originally found. Shetland ponies weren't always just ridden as a child's pet. For many years, their ancestors pulled carts or little wagons in coal mines.

Miniature Horses

The people who raise miniature horses want to raise tiny horses that are proportioned just the same as a big horse. It is thought that the Europeans brought the original horses to the New World with them. Eventually they escaped into the wild and gradually grew smaller, as the other wild horses did.

Ranchers in South America found the little horses and kept raising smaller and smaller horses from them. Some of them are now less than thirty inches tall so a very small child could ride them, but they are mainly used to pull carts. Have you ever heard of seeing-eye horses? Sometimes miniature horses are used instead of dogs to assist people who cannot see well.

Try This

Barrow Race

Like the Shetland pony, you could have your own wheelbarrow or wagon race. You need two wheelbarrows or two wagons, two people to drive and two people to ride. The object of the game is to see who can cross the finish line first. Try switching drivers and riders to see if the race ends the same way the second time.

What am I?

My name sounds more like a place for a bird to sit rather than a type of horse. One of my main purposes was to help out on the farm.

What am I?

Percheron

Fun Fact

Three Crowns Are Better Than One

A great honor for a racehorse is winning the Triple Crown. The only way to do this is to win the Kentucky Derby, the Preakness, and the Belmont Stakes, all in the same year. Only eleven horses have accomplished this in the last 125 years.

Larger Than Life

Did you ever wonder why there are enormous horses and why anyone would want one? During the Middle Ages, more than 600 years ago, these horses were used to carry armored knights. The knights weren't the only ones who were protected; the horses also wore armor, so they had to be very big and strong. Some of these horses measured between seventeen and eighteen hands or approximately seventy inches. Many years ago people used the length of a man's foot, the distance from the tip of a middle finger to an elbow, the length of a palm, and even their finger as types of measuring sticks. There are three feet in a yard and four inches in a hand, so how many hands would there be in a yard? One way to find out is to make your own stick to measure to see how many hands there are in a yard:

1. Ask your parents if you can have an old wooden yardstick or cloth tape measure.
2. Measure off four inches and write one hand at that mark with a black marking pen.
3. Continue marking hands on the stick or tape. Now measure your height with your new measuring tool. How many hands tall are you?

Tell your friends you want them to guess how tall you are and then see if they can convert it into hands. See who gets the right amount!

Big Enough?

There is no way that this tiny horse can support a full-sized rider! Can you make it bigger? Copy the pattern in each of the small squares into the corresponding big squares. When you are done, this rider will have a horse that is more comfortable!

EXTRA FUN: Use colored pencils to make the finished picture more interesting.

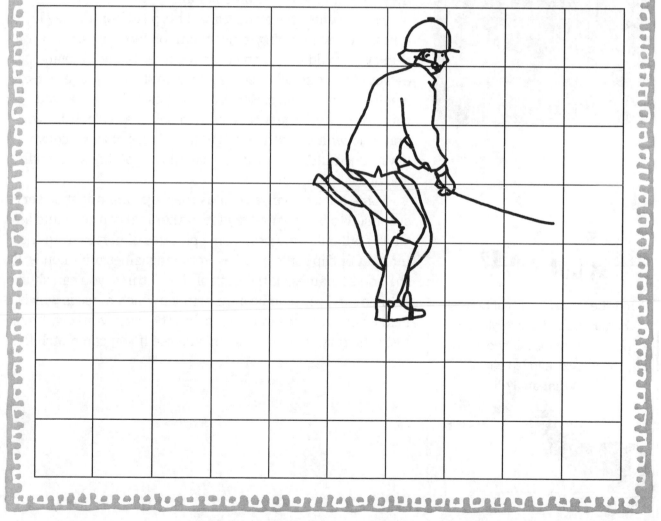

Fun Fact

Itty Bitty Horses

Did you know that the smallest horse in the world is named "Black Beauty?" This tiny horse has made its way into the record books simply by being so small!

I may be one of the finest Spanish horses around, but in Mexico, part of my name might only be worth close to ten cents.

What am I?

Paso Fino

What Kind of Horse Is That?

There are more than a hundred breeds of horses and they vary in size, shape, and color. They also vary in the type of work they do. A breed, like the Morgan, Thoroughbred, or Belgian, is a mixture of horses; there are no purebred horses. Through the years, breeders have thought about what they wanted a horse to do and kept mixing the horses until they got the result they wanted. Now, they try not to vary the breed at all.

Many owners have no idea what type of horses they have, unless they're planning to use them for show horses. Do you think you could tell a pony from a horse? Many Arabian horses would be as small as some ponies and some ponies look just like a small horse. How many colors of horses do you think there are? The most common colors are black, brown, gray, and white, but there are many shades of these colors like bays, chestnuts, sorrels, duns, palominos, perlinos, cremellos, and buckskins.

Some horses change color as they age; you might be very surprised to find that a gray Lipizzaner foal can turn into a white stallion! If you print some pictures of horses from the Internet or clip some pictures from magazines and then write the horses' names on the back of the pictures, you can shuffle them and see if you can remember which horse is which. Before you write the information on the back, you might make two sets, turn them face down, and see if you can match the pictures.

Painted Ponies

When you think of painted ponies, you probably think of a Native American rider on a pinto blending so perfectly into scenery around it that they look like they are wearing camouflage. Maybe you have heard of a breed called the Paint Horse. This unusual horse looks like someone threw a bucket of white paint over its colored coat.

Other horses that look a lot like them are called Piebalds and Skewbalds. Some horses with small spots are called dappled. The roan horse is spotted, but the spots are so close together that they seem to be one color. Appaloosa horses

What am I?

No matter the question on the test, I will never answer false. I am really "wild" about being the last of my kind. **What am I?**

Przewalski's Horse

Hidden Paint

Both Appaloosa horses and Pinto ponies are covered with beautiful spots. But these two horses have more than that—can you find the 16 items that are hiding in the patterns of their coats? Look for an arrow, sock, heart, teacup, bowling pin, car, smoking pipe, fish, mitten, balloon, flower, pine tree, hammer, kite, question mark, and capital H.

many times start out as a horse with a white coat, but as they age they develop spots in different patterns. One of the more interesting color combinations is the Grulla horse. It looks like it has a broad stripe running down its back, with stripes extending down its sides.

If someone says your horse has a snip, star, stripe, or blaze, they are usually talking about white areas on his face. Areas like these on its legs are usually referred to as stockings or socks. Although true painted ponies just look like they are painted, some of the old-time horse traders or racehorse owners really painted ponies. They substituted one horse for another and covered up distinctive markings with real paint to trick the horse's buyer.

Family Trees

The horse is valued very highly by people, even though other members of its family tree like onagers, donkeys, burros, and mules are much better workers and some say even more intelligent. Throughout history, a man's value was judged by the number of horses he had. A reason for this is that horses are expensive and another is that a person riding a horse really could look down on a person walking or riding in a coach. If you want to see how short these walking people seemed to be to a person riding on a horse, you can try riding piggyback on your parent's shoulders.

A Horse in Striped Pajamas

What do you call a horse in striped pajamas? A zebra, of course! Other people have called zebras the referee animal. Can you think of other things or animals that remind you of a zebra? Getting a zebra to work for you is almost impossible, so you rarely see them except in a circus or a zoo. Depending

Try This

Paint A Pony
Would you like to try and make your own painted ponies? Have an adult pick up some refrigerator sugar cookies from the store, cut them into the shape of horses, bake them, and then frost them with different colors of frosting and sprinkles.

Fun Fact

Don't Slurp Your Soup!
Unlike cats and dogs that lap up their water with their tongues, horses drink by sucking the water up into their mouths as though they were using a plastic straw.

Fun Fact

*Do You See
A Pattern to This?*
Each zebra has a different pattern to the stripes that cover its body. No two zebras' stripes are the same, just like no two thumbprints are alike.

on where you live, it might be easier for you to see a zebra in a zoo than a horse grazing in a pasture.

Did you know that there are three kinds of zebras and they all look very different? One has stripes all over its body, another has a light-colored belly, and one has no stripes on its legs. The stripes seem to run in the same direction on its hips, another way on its stomach, and many different directions on the rest of its body. These stripes allow it to hide in the areas of bright sunlight and the dark shadows of the African jungle. Now that you know not all zebras look the same, you may want to start your own collection of zebra photos from the different zoos you visit, then you can sort them into the three groups.

Try This

Safari Slumber Party
Have a striped pajama party where you eat striped food like chocolate and vanilla pudding cups, paint your faces like different animals, and camp out on the floor.

Tons of Things You Can Do with a Horse

Do you ever wonder what people do with their horses after they buy them? Many people take classes to learn how to become better at competing at horse shows and other events. Others learn how to play games at gymknana (horse sporting competitions) like pole bending and barrel racing. If you decide to compete at these games, there are many rodeos and special local and international gymknana events that you can enter.

Some people describe pole bending in gymkhana as being like skiing in a slalom race. You and your horse twist and turn around poles, cutting as close to them as you can, hoping to finish in the shortest amount of time. Some riders join drill teams and learn how to perform maneuvers in a group.

If you play polo, you'll be riding a horse while you swing a mallet at a ball. The horses move at a fast rate around many other players in this ancient game. Do you know someone who has a croquet set? Try playing it, using the usual croquet rules. Then you could try playing it using in-line skates or using a scooter to see how playing polo might feel.

Careers with Horses

Would you like to spend the rest of your life working with horses? If you decide that just riding a horse for fun doesn't let you spend as much time with a horse as you would like to, it's time to talk to an adult that you can trust and start planning how you can work around horses for your career. If you want to be around racing horses, you probably should get a job as a groom. In the beginning you might spend time cleaning out stalls or polishing the metal on the horse's harness. If you sign on as an apprentice, you pay for your education with the work that you do. You'll be doing everything

Words to Know

Rodeo
One type of competition for cowboys and horses is called a *rodeo*. At a rodeo, you can see everything from riders riding a bucking wild horse (called a bronco) until they are thrown off (called "bronco busting") to barrel racing.

Fun Fact

Put to Work
What if a football coach asked you to go onto the field and stamp on the chunks of grass the players had dug up with their spiked shoes? At a polo match, they ask the crowd to replace grass that the horses tear out of the ground with their hooves!

Words to Know

Harness

A horse's *harness* is a combination of devices or objects that are used to control the horse and connect it to the carriage, wagon, or plow that it is going to pull.

with a horse and can learn the good and bad things about the business.

If you decide to follow the rodeo circuit you could attend a few rodeos and ask them if you can give them any type of help that is needed. You might be surprised at how many hours they practice, polishing their roping and riding skills, and caring for the horses that help them. How about asking a farrier or blacksmith if you can watch them while they work for a few days?

If you like helping people, you can go on the Internet or consult your library to see if there are jobs for police officers or rangers on horseback that are located near your home.

Horse Work

There are many careers that would allow you to work with horses. Can you fit these seven into the grid? We left a few O-A-T-S to help you out.

FARRIER   VET

STEWARD   GROOM

ARTIST   COWBOY

JOCKEY

Going to the Fair

Have you ever wanted to learn how to braid hair? It can be a lot of fun if you want to practice on your friends. Some people make pigtails, French braids, or even just one big braid down the back of their heads. Many horses have their manes and their tails braided when they are going to a horse show or the fair. There is usually a certain way that it must be done for many of the events.

You don't want to make the mistake of braiding your horse's mane and tail only when you take them to the fair or a show. If you do that, they will link the braiding with taking a trip and get too excited because they know something special is going to happen!

Have you ever been to a state fair? There are many events for a wide variety of horses. If you can't actually go to the fair, some public television stations broadcast portions of the fair. You might want to watch to see how many of the horses have their hair braided for the show.

Many horse terms have the same name that can mean more than one thing. If your horse was plaiting, you might think he was braiding his own hair, but in horse language, you're describing a horse that crosses its hoof in front of its other hoof!

The Open Trail

Have you ever wished that you could spend some time alone, just you and your horse? Many people decide that a trail ride is the best way to do this, but the old rule about riding your bicycle is also good for horse riding: Never ride any farther than you can walk back! Never take a trail ride alone, especially one that is not used by a lot of people. The best horse can jump away from what it thinks is a snake and leave you sitting on the ground. One of the best places for a beginning rider to be is on a trail with a professional guide.

Try This

Be a Rodeo Clown

To pretend to be a rodeo clown, paint your face and put on some brightly colored clothes. Then have your friends pretend to be bulls. Give each one of them sticky circles, made out of doublestick tape and paper, and see who is the first one that is able to leave their "mark" on you.

Fun Fact

Walking On Air

When a horse canters or gallops, there is a time that all four of their feet are off the ground at the same time. Do you think this might have been where the term "flying horse" may have started?

To find a trail that is close to you, look in the telephone book or go on the Internet. There are many trails located in cities. You can even go trail riding in Central Park in New York City! Some pony clubs and 4-H clubs organize trail rides.

You could also go to a horse ranch in the mountains for a vacation. Many horses spend all day out on the trails at ranches giving rides to both children and adults. Some of these ranches are called dude ranches. A lot of ranches let you care for your horse so you can learn if owning a horse is what you really want to do. If you're feeling really adventurous, you could go with an adult on a trekking trip. Some groups take you out and let you ride a horse during the day and camp out every night for about a week.

Giddy Up

Together Is Better

For safety's sake, it is always best to go riding with a buddy. Two heads are usually better than one and you never know when something may "spook" your horse, possibly leaving you in need of a ride home.

Chapter 21

Caring for Your Horse

Words to Know

Veterinarian

An animal doctor is called a *veterinarian*. A veterinarian can specialize in caring for small animals or big animals like horses. Veterinarians are one of the few types of doctors that still make house calls.

Giddy Up

Staying a Step Ahead

When you are riding horses for competition or events, always remember to wear a helmet. If you are riding a bicycle, motorcycle, or four-wheeler, protection for your head should always be at the top of your safety checklist.

Horse Care from A-Z

One of the big questions about horses is how can you find out whether buying a horse is the right thing for you to do? If you aren't already taking riding lessons at a stable, it would be a good idea to start them and let your teacher know that you are willing to do all the care for your horse. Ask the person who is teaching you to ride what they would look for if they were buying a horse. Most would say you should try to find a horse to match your temperament and size.

If you still want to own a horse, try calling around and start finding out how much it will cost. You will need a veterinarian and farrier or blacksmith who is willing to check out the horse you are thinking about buying and able to care for it afterwards. Then total up their fees, the stabling fee, feed bill, insurance, and buying the necessary equipment.

Make a checklist for yourself before you contact the horses' owners by phone. Ask yourself what things do you want in a horse and then see if their horse matches your list. Will your horse be used just for riding or show? What is its gender, age, size, price, and experience? If you find a horse you are interested in, ride the horse, after the owner does, to see if it will do the things that you want it to do and if it looks like a horse you would want to ride.

If you find the horse of your dreams, take things slowly until the horse gets used to its new home. If you decide you don't want to buy a horse, pretend that you are buying an imaginary horse and write up what it would look like!

The Basics

Horses show how much they trust another horse by grooming each other with their teeth. You can earn their trust by being gentle and soft-spoken whenever it's time to groom your horse; this should be an enjoyable experience for both of you. A foal should start being groomed at an early age. Most people groom their horse in the morning; some groom them twice a day. Grooming gives you a chance to look closely at your horse's skin, checking for insects and cuts. Most riders try to groom their horse following the same routine each time. Here is a sample of how you might do it:

1. Use a hoof pick to make sure he hasn't picked up any rocks on your rides.
2. Rub his body, neck, and upper legs with a rubber currycomb.
3. Next take a stiff-bristled body brush to these same areas.
4. Use a softer body brush to finish cleaning his coat and his lower legs; also on his head, if he will let you.
5. A sponge and water may be used to clean around the eyes and ears.
6. Use a special comb, called a mane comb, to remove tangles from his mane and tail.
7. Finish by wiping the horse's body down with a damp cloth or towel, going with the hair, not against it!

You might think that a horse, like you, needs to have a bath every day. Luckily, the horse only gets two baths a year, when losing and gaining its winter coat; that is considered often enough. If you wash horses too frequently, they lose the natural oil in their hair and they will no longer shed water in a rainstorm.

Try This

A Horse You Can Eat

For this treat you will need an 8" cake someone has baked for you. Mark two lines on each side like the seams of a baseball. Then cut on the lines so you have two ears to frost and place on the horse's head. Use two cookies for eyes, two candies for nostrils and more frosting for the mane.

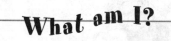

What am I?

You may know me from the television, as I like to appear in a lot of commercials. You will usually see me with the rest of my team, pulling a wagon. To some, I am a horse of grace and beauty.

What am I?

Clydesdale

It is important to wash a horse in warm water and warm weather; be sure to use horse shampoo and conditioner, especially on their mane and tail. Sweat scrapers work well after a shampoo or a hard ride to get extra water off the horse's coat and keep it from catching a cold. If it helps you to remember the order to use in cleaning your friend, say this sentence under your breath: Horses Curry Best Soon, So Clean This Horse! This will help you remember the order of grooming because the first letters of the words in the sentence will remind you:

Horses: hooves
Curry: curry comb
Best: bristle brush
Soon: soft brush
So: sponge
Clean: comb
This: towel
Horse: now you have a clean horse!

A Home for Your Horse

Sometimes families decide that renting a home for your horse in a stable is a good idea, because some neighborhoods won't allow you to keep a horse! You can choose how much care the stable will provide and you won't have to worry about storing the things you need to care for your horse every day. Your horse will probably be around other horses and this will keep them happier if you aren't able to visit every day.

At a stable you also will be around other people who know about horses and can answer a lot of your questions. You probably won't have much to say about it when it comes to building a home for your horse. If your family does ask for suggestions, many of the things that make for a comfortable

Fun Fact

Hoofed Company
Have you ever noticed a horse and donkey standing together in a pasture? Horses seem to prefer being with another horse, but living with any other hoofed animals will still make them happy.

Where's My Horse?

Admiral, Dapple, Jumper, and Gypsy are all boarded in the same neighborhood. Using the clues, can you figure out which horse is in which field?

— Admiral's field is on Pine Street.
— Gypsy's field is diagonally across the street from Jumper.
— Dapple's field is down the street from Admiral, but on the opposite side.
— Jumper lives in a field across the street from Admiral.
— Dapple and Gypsy's fields are on the same block, but not the same street.
— Jumper's field is not on Pine Street.
— If Admiral jumps his fence, he must cross Pine Street to visit Jumper or Gypsy.

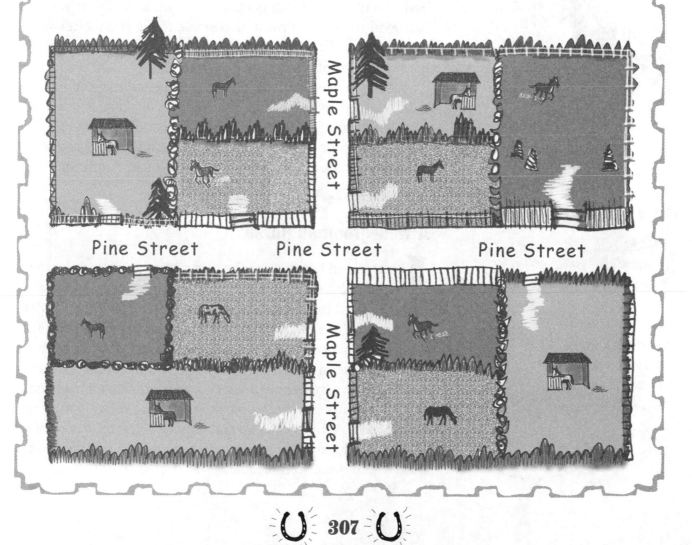

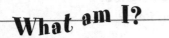

What am I?

I am a small horse from the land of Wales. Because of my smaller size, I have been known to work down in the coalmines.

What am I?

Welsh Pony

home for humans also apply to a horse's home, although this does not apply to the floor! Horses like dirt floors, because wood or cement floors can become slippery when they are wet. When you get your horse, the floor will need to be cleaned at least once a day and the wheat straw or other bedding will need to be replaced daily in order to keep your horse's hooves dry and free from the injuries and diseases wet hooves can create.

If you want to see how water can soak into your fingernails the same way it does in a horse's hoof, take a very long bath. Eventually your fingernails become so soft that you can bend them. It's almost impossible to file them after you get them wet. Now you understand why it is very hard on a horse to have soft hooves!

Most barns are built on higher ground and have doors and windows to provide fresh air and allow your horse to see outside. The rooms for your horse are called stalls and should be big enough to let the horse lay down. Yes, horses do lay down to sleep at times if they are happy in their surroundings!

Words to Know

Stable

A *stable* is a type of house for a horse. A horse's stable usually contains the horse's food, water, bedding, and all the other things that are needed to care for the horse.

A Well-groomed Horse

It may seem like you are the first person to have to learn so much about caring for and training your horse. It may also seem hard to do, but history tells us that more than 2,000 years ago, a Greek named Xenophon wrote down the rules for taking care of horses that many owners still follow today!

A rule like making sure that your horse's actual coat is in good shape are not enough. Since a horse doesn't know what is good for him, his owners must learn what other clothes he should wear. When horse owners buy clothing for their horses, they are looking for something to protect the horses and make them more comfortable.

Most owners buy bell boots that fit over the top of their horse's hooves and shipping boots that fit other parts of their legs to keep them from getting injured when they are at work or being hauled in a trailer. Some owners, like those with polo ponies, just wrap the horse's legs with pads and bandages.

Because horses do different things, they have more than one type of blanket: A light sheet blanket is used to cool a horse slowly after a workout and sometimes a heavier one is used when they ride in a trailer or stay in a cold pasture. Saddle blankets are used under the saddle to provide a soft layer that will protect the horse's skin.

Another way to protect a horse's coat is to trim it. This helps decrease sweating; the way they are clipped varies with the type of work they do and where they live. A blanket clip that looks like a blanket is only one of the many shapes left on a horse after it is trimmed.

Fun Fact

Really Big Horses
Did you know there are horses that weigh over one and a half tons? That is close to a compact car. Horses weren't always this size, but over time, several breeds have grown larger.

A Well-groomed Rider

Have you ever noticed that the riders of racehorses have a helmet on underneath their fancy caps? They also wear racing silks in special colors that the owner of the horse chooses. All riders should wear a safety helmet, but in some of the events in which the riders compete, they don't. The rules require the rider to wear a certain type of hat and a certain style of clothes.

Competitors in some horse shows are required to wear three-piece suits and derbies. If you watched people performing dressage, you might see a long-tailed coat, top hat, and white gloves! All of the riders wear shoes or boots with some type of heel, so that their foot doesn't go all the way through the stirrup. Girls and women should wear a ponytail or a bun, because you don't want your loose hair to move and frighten

What am I?

I am one of the largest of all horses and my name starts out with a jingle. I am one of the hardest working horses known.
What am I?

Belgian

the horse. This is also true when you are deciding on what type of clothes you should wear. Any thing that might "spook" your horse should not be worn, including jewelry.

Of all the horse events to see, you probably would enjoy the rodeos most of all, because the clothes they wear are like your everyday clothes: blue jeans, shirts, and a bandanna. The bandanna was a cowboy's all-purpose tool, used as a towel, a strainer for his drinking water, or protection for his nose in a sandstorm. Some rodeo events require vests, coats, chaps, and spurs, and most riders top off their outfit with their favorite Western hat.

Hungry Horses

What would you say is a horse's favorite food? If you said grass, you're right. Horses only drink milk from their mother for around three weeks and then they start nibbling on grass. Horses in the wild only eat grass and they eat it all day long, because they need lots of grass to get enough to eat! They are always moving—which helps their digestion of food—and the chewing helps to calm them.

You wouldn't think that you would have to worry about feeding your horse too much food, but it can happen. Too much new grass or other rich foods can cause a horse to founder, causing its leg bones to grow too long and stick down below its hooves. Even feeding alfalfa or clover hay can cause a horse to have problems.

It's amazing how many of the snack foods that we eat taste good to horses, too. Why not take a picnic lunch on one of your rides? You could bring along breakfast bars that contain all sorts of grains and chewy fruit strips for you and if you bring along carrots and apples, you can share them with your horse.

Try This

Make Some Noise
You can make a set of spurs by using six tin lids off of frosting for refrigerator rolls and two leather laces to tie them onto the backs of your shoes. To make a hole to string your leather laces through, have an adult hammer a large nail through each lid while they are sitting on an old board.

Fun Fact

Grazing Grown Ups
When people say someone is eating like a horse, they mean the person is eating all day. Some grownups eat lots of snack foods all day and they call it grazing!

Feed Me

Has your mother told you to eat your fruits and vegetables or cereal for breakfast because you need fiber or roughage? Hay is a horse's roughage. Smaller sections of a bale of hay are called "flakes." If you are buying a horse from someone else, they can tell you what the horse is used to eating. Your horse usually needs grains like barley, bran, corn, and oats; how much of them the horse needs will depend on the type of work it does and how much.

Sometimes horses do not get all the nourishment they need from their food so you may need to talk to your family or the veterinarian to see if they think supplements like minerals are needed. Have you ever tried eating foods cooked without salt? A horse craves salt so much that it will even lick salty ground for it! Horses can get worms this way and also lick up sand, which can make them sick. You've probably been told, "Don't eat food that has fallen to the ground!" The same is true for a horse. All you

Giddy Up

Watch Your Fingers!

It is important to remember whenever you feed a horse that you will always want to hold your hand opened out flat with the food on your palm. Horses don't eat like people; horses use their lips and teeth like fingers to pick up their food and may mistake your fingers for the food.

Apples for All

Mark takes care of 3 horses who all like apples. Today he has brought 13 apples—some are big and some are small. Use the puzzle grid to help Mark figure out how to divide the apples equally among his horse friends. Here are the rules:

- The answer starts in a corner.
- The answer reads logically, one letter after the other
- The answer path does not cross over itself.

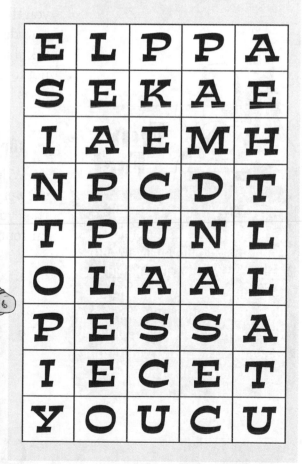

E	L	P	P	A
S	E	K	A	E
I	A	E	M	H
N	P	C	D	T
T	P	U	N	L
O	L	A	A	L
P	E	S	S	A
I	E	C	E	T
Y	O	U	C	U

Words to Know

Founder

When a horse *founders*, it becomes very ill from some food that it should not have eaten. This condition can cause the horse to go lame or even die.

Fun Fact

Hold the Ice, Please!
Horses drink more water if it isn't too cold. If you live where water can freeze, you should use a heater. Even if where you live doesn't get cold enough to freeze water, your horse might still want a heater to keep the water from getting too chilly!

have to do is make sure your horse has a salt block that it can reach.

Leading Your Horse to Water

One thing a horse needs is to have access to water. A horse doesn't necessarily need lots of water all of the time, but like all animals, it should be able to drink cool, fresh water whenever it needs it. On the average a horse drinks between five and ten gallons of water a day. Horses, like people, need their water to be free of bacteria and algae, so you will want to be sure the water is changed every day.

Horses will also drink from streams, but be sure that the stream's water is constantly moving so you know it is fresh. If you think about crossing a stream with your horse, consider how deep it might be. The deeper the water, the more effort it takes for the horse to cross it. Another thing to remember is not to allow your horse to drink too much water after it exercises because this can also cause a horse to founder.

Timing Is Everything

When you get up in the morning, you probably take a shower and get dressed. You might visit with your family and then you sit down to eat your breakfast. Horses follow a similar routine each day:

1. Horses need to move around a little before they eat in the morning. They also should have a drink before they have their breakfast.
2. You will need to feed them at least twice a day; three times a day is better for your horse, if you are at home. They don't need to eat all day long, because you are feeding them more nourishing food.

3. Never exercise your horse immediately after feeding them and never feed your horse immediately after exercising, because this can cause colic.

4. You can give your horse some oats, but most people recommend giving them no more than one or two times a week; if the horse is doing more work, this can be increased. Has anyone ever told you that you don't need any more candy because they thought it made you "act up?" Oats contain lots of carbohydrates and can affect some horses in the same way!

5. Some books recommend adding vegetable oil to the oats to make your horse's coat shinier.

6. If you change the way you are feeding your horse, you need to do it gradually, over a two-week period.

It might be fun to grow your own snack food to feed your horse. Ask your parents if you can use a small space in their garden to try growing some vegetables, like carrots, that both you and your horse would like to eat.

Is There a Doctor in the House?

From the time you were born, you have had many shots and appointments with the doctor for check-ups. Horses, just like people, need many shots every year. They also need to be weighed and measured. You can find a tape that measures a horse's height in hands in a horse tack shop. Then you can use it to measure how big a horse is by measuring around the horse (in the area just behind its front legs or elbows). Once you know this measurement, you can use it to estimate how many pounds the horse weighs. To obtain an accurate weight, machines called weighbridges are used.

Try This

Measure Your Friends Like Horses

Ask your family if they have a tape measure you can use. See if measuring how big your friends are under their armpits will give you an idea of how much they should weigh.

What am I?

Some people like to ride in my horse drawn carriage, rather than riding in a taxi or a hack. The second half of my name sounds like the middle of your leg.

What am I?

Hackney

Have you ever heard anyone call a veterinarian a horse doctor? Most veterinarians usually treat many different kinds of animals and illnesses. Horses have many of the same illnesses as people do. Some of the more common ones are thrush, arthritis, tendonitis, pink eye, and ringworm. Should you notice any of the following things with your horse, you will want to tell an adult:

1. If you have seen any bleeding or your horse seems to be in pain.
2. If the horse refuses to eat or can't stand up.
3. When in doubt, always tell an adult if you notice anything unusual or if you are not sure if what your horse is doing is normal.

Some horses go to the doctor for such things as broken legs, and some even go for surgery. If the horse can't get into a trailer to go to the hospital, the owner can call a horse ambulance for help. A lot of people believe that true horse ambulances were invented before people ambulances! Horse ambulances have all kinds of equipment to help people get an injured horse to a veterinarian. These ambulances have mats that veterinarians put under a horse that can't walk, so they can drag the horse safely into the ambulance. They also have slings like the ones you would need if you broke your arm, except much bigger! If you know a veterinarian, see if she will let you watch her at work.

Horse Pills

Horses take vitamins like people do, and horses can even get the flu! Have you ever heard your family talk about medicine that is the size of a horse's pill? What they are describing is a really big pill. For horses, pills can be about the size of a quarter or larger. When you have to take a big pill you can usually break it into pieces or crush it up and mix it in something. Horses don't have it that easy, but it helps that they have a larger mouth and throat. They usually have to be taught that taking medicine is fun. This is one of the ways that you can help your horse and your veterinarian, too.

Some of the horse's medicine can be given in a big tube that looks like the syringe that a nurse uses to give you your shots.

Shoe Doctors

If your horse was having trouble with his feet, you might think of calling the veterinarian. Many times what it really needs to see is a horseshoe doctor. Horses get corns on the bottom of their feet just like humans do. They get them the same way as people, which is from badly fitting shoes or the type of shoes that they wear.

Blacksmiths and farriers both work on horse's feet so that a horse can be comfortable running around and so that the horse won't get hurt riding on hard roads or on small rocks. A blacksmith uses a type of stove called a forge to heat a horse's metal shoes until they are red hot and soft and then he shapes them to fit the horse's foot exactly.

A farrier cuts and trims the horse's hoof (which is like a great big toenail) every four to eight weeks. This is done less frequently in winter because a horse's hooves don't grow as fast during that time. There are many different types of shoes and the farrier chooses the best one for the work your horse must do. Have you ever heard of someone "riding roughshod" over

Fun Fact

A Spoonful of Sugar
Train your horse to take medicine by putting honey on the tube and letting the horse lick it off. Practice this until the horse comes running when it sees you with the tube, then squirt more honey into his mouth while he's licking the tube. Mix the medicine into the honey next time, and he won't even notice!

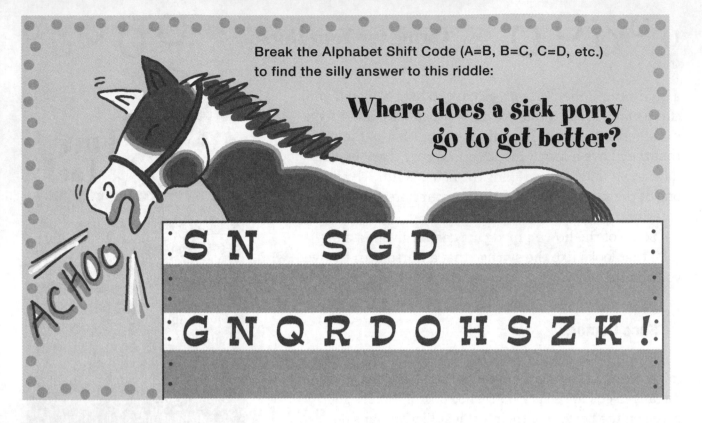

Break the Alphabet Shift Code (A=B, B=C, C=D, etc.) to find the silly answer to this riddle:

Where does a sick pony go to get better?

S N   S G D

G N Q R D O H S Z K !

ACHOO

Giddy Up

Check it Out

The next time you look at a horse wearing horseshoes, look to see how the nails come through the hoof and are bent over like a staple.

another person? This means they are bullying them, but for your horse it means they are nailing its shoes on with a very rough nail, so the horse won't fall on slippery roads.

House Calls

The best way to keep a veterinarian from making a house call is by taking good care of your horse. Look your horse over, side to side and front to back, every day. Know what it should look like, so you can tell if the horse isn't feeling well.

Any problem with a horse's hooves can affect his whole body, so be sure to pick up his feet and check them for problems every day. Horses have what is called a "frog" inside their hooves and your job is to make sure there aren't any rocks wedged in around it. Think about how it feels when you just get sand in your shoe, and imagine how it feels to have rocks stuck to your feet!

Chapter 22
Horse Sense

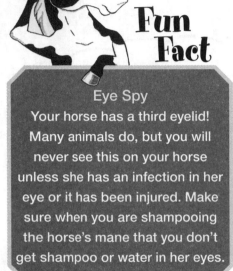

Fun Fact

Eye Spy

Your horse has a third eyelid! Many animals do, but you will never see this on your horse unless she has an infection in her eye or it has been injured. Make sure when you are shampooing the horse's mane that you don't get shampoo or water in her eyes.

To See or Not to See

Have you ever seen a horse with glasses? Some horses may lose their ability to see very well as they grow older, so it is important to pay attention to how your horse acts from day to day. A horse's eyes should be clear and bright. If their eyes appear foggy, they may have a condition called cataracts that needs the attention of a veterinarian.

Like a cat, a horse has whiskers around its face that help the horse find its way in the dark; they also keep him from bumping into anything that is close to his head. A good way to find out how important it is to be able to see well is to have one of your friends put a blindfold on you. Now sit down on the ground with a circle of your friends around you. Gently feel their heads and see if you can tell who it is from the shape of their head, nose, ears, and hair. Then try to identify them from their voices. You can take turns testing your horse senses!

Giddy Up

Give Me A Sign

Show someone behind you what you plan to do when riding: When turning right, place your left arm straight out from your side, bent upward at the elbow, fingers pointing up. For a left turn, place your left arm straight out from your side. If stopping, let your left arm drop straight down, with your fingers pointing downward.

Nearsighted and Farsighted

How can you tell if your horse is going in a straight line while you are riding it? Look between her ears; if you can see both of her eyes, she is. Horses can see almost all the way around themselves and it can distract them from doing their job. Imagine what it would be like if you could see your shoulders while you are looking straight ahead! It might make it hard for you to concentrate on what is in front of you.

Even though a horse can see objects that are close to it, not too far away, and things that are a long distance away, his head must be raised or lowered to see them. Horses can't see things that are about three or four feet in front of them without turning their heads to look out of one eye, and they can't see about ten feet behind them. This is why horses sometimes bump their hooves on the bars as they go over jumps; the horse can see the jump until it is in front of him, but then it disappears from his view! For this reason, sometimes a horse wants to stop right before it is about to go over a jump, and it has to trust its rider very much to try jumping over something it can't see.

Riders on packhorses say that horses definitely see better at night than people do, but they cannot see in complete darkness. Nobody seems to know if horses see in color. Some trainers feel that horses are able to choose colors when they are running through obstacles.

With Your Blinders On

Has anyone ever snuck up behind you, covered your eyes and said "Guess who?" You laughed, but it probably startled you, for just a minute. Horses don't like this either. They don't see directly behind or under their heads and can see one image with both eyes only for a short distance in front of their foreheads. When the images seen by two eyes appear as

Words to Know

Trainer

A *trainer* is someone who trains a horse how to race, do tricks, or basic skills. It is a trainer's job to get the horse ready for all activities by teaching it what it needs to know.

What am I?

I could be the horse of choice for an artist because of my special markings. It is easy to see that no one has used a brush on me, just splashes of color.

What am I?

Paint

one, this is binocular vision and humans have it all the time. Cover one of your eyes and then cover the other one. Don't things look different when you are only using one eye?

Try putting your hands up, palms facing each other and your thumbs touching your cheekbones, on both sides of your head. This is what a horse sees when riders put blinders on their bridles. Have you ever seen a horse in a horse show with blinders on? Do you think some horses might try to take them off? Wouldn't you?

Horses can't see anything behind their back legs, so if they feel anything around their feet, the first thing they will do is kick! Horses that don't like other horses following them too closely on trails will also kick out at them. These horses' riders tie a red bow around their horses' tails, so other riders will beware!

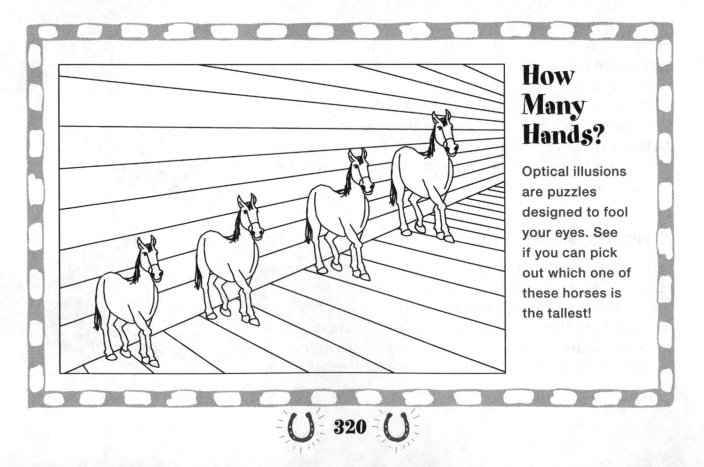

How Many Hands?

Optical illusions are puzzles designed to fool your eyes. See if you can pick out which one of these horses is the tallest!

Optical Illusions

Some horse trainers believe that they can look into a horse's eyes and tell whether it will be a good candidate for schooling. Others look at the physical characteristics of their horse's eyes: When you look into an Appaloosa's eyes, it's like looking into a human's eye. They are the only horse with a white sclera, which is the area around the colored part of your eye. Some horses like the Walleye have no coloring in their eye at all!

Did You Hear That?

Here are some tips for helping your horse to hear what you are trying to say to him:

1. Most trainers recommend using a soft voice when you're talking to your horse.
2. When you're giving commands (aids), use a louder voice.
3. Use a loud, not angry voice to let him know when he is doing something you don't like!

Cowboys always liked quiet horses because they didn't scare the cattle and make them stampede. Cowboys would also sing to the cattle to keep them calm. Do you know any of these old songs like "Goodbye Old Paint" or "Bury Me Not on the Lone Prairie?" Horses have excellent hearing that you want to protect. It is always best to keep them away from loud noises and take good care of their ears.

Make Your Own Binoculars

Make a pair of binoculars out of two toilet paper rolls taped together. What happens if you take off the tape and hold the two rolls apart from each other while you look out to the sides? This is what it is like for a horse without blinders on.

Try This

321

What am I?

My name gives you a clue to where I came from. The land that I live on is a windmill-covered peninsula that extends out into the ocean in Northern waters.

What am I?

Jutland

Try This

Horse Ear Experiment

To show how a large container transmits sounds better than a smaller one, tap different metal measuring cups with the bottom of a tablespoon. Notice how the larger cups ring for longer? If you hold them, open side up, near your ear, the big ones really conduct sound into your ears. Try both ears. Can you hear the same with both?

Amazing Ears

Have you ever watched a horse move its ears? They look like a pinwheel in a breeze. They seem to be able to swivel in every direction and oddly enough, one can point forward while the other is pointing backward. Horses also seem to be able to hear different things in each ear at the same time.

Have you ever known anyone that can wiggle his or her ears up and down? Can you? Horses move their ears when they itch or to keep the flies away. A horse's ears look sort of like the ear trumpets old timers used to use before they had hearing aids—you might have seen these in cartoons! Horses' ears are big on the outside then get smaller as they go into the horse's head. As an experiment, roll up a stiff sheet of construction paper until it is shaped like a trumpet and see if it helps you hear better.

How Horses Communicate

Have you ever been around a few horses or a whole herd of them? If you have ever heard a horse whinny, nicker, neigh, snort, or squeal, you know that they use their voices to communicate with each other just like people do. Each of those sounds is used only in a certain situation. The more you are around a horse, the more you will notice they also use pitch and volume to make their point; they use sound in a way that is similar to the way you do when you are scared, nervous or excited.

A horse shows that he cares for his rider by pushing his head against the rider's chest, whinnying to her when he catches sight of her, or nuzzling her with his nose. Over time, many riders feel that they understand what their horse is thinking just by seeing how they react to the things that happen to them.

Who is a horses' favorite storybook character?

1C	2D	3D	4B	5C	6B
		7A	8A	9C	
	10B	11A	12B	13C	

A. Not cold.

$\overline{8}$ $\overline{11}$ $\overline{7}$

B. Small horse.

$\overline{10}$ $\overline{12}$ $\overline{4}$ $\overline{6}$

C. At what time?

$\overline{1}$ $\overline{13}$ $\overline{9}$ $\overline{5}$

D. Quick hello.

$\overline{2}$ $\overline{3}$

Answer as many clues as you can and fill the letters into the grid. Work back and forth between the box and the clues to find the silly answer to the riddle.

Listening to Your Horse

Like cats that purr when they are happy and arch their backs when they are scared, or a dog that wags its tail when you pet it, horses have ways to tell you how they feel. Horses use their ears to tell you to "Back off," when they pull them back tightly against their head. They show the whites of their eyes and stamp their feet a lot, for no apparent reason. A horse will also let you know when she is tired of being cooped up in her stable or just bored, by weaving around and biting the wood in her stall.

If your horse starts limping when you're out on a ride, check his hoof for a stone. If he continues to limp after a stone is removed, hop off the horse to walk him home. If

Words to Know

Communicate

To *communicate* is to share how you are feeling or what you are thinking. One way to communicate with someone is to talk. Horses communicate through different sounds such as whinnies or neighs. Another way a horse communicates is by using body language.

Try This

Sugar Cube Art

If you have sugar cubes, you could try building a sugar cube barn or stable out of frosting and sugar cubes. Or you could use peanut butter to stick them together as well. If you don't have sugar cubes, try building with graham crackers or chocolate bars. When you're through, you can also taste it.

What am I?

I was named for the first person who raised my breed. To some, I am the All- American horse. You may know me by my small size.

What am I?

Morgan

your horse is curious, it will tip its ears forward. If it is very affectionate, it will lean toward you and rub its nose against you, especially if you're giving it a carrot, apple or a sugar cube.

Have you ever been told you eat like a horse? Get out some of those favorite horse foods like carrots and apples. Have a competition with your friends to see who can eat the most of them. Now try to eat like a horse, using only your lips and teeth while your friends hold the food on their palm of their hands. Not so easy, is it?

A Sixth Sense

Have you ever heard of someone having a sixth sense? When a person has a sixth sense they are said to be able to gain information or know things, but not by using any of the usual five senses of seeing, hearing, smelling, touching, or tasting. Many horse owners believe that their horse is able to read their mind. Others feel that if a horse and its rider have traveled for many miles together, the rider unconsciously starts to make a movement, like he has many times before, and the horse does the rest. A new horse purchased by this same rider probably takes awhile to learn how to read his owner's mind.

Can you guess what your friend is thinking? To try out-guessing them, place a few items on a table such as a bowl of chips, a cup of soda, and a candy bar. Can you guess which item they will reach for first? What will they want second? Or last? Were you right? Now, you can have them try the same experiment on you.

Sixth Sense

Find the 16 times the number 6 or the word six is hidden in this picture.

Instincts and Hunches

Some people think that horses have homing instincts. Stories of horses returning to their homes after losing their masters are attributed to years of training rather than instincts; most people believe they were just following the same road. We know that fish, geese, butterflies, and numerous other animals travel many miles to return to their homes, so maybe horses do the same.

Horses seem to know about coming disasters like fires, storms, tidal waves, and earthquakes. Maybe their senses are so much more in tune with their surroundings than ours that they can feel the changes in the atmosphere and the movements of the earth!

Horses also seem to have instincts passed down from horse to horse for millions of years that affect their behavior. Is it instinct or sixth sense that warns a mare when her foal is in danger? Even foals that are born in the safety of their own stable are usually born at night. Do you think that it is a mother's instinct that tells her this is still the safest time to have a foal, just as it was millions of years ago?

What Are Horses Afraid Of?

Have you ever been afraid and yet it seemed like you didn't really have a good reason to be? Do you dislike garter snakes, bats, and earthworms? Does the thought of picking them up make

Words to Know

Instincts

Instincts are natural-born senses given to all kinds of animals. A horse's instincts may tell it to be afraid of certain noises or to seek cover in a storm.

Fun Fact

First Steps

When a horse is born it sometimes appears to be knock-kneed or pigeon-toed. Horses weren't the only ones that had problems with their legs. Many cowboys became bow-legged after riding a horse for so many years.

a chill run down your spine? All of these creatures move quickly, and without warning they're under your feet or in your hair. We're trained to fear them because they're usually seen as the bad guys in movies, television, and books.

Horses get scared of things for many of the same reasons people do. Horses may be afraid of dogs barking at their feet because they see them as wolves that nipped at their ancestor's hooves. Horses might shy or jump when they hear the crackle of paper because they think that same wolf is creeping through underbrush. All kinds of noises can alert horses to the danger of another animal that might be trying to hurt them.

Horses sometimes seem to be scared for no reason that you can see. They have a much better sense of smell than humans do, so they may know there is an actual wolf lurking nearby before you do! You can help calm a horse that doesn't know you by slowly holding out your hand and letting him sniff it. Don't make any quick moves that will startle a horse—even flapping chaps can make a horse jump!

Would you like to make your own set of chaps? You can make a pair out of paper, cloth, or chamois (something people use for washing cars). All you need is enough material to cover the front of your legs and a way to attach it to a belt that goes around your waist. If you are using paper you can probably make your belt out of paper also and tape the chaps on to it. If your chaps are made out of cloth or chamois, you may want to use a real belt and have someone help you sew several loops for the belt to go in. When your chaps are ready, you can cut part of the way into the material to make it have some fringe around the edges.

Fun Fact

Going For Gold
Did you know there is a special kind of Olympics especially for horses? They are called gymkhanas and are a type of competition held all over the world. Some of the events are barrel racing and pole bending.

Words to Know

Fault

Have you ever said, "It's not my fault?" Something can be your fault if you make a mistake. In horse competitions, a *fault* means almost the same thing. It is a penalty you are given when you make a mistake in competition.

Is It Magic?

Have you ever heard the fairy tale about the horse called Clever Hans? Its owner had taught him to paw the ground when people asked him simple questions. He always had the right answer, even though his owner was hidden out of sight. After many tests, people decided that it must be that the people asking the horse the questions were accidentally giving him hidden clues. As he neared the correct answer, they would act excited, only to relax when he gave the right number.

All horses seem to be able to do this type of thing where they can "read their rider's mind," or sense what is going on around them. Many horses can even tell if you are afraid of them or if you are just not used to riding a horse.

Where in the World Are They?

Horses are everywhere, from history and movies to real life horses that live all around the world. If your brother or sister was born in 2001 and if they lived in China, you would say they were born in the year of the horse. The horse is one of the twelve animals after which the Chinese used to name their years. If you were going to use this method, what animals would you use and would this make it easier to remember when you born?

The Chinese aren't the only group of people to have horses in their history. The Greeks sponsored contests for horses thousands of years ago in the Olympic games and they continue this tradition to this day. Horse-drawn carriage rides are popular in England, Canada, Australia, and throughout the United States. You may

How many?

Answer each question with a number, writing the answer in the correct box. Then, work the math equation from top to bottom to get an amazing answer!

Whoa! That sure is a lot of horses!

How many...

☐ ...hooves on a horse?
×
☐ ...horses in a dozen?
×
☐ ...races in the "Triple Crown"?
×
☐ ...horses in a pair?
+
☐ ...saddles give you 24 stirrups?
=

There are ☐ different breeds of horses!

have seen police officers in the United States patrolling on horseback in cities. The Royal Canadian Mounted Police are the most famous officers on horseback.

The world famous Lipizzaners of Austria travel on tours with horses that are known for their ability to do "airs above ground." Some people have compared the tricks and spins that these horses do to those of an ice skater or a ballerina. If you would like to see them perform you might be able to attend one of their actual shows or just watch the movies *The Miracle of the White Stallions* and *The Sound of Music*.

Hunting for Horses

When you go searching for horses, it's hard to know what you will find! One place to look might be Arabia, where some people think the best horses come from. Not so long ago, camels were the only animals that were seen by most visitors to Arabia. Horses were ridden by wandering tribes and seldom seen in except in the desert.

Try This

Glow in the Dark Mural
See if your family will let you use an old sheet or piece of cloth, a few markers, and some glow in the dark paint. Lay the sheet over a large piece of plastic on the sidewalk and draw or trace several horses running in the open. You can add grass, sky, flowers, and stars that will glow in the dark!

Giddy Up

When working around or riding a horse, always wear hard, closed-toe shoes or boots. It is also important that your shoes fit loosely in the stirrups and have enough heels to prevent them from sliding too far into them. There may be times when your feet may need to come out of the stirrups quickly!

What am I?

When you hear my name, you might think of Aladdin and his magical lamp. Although I don't have a magic carpet or blanket, I am the choice for most riders.

What am I?

Arabian

You could also trace the tracks of Brumbies, wild horses that many people thought were brought to Australia many years ago by a man called Brumby. Horses or replicas of them have been found almost everywhere. People found thousands of life-sized clay horses and soldiers buried in China. These statues belonged to an emperor that lived in China thousands of years ago.

Warm-blooded and Cold-blooded Animals

Different kinds of horses are grouped in categories of hot-blooded, warm-blooded, and cold-blooded. These groups are different from how you might have learned about warm-and cold-blooded animals in school, though. You probably learned that warm-blooded means that a person or animal's temperature doesn't change much because of the weather. Some animals that are considered warm-blooded are cows, dogs, cats, and horses. These animals do things to stay warm when the temperature gets cold and to stay cool when it is hot, like a dog panting to stay cool, and like birds having feathers to stay warm. Cold-blooded animals, like snakes, frogs, and turtles, change temperature so that their body is cold if it is cold outside and it is hot when the weather is.

Words to Know

Warm-blooded
Horses that are *warm-blooded* are usually faster and more active than their cold-blooded counterparts. There are more warm-blooded breeds than there are cold.

Hot-blooded Horses

Horses are grouped with names like "hot-blooded" and "cold-blooded," but they mean something else! Hot-blooded doesn't refer to the temperature of these horses—horses that came from the warmer regions of the world are called hot-blooded. Hot-blooded horses, like the Arabians from the near East, are usually smaller horses; some are not even much larger than a pony! They can move quickly and are very spirited horses.

Warm-blooded horses are the result of mixing hot-blooded and cold-blooded breeds of horses and are usually the type of horses seen at horse shows and other events featuring horses.

Cold-blooded Horses

Most people believe that horses were called cold-blooded because they originally came from Northern Europe. Others think it is because of their easy-going temperament. A horse of this type that you would recognize easily would be the huge Clydesdales. They were used as draft animals on farms because they were big and strong. They pulled the farmer's plow, hayrack, and corn wagon. Many are still used today in parts of Europe where a tractor might cost a lot of money and a horse is cheaper.

When people first started talking about horsepower, they were really measuring how much work a horse could do. Have you heard your friends talk about the horsepower of their parents' cars or trucks? People still compare how much work these modern vehicles can do with that of a horse! Years ago, farmers tried to find out who had the strongest horses so they started having horse pulling contests.

Wild Horses

When you think of wild animals, you probably think of lions, tigers, and bears. Some people think of the millions of wild horses that used to live in the West. Have you ever heard people talk about "hightailing it right out of here?" When something startles a herd of wild horses, their tails do fly up! This is where that saying comes from. White-tailed deer do this and beavers slap the water

Fun Fact

Simply Hair Raising
People have used horse hair to make all kinds of things over the years. Some of the places where you can find horsehair (other than on a horse!) are in horsehair brushes, cinches, and plaster.

Words to Know

Cold-blooded
A *cold-blooded* horse is considered to be cooler in nature than a warm-blooded or hot-blooded horse. These calmer horses are believed to have originated in the colder climates of the world.

with their tails to warn the rest of their family of danger. Can you think of other things that animals do to communicate to each other if something is wrong?

A wild stallion's ears seem very large in proportion to the rest of its body—this might be because a wild horse must always be listening for dangerous sounds. While the wild horse's ears have grown bigger, the rest of its body seems to have grown smaller. When they don't get enough to eat, animals usually are not as big as their parents, so wild horses have become smaller than regular horses. If they are adopted and fed well, young wild horses will grow to be full-sized.

Herds of Horses

Horses in the wild live together in herds because they like being with other horses. When you think of a herd, do you imagine a stallion, living a life of freedom, standing on a high hill looking after his herd? Sometimes when one stallion tries to take away the herd of another, they will stare each other down, like kids in a schoolyard, to see who is the boss.

Every adult horse in the herd knows who is stronger or weaker than they are. They know it is important to decide who is the leader, so if danger comes, they will know who to

What am I?

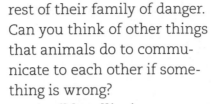

Black Beauty has been one of my favorite kinds of horses. My family history goes back thousands of years. **What am I?**

Fresian

Horseplay

Look carefully at this herd of horses and see if you can answer the following questions:

Are there more dappled and painted horses, or more solid horses with stockings?

Are there an even number of horses with blazes?

Which horse belongs to Ben Blair?

Fun Fact

What Did You Say?
When television first started, there were several horse stars, mainly in Westerns. The only horse that spoke on television was in a comedy and he was known as "Mr. Ed."

Words to Know

Domestic
A *domestic* animal or horse is one that has been tamed, allowing it to be more comfortable and useful around people. The opposite of a domestic animal is a wild animal.

follow. The stallion is usually trailing after the herd, protecting it from harm and making sure that none of the horses stray, while an old mare in front of the bunch chooses which direction they will take.

There are still a few herds of mustangs roaming free with the mares circling around their foals. If the foals stray from their mothers, the horses' keen sense of smell soon lets them find each other again. Some mares that don't have their own foals act like an aunt and help care for the new babies. If you want to form the right kind of relationship with your horse, he will need to feel that you are the one protecting him; he will let you be in control.

The Horse's Cousin

Have you ever heard of a quagga? This relative of the horse disappeared from the earth more than a century ago. It looked like a cross between a horse and a zebra, with stripes only on its front half. Spaniards brought another cousin of the horse, the burro, to the New World. Many still live free in many parts of the West, but others are adopted through government programs every year. Male burros are called jacks and females are called jennies. Male deer are called bucks and females are called does. Can you think of other names for male and female animals? What do you think a cob is? What about a pen? A cob is a male swan and a pen is a female swan.

There are also wild mules. Mules are one-half horse and one-half burro. Some people describe their friends as being as "stubborn as a mule," but many people believe that mules are very intelligent and just are thinking things through before they take a step. Domestic mules are used to carry people into the Grand Canyon, because they are careful before taking a step.

The Only True Wild Horse

Have you ever been to a zoo and seen a Przewalski's horse? This horse differs from all other wild and domestic horses and seems never to have changed in appearance. In fact, some of those horses in the cave paintings look almost exactly like it! This horse could probably also be called the only purebred horse, because all of the other breeds seem to have developed from a mixture of other types of horses over the years. The Przewalski's horse still lives as a wild horse in remote parts of Asia.

Some scientists wonder if millions of years ago, a combination of the Przewalski's horse and the zebra produced the new varieties of wild horses, since many of them have stripes on their legs and bodies.

What am I?

You might think of a bean when you first hear my name, but I really am a horse. Because of my camouflage type of markings, I was the favorite horse of the Native Americans.

What am I?

Pinto

A World Changed by Horses

Horses and their cousins were the only way that people could travel back in the horse and buggy days. Everyone could ride and did ride a horse then, just like they drive cars now.

Before car engines were invented, mules and horses were used to pull barges along the Erie Canal. Traveling ministers, in pioneer days, rode their horses to all the churches in the area. Teachers and pupils attending the country schools rode their horses in good and bad weather. The original milkman was driving a milk cart, pulled by a horse that knew his route from memory. Horses hauled all the cargo to and from the ships that supplied the stores and then delivered these things to their customers. Fire horses were so well trained that when the fire alarm sounded, they got in front of the fire engine by themselves. The firemen dropped the harness that was suspended above them onto their backs, buckled it up, and they were ready to go!

Fun Fact

Taming the Wild Horse
There are two kinds of horses, wild ones and tame ones. The difference is that the tame ones have been domesticated. Animals like the cow and the sheep were domesticated many years before the horse was.

Cowboys and Indians

Cowboys didn't have parking lots so the riders stabled their horses in livery stables in the old West. They wore ten-gallon hats to keep the sun off their faces on their long rides and used them as a pillow when they slept on the ground by their horse. Everything changed as more and more people had their own horses.

Just like the Europeans, Native American life changed completely when they learned how to ride the horse. They could hunt buffalo more easily, carry their belongings on the horses, and also go farther to fight with their enemies! Horses helped the people to get everything they needed for food, comfort, and safety. In return, the horse received food, water, a blanket, and sometimes a roof over its head.

In The Shadows

Can you find the one shadow that exactly matches the picture of this cowboy on his horse?

All you need to make your own fringe blanket is cloth, scissors, and an adult to help:

1. Place two pieces of fleece cloth together.
2. Make cuts four inches long that are about one inch apart, toward the center of the cloth, all the way around the edges.
3. Then you tie one fringe from each blanket together until the whole blanket is tied.

Wagons West

Maybe you have seen pictures of some of the pioneers driving their horses and floating their wagons across the rivers. Many horses don't even like to cross a small stream when you're out trail riding!

Modern roads eventually followed the same trails that were used by the trappers and pack mules. You can still see the tracks carved in the rock by the old wagons' wheels if you travel some of the back roads in the West! If you look on the Internet under the Oregon Trail, you may be able to see some pictures of the ruts. The wagons were not very big and had to hold all of the pioneer's supplies to start a new life in the West. Imagine putting everything you owned inside a small minivan and traveling for months across thousands of miles.

Pioneers usually used oxen to move their belongings across the prairie, but horses were used by scouts and hunters, as well as for herding cattle. Most of these wagons had no beds in them, so people wound up sleeping out under the stars. Some of them used their blankets and slept with their head on a saddle. But you might prefer making your own tent out of several trees that are close together, some ropes, and a blanket. After you get your tent set up, it's time to fix an old-time chuck wagon supper. To fix this meal, you will need a

Try This

Cowboy Jerky or Sausage
Mix together: 2 pounds hamburger, 1 cup water, 1 teaspoon mustard seed, 1 teaspoon pepper, 2 teaspoons liquid smoke, ½ teaspoon onion powder, ¼ teaspoon garlic salt, and 2 tablespoons of tender quick salt. Stir and flatten rolls on foil. Refridgerate 12 hours, then bake at 325 degrees for 90 minutes and then at 350 degrees for 55 minutes.

skillet, a two-and-a-half-quart casserole, and an adult to help you prepare this recipe.

1. Brown ½ pound ground beef, a medium onion, cut up finely, and ½ teaspoon chili powder in the skillet. Put into greased casserole.
2. Then fry one pound of bacon, after cutting it into small pieces, in the skillet.
3. Mix ⅓ cup sugar, ⅓ cup brown sugar, ¼ cup ketchup, ¼ cup barbecue sauce, ½ teaspoon salt, one table-spoon prepared mustard, ½ teaspoon black pepper, one 16-ounce can pork and beans, one 16-ounce can red kidney beans, one 16-ounce can great northern beans, and bacon in the casserole.
4. Bake 45 minutes at 350 degrees, then bake for 45 min-utes at 200 degrees.

The Iron Horse

Strange as it may seem, long before there were any railroad steam engines (known as iron horses), there were railroads. Horses had been pulling coaches over rough roads for many years, but then someone decided that it would be a lot easier and safer to pull coaches on rails. The horse would run in the space between the rails and pull something that looked like a stagecoach on steel wheels.

Eventually the true iron horse was built, which became known as a train, and soon many of the horses and the peo-ple who worked with the coaches were out of a job. Many old iron horses still run on tourist railroads today. See if your family would like to try one out. Don't be surprised if outlaws employed by the railroad hold up the train!

Fun Fact

Weighing In
When some horses are first born, they start out their life weighing as much as you weigh now. Other foals weigh closer to the weight of a newborn human baby.

Where to Start

Would you like to help train a horse? If you are fortunate enough to be around a riding stable, ask if you can visit a newborn foal frequently and help with its care. Hand-raised foals usually respond well to consistent training. Some ways to train them are:

1. Spend time running your hands over the foal's body, head and legs, so it gets used to being handled.
2. Once it is willing to let you stroke its head, you should be able to put a halter on and then you can lead it around the corral.
3. This is also a good time to teach the foal to let you gently lift its feet, so the farrier's job will be easier when it's time to get its first shoes. Most horses have shoes before they are a year old!

Giddy Up

Scoping it Out

It is very important to know the lay of the land anywhere you plan to ride a horse. New places to ride should always first be checked out on foot to prevent your horse from stepping in a hole and breaking his leg.

Usually horse owners wait several years for a horse to grow up before they start any serious training. In the first few years you will want to teach your horse the basics and allow it to grow to know you and learn to trust you.

One of the main ways you can help your horse get to know you and start to trust you is by giving your horse attention each day and trying to be the one who handles the horse and shows it the different skills you want it to learn. Soon, the horse will feel comfortable enough with you to be properly trained.

Breaking a Horse

Have you ever seen kittens or puppies that have never been around humans? You have to be gentle and use lots of time and snacks to convince them that you are their friend. Most wild horses in the old West had never met a person until they were full-grown and their riders believed the only way they could be ridden was to break their spirit. They would tire out these wild horses until the horses lacked the

What am I?

You might have to really "rack" your brain to guess my name. I am one of the fancy steppers at many of the horse shows or events.

What am I?

Racking Horse

Try This

Walk Like a Horse

If you want to see how a horse feels when it is walking through the mud, try wearing your parent's boots around for a few minutes with pillows tied on top of them.

• • •

Boot Boogie Relay

How fast can you go in a pair of boots? How about having a relay using two teams? Each team will have a person race to see who goes the fastest putting on boots, running to a fence, then returning to the start and so on until the fastest team wins.

strength to resist being tamed. Native Americans would take a horse into water that covered their legs, then lie on the horse's back and finally sit up. The horse didn't want to dip its nose into the water, so it wouldn't buck.

Cowboys would ride their horses in a plowed field or a snowdrift to do the same thing that the Native Americans did: make a horse so tired that it would let itself be ridden. Another thing that slows a horse down, like snow or the soft dirt of a plowed field, is mud. It is always best to avoid riding your horse through mud if you can. A horse that is walking through the mud gets tired very quickly and it is very hard on the horse's hooves.

Cowboys had another way to train horses to be ridden. When the cowboys went on cattle drives, they would let the horses get used to running with the herd of cows all day. Then at sundown, they kept the horses from following the cattle until the cowboy mounted the horse. The horse would then hurry to follow the herd, even though it had a rider on its back.

One type of person who trains horses is called a horse whisperer. She wears the horses down by using soft words and patience, instead of using force or making the horse tired. A horse trained this way is usually more popular because it is not constantly trying to break its rider!

Mixed Signals

Even if you are fortunate enough to help care for a foal, you will want to learn to ride on an older horse. A young horse that is learning to be ridden needs the firm hand of an experienced rider because horses have good memories. They learn bad habits just as easily as good ones. It is best to give instructions to the horse by talking to them, always using only one word, so they don't get confused. Sometimes the easiest way to train a horse is to have him follow an experienced horse, which helps to take away his natural fear of the unknown.

You also need to lean your body forward, backward, and from side to side in the saddle and grip the horse's body with your legs to communicate. The reins are used to let the horse know if you want it to go to the left, right, or back up. These methods are called soft aids. Using a bit that fits in the horse's mouth, a whip, and spurs are called hard aids.

Horses have several different types of reflexes similar to what people have. If you gently touch their hips with a whip, this will emphasize the pressure from your legs. A well-trained horse will seem to sense what you want it to do.

Words to Know

Aids

One way of communicating or "talking" to a horse is known as using *aids*. Some of the different methods that are used are speaking softly, positioning yourself in the saddles and moving the reins from side to side.

Growing Up

A riddle and its silly answer have been put in a grid and cut into pieces. See if you can write the letters in their proper places in the empty grid!

What am I?

With my head held high, I proudly prance by. Even when I am not wearing a saddle, I have one on me. **What am I?**

American Saddlebred

Now that you know how important the rider's skill is to make the horse perform well, it is easy to feel sorry for the horses that live at the stables and have a new rider every day, especially when the rider doesn't know what he is doing!

Going to School

Most horses have to go to school just like kids do. There are many schools or academies all over the world for advanced training, but generally horses are taught the basics by people who train horses at stables or other private establishments located all over the country.

So what does a horse learn in school, you ask? Well, these schools teach horses everything from training the horse to accept a rider, how to do different types of gaits, and even the correct way to exercise. Some schools offer specialized classes in flat racing, hunting, jumping, and dressage. Usually

the riders also need to go to school, so many of the schools offer classes or know of people who will teach you how to ride and also care for your horse.

A type of graduation after all of this work is a horse show, where judges decide how well both the riders and horses have been trained. Red, white, or blue ribbons are awarded to the winners and their pictures are usually taken for the local newspaper.

Raising the Bar

If you have ever been to a track meet and watched someone do the high jump, you have a pretty good idea what it is like for a horse to jump bars in competitions. When a horse is first learning to do this, it doesn't seem that hard, because the bar is simply a log or tube lying on the ground, but as the horse gets better at each jump, the bar is raised and the work begins. Horses appear to be natural jumpers, but they usually need to learn how to jump the same way humans that become high jumpers do.

If you were the high jumper, how would you feel if you were doing this jump with a blindfold on? When a horse gets close to the bar, he can't see it, because his eyes are on either side of his head! Maybe the horses would like it more if they had a large mattress or pillow waiting for them on the other side like humans have, in case it was needed to break their fall.

Hurdles for Horses

How would you feel if after you learned to jump over those bars, someone said they were going to become four feet wide, and that you would have to turn right before you

Try This

Have a Show

If you would like to create your own horse show, you can take pictures of real horses or search magazines for pictures of horses and decide which ones should be the winners. Make ribbons, blue for first, red for second, and white for third, out of cloth or construction paper and attach them to the pictures you judged as the winners.

Fun Fact

Measuring Up
There are special measurements in the world of horses, like hands for measuring a horse's height, length for measuring a racehorse, and furlongs for measuring the distance in a racecourse. A furlong equals one-eighth of a mile.

Giddy Up

Whoa There

If you approach a stream, or any other obstacle, the horse may decide he wants to jump it immediately or not at all. You should always be ready for a sudden stop and be able to hold on to the saddle, if necessary.

jumped them, and on the other side, there was a road running downhill? Many of the horses in foxhunts, steeplechases, and other obstacle courses must do all this and more!

Are you wondering if the steeplechase riders really chase steeples? The reason they call it that is because they use the steeples as places where they must turn, in the same way you use landmarks like schools and stores to find your way home.

When either you or your horse is walking, you don't fall over because you're balanced. Your center of gravity runs from your head to your feet. To see how this works, try leaning to one side. You don't have to lean too far before you start to fall down!

When you get on the horse, you change his center of gravity, which is located toward the front of his body, whenever you move. When the horse starts jumping over things, you need to move your body to help keep him upright. Try placing a backpack on the middle on your back; it should feel pretty good. If you move it to one side it becomes much harder to keep your balance. Remember how it feels to be unbalanced and try to help your horse keep its center of gravity when you are practicing jumps.

Fun Fact

Running Like The Wind

Some horses have been reported to run at speeds in the range of forty miles an hour. One horse that became famous for running very fast in the Kentucky Derby was Secretariat.

Putting Your Best Foot Forward

When you walk, do you start out with your left foot or your right? Have you ever thought about how fast you have to be going before you decide to switch from walking to running? You can think of a horse going through its paces as if you were going out for a morning run or walk. The horse walks just like you do, one foot after the other, only the horse has to keep track of four feet.

When a horse is trotting, it moves faster. The horse is alternating touching its toes: its right hand and left foot come together and then its left hand and right foot. To trot, the horse is moving its body a lot. If you don't move up and down while riding the horse when it is trotting, it can be a pretty uncomfortable ride for you!

Cantering is more like a jumping exercise. See if you can do it! Stand on your right foot, then jump and put your right arm and left back foot on the ground; then, if you can do it (and most people can't), stand only on your left hand. Then imagine that someone tells you to switch and stand on your left foot first, while you're running at a fast rate. As you can see, this takes a lot of training and some horses are never able to do it!

If you were a horse, you would probably be glad to go to the gallop. It's the fastest pace of all, but the horse only has to put one foot after another. See you can do any of these gaits by yourself or with a friend. If you get good enough, maybe you can have races between a few teams of your friends!

Words to Know

Canter
One type of gait or step that a horse uses is called a *canter*. When a horse canters, it first lands on a back foot, then the two opposite front and back feet and then on its other front foot.

Gallop
When a horse *gallops*, it is similar to a human running. Only one foot hits the ground at a time until all four feet have taken a turn. Galloping is the fastest gait for a horse.

A Balancing Act

Finding balance is sometimes hard to do. People who teach horses have learned that horses, like people, need to have balance between work and play, so they have made many of the horse exercises, like longeing, into things that horses like to do.

Many of the jobs that horses must do require them to be able to curve their backbones as they make circles, figure eights, and change their gaits from a walk, to a trot, and then a gallop. They spend a lot of time in a large round pen with the horse on a long line and a person on the ground walking round and round in circles, changing directions, until the horse's back bends easily.

If you've ever washed a car, you know you have to rinse it off and wax it using little circles. When you're done, you might wipe it off with a chamois cloth. When you buy a chamois, it feels like velvet in your hand. After you use it and it dries out,

'Round and 'Round

Start at the letter marked with a dot. Collect every other letter until you get to the last letter in the center. Then, turn around and collect every other letter on the way back out! When you are done, you will have the silly answer to this riddle:

What has six legs, but only uses four for walking?

it feels like cardboard. A horse's back is like the chamois; it can be hard and stiff before training and then it becomes soft and flexible, after the horse is done with training.

Horses can only do the exercises for a few minutes before they need to rest. After the horse has mastered the solo circle drills, the rider climbs into the saddle and the learning continues.

Working with Horses

Horses can sense if you like them or not, so it is very important for the person that is working with the horse to really like them! The person working with them should also be the person who will be riding and showing the horse.

Always try to think of your horse as being similar to a young child who weighs nearly half of a ton. It doesn't understand many of the things you are asking it to do. Be quiet and in control and never get angry at your horse. If you want to know how the horse is feeling when it tries to do something it has never tried before, you might try standing on your head, learning a new dance step, or a simple gymnastic trick. It won't take long before you will understand how the horse is feeling.

Getting Off on the Right Foot

Did you ever wonder why you are always supposed to ride your bike on the right side of the road, but you're supposed to walk on the left side? Rules make it easier for everybody to do what they should, so there are no surprises. Be consistent, so that your horse will know what to expect, too. That's why most riders are trained to get on a horse on their left side, even though a well-trained horse will also let you get on from the right side.

Words to Know

Longeing

Longeing is a way of training the horse to have a more balanced gait or to exercise a horse that can't be ridden yet. To train this way, the horse is attached to a rope and runs in circles around the trainer, who is holding the rope and guiding the horse.

Fun Fact

Now That's What I Call Tired!
Have you ever been so tired that you thought you could fall asleep standing up? Well, some horses can and they don't lay down for days! The only way you might know if they are sleeping is that they do shut their eyes.

The knights in the Middle Ages usually faced the back of their horse when they climbed on so the sword that was hanging on their right side would swing out of the way after they put their left foot in the stirrup and lifted their right leg over the saddle. Many people believe that is why we climb on the same way today. As you climb on, be sure you never bump the horse's back as you swing your right leg over the horse!

When its time to get down, slip your shoes out of the stirrup, swing your right leg over the back of the saddle and slide both legs down to the ground. Riders wanting to ride on a camel usually ask that the camel to lower themselves to their knees so the rider can get on them, while elephants let their riders walk up their trunk. You could try looking in books or going on the Internet to see how people get on mules, donkeys, alpacas, llamas, or ostriches.

Saddle Up

What is the most important piece of equipment you need after you buy your horse? It's the saddle, of course! Each saddle is made for a certain sport, a certain size of horse, and a certain size of rider. You have to try the saddle on your horse and you have to try on the saddle. Being "saddle sore" can be true for both the horse and rider! Size and fit is important, so they have saddlehorses to hold saddles that kind of look like sawhorses. You just have to keep trying the saddles that are placed on these saddlehorses until you find the right size.

If you happen to have an old sawhorse, maybe you can store your saddle on it. Saddlehorses are sometimes found in tackrooms (the place where you store all your horse care stuff). Your saddle and all your other leather equipment needs to be wiped off, cleaned with saddle soap and then oiled, if it is new.

Try This

Balance Test

Balance is important when you swing up into the saddle. One way to practice your balance is to use a large log placed on a bed of soft straw. Once you are used to climbing on, sitting down, and balancing, you can try having a pillow fight with a friend to see who can stay on the log for the longest time!

Matching Saddles

Can you find the two identical saddles?

Try This

Make Soap

If you want to make your own soap like saddle soap, ask an adult if you can use soap chips that are left over from the bathroom. Place the chips in a bowl and add water to it, letting it slowly dissolve into liquid soap. Now your new soap is ready to go in a pump dispenser!

When you put a saddle on a horse the first time, have someone hold your horse, so it doesn't move away. Carefully swing the saddle over its back after you are sure you have fastened down everything on it that might move. Then tighten your "cinch" if you're using a Western saddle, or the "girth" if you're using an English saddle. Make sure your horse hasn't taken a deep breath to keep you from pulling it tight or you might find yourself under the horse instead of on top of him when the horse lets his breath back out again!

At the End of the Day

ou probably have heard that runners need to warm up and have a cooling-off period when they work out. This is a good idea for horses, too:

1. Before you put your horse in the stable, whether you've been running a race or just taking your horse for a good run, walk him around until he is breathing slowly and is completely cooled down.
2. You could also just walk him the last ten minutes of your run. A wet horse is a cold horse and could become sick. Everyone has things that they usually do at the end of the day like take a bath or brush their teeth. The same is true for a horse—they enjoy having a routine.
3. If you know that you will be riding later in the day, you can wait to groom your horse until after you finish your ride. If your horse was groomed earlier, groom him again.

If your horse has been clipped recently, you might even need to throw a blanket over him before he goes to sleep, so he won't be chilly!

Chapter 25
Off to the Races

Words to Know

Stallion

An adult male horse over the age of four years is called a *stallion*. In herds of wild horses, there is usually only one stallion that watches over the rest of the group.

Jockey

A person who rides a horse during a race is called a *jockey*. Most jockeys are small in size to put less weight on the horse, so the horse can run even faster.

Running for Your Life

How long do you think people have been racing horses? History tells us that around 2,000 years ago, the Romans built an arena for horses called the Hippodrome, which means a "course for horses." Back then teams of horses competed against each other like our baseball and basketball teams do today.

The early settlers and Native Americans also had horse races, not too long after the colonies were established. The highlight of the racing year in the United States is the Triple Crown, which is a group of short races that started in the nineteenth century: the Kentucky Derby, the Preakness, and the Belmont Stakes.

Most winning racehorses are stallions and once they stop racing, they go on to raise a new family of racing champions. It must be hard deciding how to name a racehorse. Many of their names are combinations of their father, mother, or grandparent's names. If you want your horse's name to be registered, you need to check his breed's association on the Internet and see if its name has been registered before. Just for fun, think up a good name and have someone help you check the Internet sites for registering horse names, to see if it has ever been chosen.

Old enough to race

If you've ever wondered if horses like to run, watch a bunch of foals in a pasture. They take turns nipping other horses, so they will start to run and then they race after them. Kids do the same sort of thing when they play tag. Someone who watches over you so you don't get too wild is called a babysitter or a nanny. Horses have nannies too! Racehorses are usually tak-

Ace Horse Race

Get Ready: You will need a tile floor or a linoleum floor with a pattern of squares, a deck of cards.

Get Set: Deal out the four aces from the deck. These are the horses. Line them up side by side on four different tiles. Decide which row of tiles will be the finish line.

GO: Deal out the cards from the deck, one at a time, face up, and in a single pile. Each time you deal a card, move the ace with the same suit forward one tile. The first ace to cross the finish line wins!

Extra Fun: Keep reshuffling the stack of dealt cards to make the race longer, or use two decks of cards. Try setting up a "cross country" race track that goes from one room to another in your house, or across a brick patio or sidewalk.

What am I?

I am probably the most popular of all of the ponies. My name is the same as the islands where I originally came from.

What am I?

Shetland Pony

Fun Fact

The Push Off
Have you ever noticed how a jockey rises up and leans forward when he's racing down the home stretch during a race? They do this to help the horse so that its back legs can push harder.

en from their mothers at an early age and are placed in a lot with an older mare that is called a nanny because sometimes they may need a little extra care.

Even though the racehorses in the Kentucky Derby are called three-year-olds, they aren't necessarily that old. Most horses are born in the spring, but their official birthday is considered to be the first of January. The trotters in harness racing can't race until they are five years old and this is when most horses are considered to be full-grown.

Don't Look a Gift Horse in the Mouth

When the dentist asks you to "Open up," she can tell what age you are by checking if you have baby teeth, twelve-year molars, or your wisdom teeth. Horses also have baby teeth, but theirs are called milk teeth. By the time they are five years old, horses have lost all their baby teeth and they have forty permanent teeth.

One young horse's teeth may not arrive at the same time as another horse's and so it is difficult to tell if a horse is old enough to race just by looking at his teeth. Your teeth don't change that much as you age, but a horse's teeth gradually stick out further in front. Telltale lines also appear on some of the horse's teeth, and it usually wears off parts of its teeth as it gets older.

When someone says "they're getting it straight from the horse's mouth," they're doing what the old horse traders used to do, which was looking in a horse's mouth to see how old the horse is. If someone gives you a horse and you immediately ask to look inside its mouth, they may laugh at you or they may think you want to know how much they paid for your present! How many teeth do you have? Look in the mirror to count and see how close you are to having all of the thirty-two teeth you will have as an adult. How many teeth do your friends and family have? Do they know before they count them? If not, have them guess and then see if they are right!

A Change in Pace

Are you good at more than one sport? Some horses that compete in three-day events must be equally good at dressage, cross-country jumping, and show jumping over fences. Most horses use a variety of gaits, but others are bred to do only a certain gait; the riders of a Tennessee Walking Horse expect them to use only a four-beat running walk. A true pacing horse moves his front and back leg on the same side together, then he moves the legs on the opposite side together.

Have one of your friends grab you around the waist and see if the two of you can move like the pacer. Try to be sure to use the same feet at the same time that your friend is using theirs. Now take a little half-step as you're moving and lead off with the other feet! See if you can switch to moving one foot after another. Then start to run, then start to skip, and keep repeating these steps. Is it any wonder a horse gets confused, especially since he has four feet?

What Makes a Winner?

D o you think it is always a good thing to be a winner? Not necessarily! Do your parents play golf or bowl? Have you ever heard them talk about their opponents giving them a handicap because they are better players and your parents wouldn't be able to get close to winning if they didn't? Racehorses have a handicap, too. If they have run too well in the past or are older than some of the other young horses, then they must carry extra weight, so they can't win too easily.

Fun Fact

A Place to Call Home
Do you know what state is the most famous for its Thoroughbred horses? Kentucky! Kentucky is also the home of the Kentucky Derby and is known for the beautiful fields of bluegrass growing on its horse farms.

Try This

Mint Juleps for Kids
People who go to the Kentucky Derby to watch young horses run often have a drink called a mint julep. To make your own mint-flavored shake try blending chocolate-covered mints with vanilla ice cream and just a little milk in a blender.

How does the horse's owner find out if he "got part of the purse" or "was in the money?" This is racetrack talk that means their horse was in the "win, place, or show" position (first, second, or third place) at the end of the race. Part of the money that is bet on the horses goes into the purse. Horse breeders strive to develop winners for the money, but the glory of winning also makes them work harder to develop the perfect racer!

Sometimes the horses win by a nose or a neck, which is just what it sounds like. Sometimes the owners never know who won until they see the photo finish, a picture taken as the horses cross the finish line! Racehorses must all carry the same amount of weight; do you want to see what it would be like if you had to add weight every time you ran? Try climbing on a bathroom scale and see how much you weigh. Can you run a couple of blocks pretty easily? Now weigh yourself holding your backpack, your coat, and a couple of books. Try running with just your coat in the backpack and then add the books. Did it slow you down when you had to carry more weight?

What am I?

My pink eyes will surely give me away if my ghostly appearance doesn't. I am one of the few horses that always looks like it is blushing or "tickled pink."

What am I?

Albino

Giddy Up

An Eye on the Sky

You must always keep an eye on the weather if you plan to ride very far or for a long time. Weather can change quickly and storms or lightning are not safe for you or your horse. The safest place for you in a storm is in the stable, barn, or some other type of shelter.

Being Number One

When you see a baby horse running alongside its mother in a pasture, do you say, "Look at that colt?" Most people do. Surprise your family the next time you see one and call it a foal. Boy foals are called colts and girl foals are called fillies. When they reach their fourth birthday, they become stallions and mares and by this time some of them are old enough to have their own foals. Only certain horses are picked to become parents in the racehorse world, usually because their owners think they have the potential to become champions, just as their ancestors did.

Being born from a certain family isn't always the recipe to success, though. It also takes a great deal of training, hard work, and luck! One of the most important parts of winning is determination. The only way to know if a horse has the potential and drive to win is to race it. Have you ever seen a stopwatch? Trainers press a button on the watch when the race starts and again when the race is over; the amount of time that passed in between reads out on the dial. One way to see if your horse is getting faster is to use the watch every time your horse races. You can use a regular watch to time yourself and your friends in your own distance race.

Practice Makes Perfect

You've probably heard that practicing always makes you better at whatever you do. Horses and their riders spend several hours every day practicing and exercising for their jumps and flat racing. Racehorses usually get better as they get older, but people are much more interested in seeing how well a young, untried horse will run. Many horses that didn't do well at one sport often do well at another. Steeplechasers do their best after they're eight years old. Drivers in harness races are often more than seventy years old!

Fun Fact

With A Touch of Salt

Have you ever heard of Epsom Salts? They are used for people, including jockeys, and animals for soaking an injured body part. Epsom is the home of a famous racetrack in England where Epsom Salts are also found.

Try This

Decoupage Horse Box

Whether you need a box to hold your tools or the things you collect, you will have fun making a decoupage box. For this project you need horse pictures, a cardboard or wooden box, glue, and a brush. Start by brushing on enough glue to hold your picture down, then brush on several coats of glue over the picture.

Let's Race

Which of these thoroughbreds is the fastest? Find each horse's path to the finish line. Add up all the numbers along the way. Who ever scores the most points is the winner!

1	18	15	11	5	13	5	15	8
2	12	8	9	18	22	10	3	14
20	7	17	2	20	8	9	5	12
17	6	23	3	13	19	2	13	16
11	12	3	17	10	19	12	7	19
4	14	6	4	14	6	10	16	17
9	18	15	12	1	16	21	7	4
END	END	END	END	END	END	END	END	END

Would you say that cowboys in the old days were born in a saddle? Many of them had never seen a horse before they applied for the job so they got on a horse and learned the hard way—by practicing! Whether you are practicing dance steps or catching a ball, if you practice every day, you will get faster and stronger.

Teamwork

When you see a trophy awarded or that big rose-filled horseshoe placed around the winning horse's neck, do you think, "That horse must have come from a long line of winning horses?" Usually that is true, but no horse could win without his faithful owners to pay for this expensive sport and a jockey who knows "when to make her move" or is willing to "jockey for position," when she is racing other large horses traveling at more than forty miles an hour! Most of these horses were trained by people who believed in that horse when no one else did. Many of the trainers were there when the foal was born.

Many horse racers have what is called a "kick" at the end of the race where they go faster as they finish and sometimes that helps them win. Did any of the people in your relay team have a "kick" that helped them push ahead at the last minute?

It's All About Luck

For a long time, people have thought that horseshoes are good luck charms. This is why you sometimes see horseshoes hung up on walls or above doorways. People hang them with the open part of the "U" shape of a horseshoe facing up—they think that if you hang it upside-down, your luck will run out of the bottom!

Fun Fact

Going In Circles
Have you ever tried to count the number of horses on a carousel? Depending on the size of the carousel, it could contain a few horses or more than fifty!

Try This

Relay Race
You need four people for each team and two sticks, each about a foot long, for this race. Have each person on the team wait at a corner of the block. One person runs around one side of a block and then hands the stick to the next person. Keep running and passing the stick until one team gets back to the start and wins!

Try This

Horseshoes You Can Play With

If you want to try your hand at a game of horseshoes you can make your own horseshoes out of plastic lids or cardboard. If you are looking for something to be the stakes, you can use plastic soda bottles filled with sand. The object of the game is to try to toss the horseshoe near or around the stake.

If you are lucky enough to find a horseshoe or two, you can make your own coat rack, using a piece of wood or a barn-board:

1. Depending on how many horseshoes you use, the wood will need to be anywhere from eight to eighteen inches long.
2. You will want to nail the horseshoes onto the wood with the open ends up; your luck runs out the bottom if you hang them upside down and you will want to hang your hats or jackets on them.
3. If you want to use your lucky new coat rack for a game, you can use foam rings or cut out cardboard circles for a ring toss game.

Do you think that good luck is given to the finder of a horseshoe that is lying in the road or do you think about the bad luck of the horse that is now missing a shoe?

Things That Bring Luck

Some people believe that winning is all about luck. Others believe you make your luck through hard work. Can you list some things that bring good luck? Maybe you have a lucky number or a lucky shirt. Some people have lucky coins or lucky medals they wear around their neck; some people even have lucky underwear! If you ask most people to make a list of the things that they think bring someone good luck, most of them would list a horseshoe.

Another lucky thing you may find while walking your horse is a four-leaf clover. Although finding one is considered lucky because it is believed to be a very hard thing to do, you might try looking in a clover patch for a few minutes. If you find one, place it in plastic bag and press it between the pages of a book; that way you can keep it around for good luck.

Lucky Find

Can you find the four-leaf clover in this paddock?

Superstitions and Traditions

Racing has been a tradition in many countries for centuries. It was called the "sport of kings" in England and still is today. You have been taught to do things in a certain way because of what the people who taught you learned from their horse trainers. You learned to do everything for your horse from the left side; you even start grooming them there and work your way all the way around the horse.

Does your family have any traditions, such as celebrating holidays in a certain way? Some people believe that crossing the path of a black cat or walking under a ladder will bring you bad luck. Others fear seven years of trouble for breaking a mirror. Even horses appear to have a few superstitions about racing! Some horses will actually refuse to run if their lucky stable mate doesn't go to the races with them.

Words to Know

Superstition

A *superstition* is a belief that is unfounded. Many people believe it is unlucky to cross the path of a black cat or that hanging a horseshoe over their door will bring them good luck.

Try This

Horses You Can Wear

If you have a plain T-shirt that you can paint on, try tracing a horse onto a piece of clear contact paper. Then cut the horse out of the center of the paper and stick the stencil you have made on your shirt. Using fabric paint, brush the paint on the shirt where the opening shaped like the horse is.

What Are the Odds?

Have you ever heard someone say, "What are the odds of that happening again?" when something out of the ordinary happens? When you toss a coin with a friend and choose heads or tails, no matter which one you choose or how many times you toss it, the odds are that one half of the time it will be heads and the rest of the time it will be tails. That is why this is the fairest way to choose who gets to start a game. Try this a few times and see if it works out this way. Odds at a racetrack are determined this way:

1. The horse that wins a race usually has won one before and that determines whether people betting money on the race think he will win again.
2. Odds are determined by how many people are willing to bet that the horse will win.
3. If one person betting one dollar thinks that he will, while fifty others betting a dollar think he won't, the odds are fifty to one.

You might think that odds aren't that important, but a horse winning a race can be worth hundreds of thousands of dollars to someone who guessed the correct order of the horses that win, place and show. Most people don't win that much money very often, but the betting also makes money for the owners of the racetrack and keeps the tracks open so the horses have a place to run. Most racetracks are named after the place where they are located. Many of them have Downs or Meadows for the last part of their name.

What am I?

The state my name comes from is famous for songs about horses. My name also implies that I may not like to run.

What am I?

Tennessee Walking Horse

Giddy Up

Danger in the Dark

Riding at night is not recommended for you or your horse. Even though horses can see very well at night, no one can guess what dangers might be missed in the dark. If you ever do have to go out in the dark, be sure to wear reflective clothing and use lights that you can mount on your stirrups.

Weird Facts

Has one of your grandparents ever said "Ah, horsefeathers," when they thought you were fibbing to them? Did you know some horses have feathers? They're those big tufts of hair that are on the back of the legs of a Clydesdale (and a few other types of horses).

Do you think horses still have toes? You probably know that each hoof is like one great big toe, but does a horse have any more toes than this one? If you have an adult who is able to help you, feel the bump on the back of the horse's front leg where your elbow would be. Then check the bump under the feathers on the backside of the hoof. These bumps are called chestnuts and ergots. Don't they feel like toes? At one time, millions of years ago, they were!

Going to the Dentist

Have you ever wondered if horses have teeth like ours that need to be cleaned by a dentist or brushed twice a day? As you found out earlier, people can tell a horse's age by his teeth and they can also tell your age by looking at your teeth. Unlike human teeth, horses' teeth develop sharp edges and so they need to be smoothed twice a year by a veterinarian, who is also their dentist. A horse's teeth continue to grow throughout the horse's life, so they should never develop cavities or need false teeth like people might need when they get older.

When you go to the dentist, how would you feel if he said "Open wide," and then reached for an enormous file like the one used on a horse? Then you might wonder how big the horse's chair would have to be, and if the vet could ever get the horse to lay down for any amount of time at all. Most wild animals need to have a shot to calm them down so they can be moved from place to place because they get scared

Invisible Horses

Circle the horse word hidden in each of these sentences. Look for words from the list, but be careful! There are extra words in the list that aren't used.

1. In the stall, I only talk quietly.
2. Ken rode Opal into town today.
3. Suzy feeds Romeo at six o'clock.
4. It's true — dry hay will not rot!
5. A man eats differently than a horse.
6. Silver can't spin to the left.

hoof
mane
oats
colt
pinto
rodeo
canter
trot
stallion

and nervous when they have to leave their home. If a horse is tame or trained, it is much easier to get it to do what you want and to give it the care it needs—hopefully without a shot!

Do Horses Have Tusks?

Most horses do have tusks! Some horses' tusks just don't come through their gums. Horses' gums are never completely filled with teeth. They have empty spots between their front and back teeth that are called bars. You can reach through these openings to rub their tongues or you can place the bit of their bridle in this space.

Some horses also have teeth called wolf teeth, but they don't usually get to keep them. The veterinarian

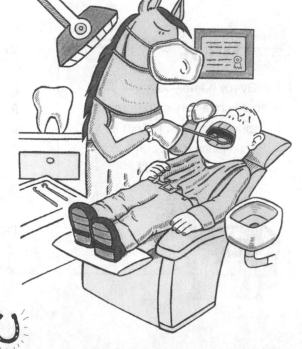

Fun Fact

Shake, Rattle, and Roll

Like dogs, horses like to roll in the grass and run around in circles. Because horses do enjoy rolling around as soon as they are turned loose, it is always best to remove their saddles as soon as you are finished riding.

What am I?

By my name you might think that I am a very cold horse, but actually I am just known for the cold place that I come from.

What am I?

Icelandic Pony

usually takes out the horse's wolf teeth because they get in the way! When you try to put the bit into the horse's mouth, the wolf teeth are right in front of the first molars in the horse's jaw.

Do Not Touch

How will your horse know that you really like him if you don't pet him like you would any other pet? Your trainer will tell you that the more you stroke your horse while you are grooming or training him, the better your relationship will be:

1. Horses just don't like to be lightly touched! Pet your horse with a firm touch so they don't think that you are one of those pesky flies and react by trying to kick you!

2. Some people say horses don't like to have their nose petted, but that they would rather have you pet them between their eyes.

3. Don't force a horse to accept you touching either its nose or between its eyes; it might make the horse jump or spook whenever you reach for its head.

4. It is also important to teach your horse to respect your space and never crowd you when you are grooming him.

5. It's a good idea to tie a horse up (at its chest level) before you start grooming it, so that you don't get hurt by the horse moving around, and so that your horse doesn't get injured if it gets startled while being groomed.

Pay close attention to how your horse reacts to the way you take care of it. You should be able to tell what makes your horse happy or what it doesn't like. Sometimes keeping a horse happy simply involves getting rid of a few flies. In some stables you may see sticky tape used to keep the flies away from the horses. For fun, how about wrapping a large box with double stick tape, making a target on it, and then throwing cotton balls at it to see who can get the most balls to stick?

Let's Go to the Rodeo

Most rodeo horses today are specialists and only compete in certain events, unlike the cowboy's working horses of the old West that had to be able to do everything connected with working with cattle.

Horses are a large part of the rodeo. They have many different jobs that range from helping to lasso a calf to performing show tricks. You can have your own rodeo by steering your bike around obstacles like cardboard boxes, throwing a ball through hoops, riding between tires, and picking flags off of trees.

Bucking Broncos

In the old West, cowboys usually wanted to celebrate and compete with each other after they finished herding the cattle to market. Have you ever been to a rodeo? Some cowboys decide they want to travel all over the country and demonstrate how well they ride cattle and untamed horses called broncos.

When a cowboy tries to ride a bronco for the first time, the horse will buck and jump straight up into the air. The horse isn't sure what is on its back and, like its ancestors, it wants to remove whatever it is. A bronco will also try to scrape off whatever is clinging to its back by rubbing against the fence.

Words to Know

Bronco
A *bronco*, or bronc, is an undomesticated or wild horse. Bucking broncos can be seen at most rodeos, waiting for a cowboy who is brave enough to try to "bust" or ride them.

Fun Fact

Can You Believe It?
For many years, people have known that when you combine a horse with a donkey, you get a mule. But what happens when you combine a zebra with a donkey or a zebra and a horse? You get a zonkey and a zorse.

Ouch!

What did the rodeo rider say when he got bucked off his horse?

Write the answer to each question on the dotted lines. Then put the numbered letters into the grid to find out

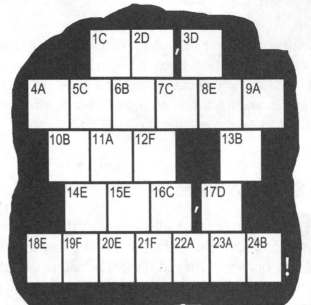

A. Causing laughter

$\overline{4}$ $\overline{23}$ $\overline{9}$ $\overline{11}$ $\overline{22}$

B. Bucket

$\overline{24}$ $\overline{10}$ $\overline{13}$ $\overline{6}$

C. Hammer and _____

$\overline{16}$ $\overline{5}$ $\overline{1}$ $\overline{7}$

D. Short name for pet doctor

$\overline{2}$ $\overline{3}$ $\overline{17}$

E. Kept in a wire box, like a bird

$\overline{14}$ $\overline{15}$ $\overline{18}$ $\overline{8}$ $\overline{20}$

F. Past tense of "do"

$\overline{12}$ $\overline{19}$ $\overline{21}$

Even though the same broncos may be used in a few rodeos, most of them remain untamed. In fact, the more the broncos buck, the better the cowboys and the rodeo crowd like it. Sometimes they try to rear up and stand on their back legs. Cowboys never pull back on the reins when the horse does this; it could make the horse fall over backward and injure its rider.

All Tied Up

Cowboys have to learn how to do many jobs so that they can catch and herd cattle; they use most of this knowledge when they compete at their rodeos. The cowboy's horse is his most important tool. When you go to the rodeo, notice that the horse seems to do many jobs without any instruction from the rider—this is because the horse is so well trained! A good cutting horse can separate a calf from the rest of the herd as soon as it is shown which calf the cowboy wants.

Sometimes, horses are too smart—they can learn how to untie their ropes from their tie-down using their teeth! Have you ever seen a cowboy lasso a calf? After the rope is around the calf's neck, the horse will stop and slowly back away, while the rider jumps down and ties the calf's feet together. A cowboy doesn't always use the same knot for every task. Would you like to learn to tie some knots? You can look up knot tying in encyclopedias, books, or on the Internet.

Fun Fact

Cowboy Slang
When a horse bucks, some cowboys say it is "sunfishing." Some other cowboy words for riding their horses are ambling, loping, and jogging.

Words to Know

Lasso
A *lasso* is a rope formed into a circle by tying a special knot in it. Cowboys use these lassos to catch both horses and cows. Another name for a lasso is a lariat.

Try This

Lasso knots

To make a lasso type of knot: Take a piece of yarn and on one end make a circle, then pull the same end partway through the circle. Before you pull it tight, feed the other end of the yarn through the circle, leaving a big loop that you put your finger in. Now pull the first end tight.

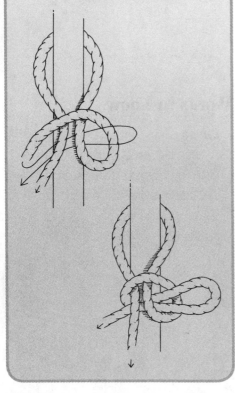

One knot you should learn how to tie well is a "quick release knot." This knot is safe for when you are grooming your horse, because if something happens to scare your horse, you can untie the knot just by tugging on one end of the rope. This way, your horse won't hurt his back or neck by moving suddenly while tied to a post.

Learning a New Trick

Do you think that there are many people who wish that they had grown up to be cowboys and cowgirls? Lots of people attend barbecues, go line dancing, dress up for square dances, go on hay rides, and tour ranches and horse farms—all of these are activities cowboys and cowgirls would like too! Have you ever gone on any trip like this?

Eventually many of the people who want to be cowboys and cowgirls buy horses because they enjoy the life that goes with ownership of a horse. You should try some of these activities and see if you would enjoy this life too! Ask an adult to help you find square dancing lessons in your area, or to take you on a hay ride in the fall!

Horses on the Move

Have you ever moved? Most people move several times in their lives. Like people, horses don't always stay where they were born. Some horses are sold and travel only a few miles away while others go from one country to another. Horses also move from place to place to race, compete in events, and travel in shows. Some horses even get to go on vacation with their owner's family! Some national, state, and county parks and many

privately run campsites offer places to tie up your horse. Some even come equipped with stalls for you to keep your horse in while you are there.

One of the most popular ways for a horse to travel is in a special horse trailer. Maybe you have seen one of these trailers while you were on vacation or just traveling to another place. For fun, try counting all the trailers or horses you see on your next trip; you might be surprised to learn how many horses are on the road!

Some riders like to hobble their horses as well as tie them up. Hobbles are loose ropes that are tied around two of the horses' feet so that the horse can't move around so much and so that the horse learns to stand still when told. Would you and some of your friends like to see how fast you could go if you were hobbled? You can get the same effect by having a sack race or holding one of your friends up by their legs while they race on their hands.

Horses with Passports

Have you ever traveled to another country? Most of the time you need a passport to leave the country and also to re-enter it. Horses that travel from country to country need passports for the same reasons people do. It tells what the horse's name is, who its parents are, some of its grandparents' names, when and where the horse was born, and its registry in the studbook.

You may know someone who has a tattoo. But did you know that horses also wear them, to help their owners prove the horses are who the owners say they are. You probably

Fun Fact

No Bones about It
Although there are horses in Australia now, this wasn't always the case. Australia is the only continent on the planet where no horse fossils have ever been found!

Words to Know

Passport

When you travel from your home country to another country, most places require you to bring a special identification card with your picture on it, called a *passport*. When horses travel, their owners have to show passports for the horses as well.

have heard of housesitters and babysitters. Sometimes horses need someone to look out for them, just like you. When people travel with these valuable animals, someone has to stay with them all the time—so you could say they have horsesitters!

Shipping Horses

Did you know that you can enter your horse in events located all around the world? Transporting horses for long distances by trailers, boats, or planes can be difficult, expensive, and involves a great deal of paperwork to make sure your horse is allowed to run after it gets there.

If you ship your horse by boat, you are part of a long tradition going back to the ponies that were brought to Iceland by Vikings. After the time of the Vikings, Spanish horses were transported in boats so that their riders could fight against English soldiers. Many of the Spanish horses had to swim to shore when the battle was lost and the Spanish ships started to sink.

Have you ever ridden in a sailboat? If the winds don't blow, you have to wait until they do before you can move.

Giddy Up

Kicking Up Your Heels

For a horse, kicking is more of a reflex than a choice. Like any other large animal, it is always best to stay off to the horse's side. Never stand behind him or bend over and go under the horse's neck where he can't see you; it's much safer to walk around in front of him.

376

Many horses died aboard ships that were bound for the New World because the ships had to wait for a breeze to reach an area of the ocean east of Mexico and the horses couldn't survive on the boat that long. Because of this, the sailors called this part of the world "the horse latitudes."

Even when horses travel, they compete with other horses to arrive first to their competitions. Have you ever thought about holding your own horse race at home? All you will need is a chessboard and the chess pieces:

1. Line up your knights, bishops, castles, queens, kings, and pawns on the board. You can use both colors and assign a piece to each player.
2. Roll one die to determine how many spaces the players can move.
3. Keep rolling the die until one player reaches the other side.

What am I?

I have been mountain climbing in Spain for many years and my name sounds like I could have been missing something.
What am I?

Andalusian

Where In The World

Figure out the six rebus puzzles to see where your horse could travel.
HINT: The answers will sound correct, but may not be spelled correctly!

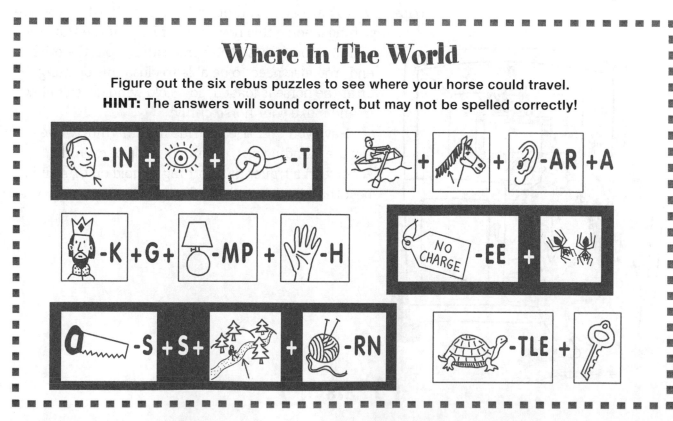

Trailing Along

Whenever you move your horse, be sure to put its shipping boots on it, so it won't be injured and be sure to have a first-aid kit for you and your horse whenever you travel. Shipping boots are padded boots that wrap around your horse's lower legs and protect them while your horse is being moved in a trailer.

Many horses do not like to cross bridges or enter a dark barn or trailer. Maybe they think that they are going to be trapped and unable to use their best defense, which is running away. Horses will fight, if they can't avoid it, by using their hooves and teeth as weapons.

If you are thinking about buying a horse, ask to see a demonstration of how willing he is to enter a trailer. The best way to avoid a traveling problem is to take a foal, preferably with his mother, on frequent trips as he growing up. If this is not possible, try to load him with another horse for a few trips. Always have an assistant and lots of time when you are teaching a horse this new trick. It helps if the trailer is well lit, especially so the horse can see out the other end. You also need to be able to close this opening after the horse is loaded, so a cold wind doesn't blow in and make your horse chilly!

Have you ever tried to ride in something while you are standing up? You might slide or even fall. A horse in a trailer has nothing to hold on to, so it is best that the driver slows down for turns and curves.

Try This

Happy Trails

See if your family can take a day sometime to take you somewhere where they offer trail rides or a pony ride. If you don't have any horses nearby, how about going for a day on a walking or biking trail? If you have time, you can have a picnic along the way.

Try This

Horse Sculptures

If you want to make your own horse statue, you can use clay, play dough, or you can form your horse out of several cardboard horse shapes glued together. Once your horse is formed or dry you can add decorations, paint, eyes, saddles, and more. You can also make soft horses out of stuffed and hand-sewn socks or fluffy pipe cleaners.

Horses That Rock

Horses are so loved that they have been re-created in marble, glass, and wood. Statues of horses can be found everywhere from parks to museums. Horses are fun to look at whether they are alive or carved out of stone. There are horse replicas in stores, homes, and parks throughout the world.

Carousel Ponies

If you ask a horse trainer what he thinks a carousel is, he would say it's a horse trotting in a circle around him! When you hear the word carousel, you probably think of a merry-go-round. Carousels with horses were always more popular than those with other animals on them. Children didn't want to ride on merry-go-rounds with cats, dogs, and birds nearly as much as they did a horse.

You might think that someone decided long ago that their child would enjoy riding on a play pony that twirled in a circle, but most toys are modeled after things we use in real life.

When knights were practicing for carousels or tournaments, they decided that they didn't want to tire out their horses, so they built horse-shaped moving targets. Their wives and children thought it would be fun to ride on them and soon the carousels were decorated and played music.

You can make your own carousel pony from a children's jumping horse toy. If you don't have room for this, most hobby stores will have models of carousel horses that you can buy, decorate, and put somewhere in your room. If you want to make one, it is best to leave the pony on its stand until you are done decorating it:

1. First, ask an adult to help you spray paint your horse outside.
2. Once the horse is dry, you can add other colors to its saddle and mane or anywhere else that you would like.
3. Then you can paint the eyes, and add a mane and tail made from yarn or ribbon.
4. Finally, you can decorate your horse with pearls, jewels, small flowers, and gold touches.
5. Once your horse is finished, you can see if an adult will help you mount it on a golden pole.

Stick Ponies

For years, children have been pretending to be equestrians or people who ride horses. A true equestrian rides a real horse, but most children ride horses that are made out of cloth and poles. Over time, these stick ponies were eventually made out of plastic, leather, and yarn. They have the head of a horse, a place for the rider and a tail or a wheel on the end.

You can even make a broomtail horse, which is what the Western riders called their horses, by using a broom for the

Words to Know

Tournament

A *tournament* is a type of contest or competition. Tournaments date all the way back to the times of the knights on horseback.

Equestrian

The word *equestrian* is used to describe all things related to the riding of a horse or the name of the rider himself.

Wild Ride

See if you can wind your way from START to END through the carved and gilded curls of this fancy carousel horse.

Start

End

stick and an overly stuffed sock for the horse's head. You can also make miniature stick ponies by using a lollipop and a piece of cloth or tissues with a piece of yarn to tie it on and a marker to draw the face.

Rocking Horses

Rocking horses have been around for many years. You can see how people still love to swing or move in a rocking motion if you go to a playground and look on the swing set. Both children and adults love to swing and rock—it can be very relaxing! Rocking horses can rock, bounce, and swing. So what do you think came first, the rocking horse or the rocking chair? Did someone outgrow their rocking horse, so they invented the rocking chair or did they decide a horse that rocked would be a great toy for a child who used to be rocked in a cradle or chair?

Try This

Trojan Box Horse

You can make your own Trojan horse out of a large appliance box with smaller boxes taped on it to be the horse's head, neck, and legs. Then you can make a place to hide in the horse's body and add decorations like eyes, a tail, and a mane.

Giddy Up

Keeping Control

Always keep your horse's reins in your left hand. Never release the reins at any time while you are mounting or dismounting from your horse. Don't keep the reins too tight or too loose; just move your hands that are holding the reins together gently from to one side to the other to turn the horse.

What am I?

By my name, you might think that I am a cow rather than a horse. I am a warm-blooded horse that originally came from Germany.

What am I?

Holstein

Words to Know

Mythological

If something is *mythological*, it is believed to be untrue, has not been proven to be true, or is something from a story. Two mythological types of horses are the unicorn and Pegasus.

One of the reasons people like to ride horses is to feel the calming rocking motion as you ride. Maybe you like to ride on a roller coaster or a speedboat for fun? Some of the first rides for fun were in wagons pulled by horses.

One way to rock like a horse or a boat is to have a friend sit on the floor facing you with the bottoms of your feet touching. Now stretch out your legs as far as they will go and grab a hold of each other's hands. To start rocking, one person must lean back while the other one leans forward, then you do the opposite going back and forth.

Mythological Horses

Ancient people in many lands believed the sun was a god. They also thought that mythological horses were also gods, believing that these horses carried the sun across the sky each day. Other people believed that the horses they heard about in myths also carried young maidens into the sky and that these maidens became the Northern lights. If you would like to see the Northern lights you might be able to find a tape about them at the library or look at them on the Internet by typing "Northern lights" in your search box.

Centaurs are a kind of mythological animal. In Greek mythology, centaurs are creatures that have the body and legs of a horse and the torso, arms and head of a human. Unlike the other monsters in these tales that humans were afraid of and tried to kill, centaurs were usually respected by humans for their intelligence and good intentions. People even believed that it was centaurs that taught humans how to hunt!

When the Indians of South America saw Spanish explorers on horseback, they believed they were looking at gods in real life. They had never seen horses before and they believed that the man and the horse were one animal. After the South

Americans found out this wasn't true, they were still amazed at the fact that the explorers could control these fantastic beasts, even if they really weren't part of them.

Finding the Unicorn

Many people spend their lives searching for rare birds, insects, and plants. What rare things do you look for: a rainbow after a summer storm, the pearl in the shell of the oyster, or that especially beautiful sand dollar on the beach after a big storm over the ocean? Some people hope to be the one who discovers an animal that has never been seen before, like the unicorn—an animal that many people have read about in stories and myths.

Can you imagine what the first person thought when he saw a platypus or an ostrich? There are many strange and exotic animals that are rarely seen or haven't been seen for a long time, but people know that they are still alive today.

In the olden days, you might have spent a lot of time looking for that elusive creature known as the unicorn. A unicorn looks like a regular horse with a single, shiny, twisted horn sticking out from its forehead. People believed that unicorns symbolized purity and wisdom, and that they were calm and beautiful animals. Many people say that the unicorn never existed, but have you ever seen a moa, a rhea, or a saber-toothed tiger? Just because they aren't here now doesn't mean that they never were!

How about conducting a search for the horses that are alive today? Some people say they number in the

What am I?

You may expect to find me trotting past the Eiffel Tower unless, of course, I am feeling a little "sulky." France isn't the only place you will find me, though.

What am I?

French Trotter

Can you spot the unicorn?

If you think it is hard to find a unicorn deep in the forest, try to find the one time that UNICORN is spelled correctly in this letter grid! Search up, down, side to side, or even backwards.

```
C R N U N C I O R N
U R U N U U U N I C
R O I C N U N U C R
N I C R N N I N O O
I O C N U I C I R C
C C U I N C R C N I
I N R O C I N U U N
O C O R N O U O N U
R C I N U R N R I N
N N R C I N U N C I
```

What am I?

I am the type of horse who is the most preferred for racing. My family tree is very important to me. Year after year, my breed makes a "run for the roses."

What am I?

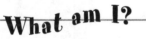

Thoroughbred

hundreds and you might be surprised at the varieties you find. You and your friends could make lists and see who can find the largest number of horses. Start by looking in books at the library and then go on the Internet to see the horses that are scattered all over the world.

Horses with Horns

Some people believe that the unicorns were magical creatures that lived in the world for many years. Legends of pure white horse-like animals with horns have been around for centuries. For some reason, even though many people would still believe that the joy that horses bring to their owners is almost like magic, eventually unicorns lost their magical powers and their horns and then they became known as horses.

True white horses themselves are hard to find; their eyes can be pink, blue, or brown. Some of them are called albinos or perlinos. In an effort to figure out if there actually were unicorns roaming the earth years ago, explorers have searched all over the world hoping to find evidence that these magical creatures really existed.

Long horns have washed ashore from the ocean and most scientists think that these horns found over the years may have belonged to a creature known as the narwhal. This is a type of whale that grows a huge tooth (like the tusk of an elephant) that looks like a horn on its head!

Horses with Wings

If horses could have horns, why couldn't they have wings? Wouldn't you like to have your own personal flying horse that you could put in a stable in your backyard? It would be much quieter and cheaper than a helicopter parked on a pad on the top of your house!

Pegasus is the most famous winged horse. Greek legends tell of Pegasus carrying gods, and describe him as a beautiful white horse who wore a golden bridle that was given to him by a Greek goddess named Athena. Sometimes Pegasus is even described as having golden wings!

If horses had wings, would they be made out of skin like a bat's, feathers like a bird's, or would they made out of a framework with scales attached like the butterfly's? It would take enormous wings for a horse to fly. Even a bird like the ostrich is too big to fly, because its wings are too small. Humans are the only creatures who have managed to fly even though they don't have wings.

Try This

Make a Winged Horse

Do you think the horses would make wings for themselves if they could? One way to find out if a horse might be able to fly is to try attaching different kinds of wings or some type of a paper airplane to a plastic horse and testing it to see how well it would work. What did you find out?

Horses You Can Collect

The first examples of horses in art were made around three thousand years ago (and if you count the European cave paintings, it was thousands of years before that). Buildings were decorated with images of horses being used in sport and battle. Have you noticed that presidents are frequently shown on the money you use? The ancient Greeks showed how much they valued their horses by decorating their coins with pictures of horses. Some Greek coins featured a picture of Pegasus, the companion to their gods.

Model Horses

Have you seen bronze statues of horses for sale in a store? Frederick Remington lived in the West and created statues, drawings, paintings, and stories of the life of the people living during the nineteenth century like the cowboys and Native Americans. One of his most famous horse statues is called "The Bronco Buster" and it is on display in the Oval Office, where the President of the United States works every day! Remington molded his statues out of clay and then used these to make the castings in bronze. You can make your own horse plaque to hang on your wall. You will need a plastic horse, a can of play dough, a sack of plaster of Paris, a small paper plate, and some color of paint:

1. Spread your dough out on the plate until it is about one inch thick.
2. Press the horse half of the way into the dough and then gently lift it out.
3. Mix about a cup of plaster of Paris according to the directions.

Fun Fact

Horses With Hairdos
Horses have manes and tails braided for most competitions and shows. They should have their hair braided most of the time to keep them from developing new tangles in their hair.

My Crazy Collection

Ask a friend or someone in your family to help you finish this story. Don't show them the story first! Ask your helper for the kind of word needed for each blank line (a description is written underneath). Write in the words your helper gives you, then read the story out loud. Be prepared to laugh!

I collect only _____ _____ horses. I have _____
                                color   *material*   *number*

in my collection. I found my favorite horse in _____
                                                           state other than your own

at a _____. It only cost _____ dollars!
               kind of store   *number*

4. Pour the prepared plaster of Paris into the mold the horse made in the dough.
5. When the plaster dries, carefully remove your plaster horse and paint it.

Charles Russell was another famous painter and sculptor who used his time in the West to help us see what it was like in the early days. Many of his artworks are displayed at the Yellowstone Museum. This would be a good place to visit on vacation or you can view much of the art on the Internet.

Glass Ponies

Another type of horse that you can collect is a glass pony. People are fascinated by glass, which is made by heating up grains of sand until they melt and form glass. There are

many things today that are made out of glass—everything from horse figurines to crystal bowls. These delicate items can be molded or made by a person gently blowing air into a tube of heated glass. There are even unicorns that are made from marbled glass!

If you aren't able to collect glass horses, one way you can have one is to make one out of a clear plastic lid like the top of an oatmeal canister, coffee tin, or deli container. You can trace the outline of a pony onto the lid and color it in with markers and outline the pony with puffy paint. Then you can hang your pony in a window or in front of a light.

True Collectors

Have you ever gone on a vacation to Kentucky? There are statues of winning racehorses everywhere, especially the ones that have won the Kentucky Derby. Some of these horses are still alive and you can tour the farms where they live. It is also possible for people living in other places to adopt them after they have been retrained for new owners. It's kind of like a recycling place for horses! Some owners keep their horses, long after they aren't able to work, just because they like to have them around.

If you can't collect a real horse, how about starting a collection of small statues of horses or ponies? Maybe you will want to collect just a certain breed, color, or age. Although collecting these kinds of ponies may not be as much fun as collecting the real ones, it can be fun planning what the next one should be! You might want to start your own collection by picking out something else you really like; whether you collect horses or something else like unicorns, coins, or rocks, collecting can be fun!

Words to Know

Habitat

A *habitat* is the natural surroundings where an animal lives or is usually found. A horse's natural habitat can be in the mountains or the prairies.

Species

A *species* is a section or part of the divisions of the animal kingdom. Horses belong to the *Equus caballus* species.

The Zoo Life

Even though people in America don't use horses to get around much anymore, there will still be lots of places for you to go see horses in the future. One of these places is the zoo! Did you ever go to the zoo and wonder if the animals like to live in pens, corrals, or cages? All kinds of animals from other countries or different habitats are often displayed at a zoo for people to see.

Many times these animals live in zoos because some of them are unable to still live in their original homelands. A few of them are called rare or endangered species and they are able to receive the special foods and treatment they need in this protected environment. The zoo also provides them with a safe place to raise their young.

Certain members of the horse family already live in zoos like the horse's cousins: zebra, onager, donkey, mule,

and burro. You can try making your own zoo collage using animal pictures from magazines, a piece of poster board and glue stick to arrange and glue down all of your pictures of animals.

Petting Zoos

What kinds of animals would you expect to see in a petting zoo? Most petting zoos include ponies. They also have cows, sheep, chickens, goats, and rabbits. Although it may seem strange to see so many different animals sharing the same barns and corrals, it isn't as odd as you might think. Herds of animals that live in the wild are many times made up of different animals like zebras, ostriches, and gnus.

What am I?

Originally, my name was used to label wild horses, but it soon became more famous for a sleek sports car that can go really fast.

What am I?

Mustang

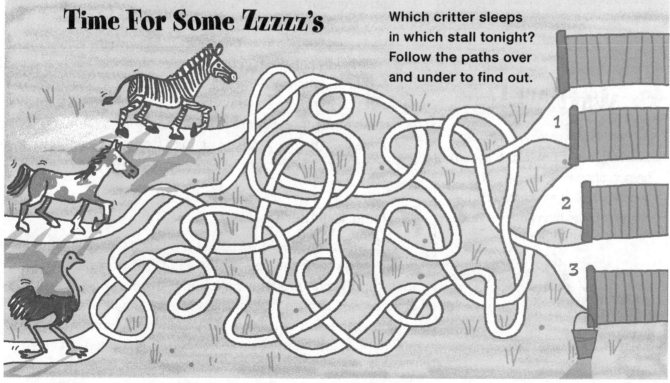

Time For Some Zzzzz's

Which critter sleeps in which stall tonight? Follow the paths over and under to find out.

1

2

3

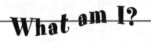

Try This

See For Yourself

Some zoos let people spend the night. Do you think zebras sleep standing up like horses? One way to find out is to see if your area zoo lets families sleep over. If so, you can camp out by the zebra house or the horse's barn and watch to see who sleeps lying down and who sleeps standing up.

What am I?

I am the favorite horse for a cowboy. You might think that I am named after a certain type of coin, when actually I am named for the length of race than I run the best.

What am I?

Quarterhorse

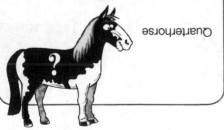

These animals choose to live together and use their special senses to protect one another. The zebra, like the horse, has a wonderful sense of smell; the ostrich is able to see movement at a great distance; and the gnu turns its head toward any dangerous-seeming sound. They all alert the herd when they fear something so the herd can move quickly away. If you aren't anywhere near a petting zoo, how about visiting the fair when it comes around? A lot of fairs have petting zoos included in their events.

Pony Rides

Children have always loved pony rides. They usually ride them at circuses, zoos, carnivals, or fairs. Many ranches also offer rides for their smaller customers. Ponies are the best choice for the beginning rider because a pony's build is smaller than a regular horse, so it is easier for the rider to climb on and stay on.

Have you ever heard of pony runs? A pony run is like the relay fund-raisers held at schools, only you would be riding your horse a certain distance to raise money for some worthwhile cause. If you're not involved in a pony run, how about joining a pony club to meet and share information with other people who like ponies? Some pony clubs organize rides for people who love horses and like to ride with other people in groups.

Living Together

What animal would you like for a pet? Most kids would say a dog. Other than the dog, a man's next best friend in the animal world would probably be a horse. People and horses have shared the Earth for millions of years, and will continue to work together in the future. They have been partners in work and in play, and many people could not have even survived

without their horse, like the pioneers, cowboys, and Native Americans in the West.

There are specialized groups that help mentally and physically challenged people adapt to their world through horse riding therapy. Just riding a horse for a short time can help people to relax and feel safe and loved by being so close to a kind animal.

As time goes on, people are providing special places for horse to live in like sanctuaries or preserves so they are able share the planet with humans in safety. Some of these places conduct tours for city dwellers hoping to see a glimpse of these bands of wild horses.

Let's Go to the Circus

The circus is another place where you can see all kinds of talented and well-trained horses. Have you ever been to the circus? The first circuses were held thousands of years ago in a special building made just for them. Eventually, the circus started to move from town to town so that more people could get to enjoy the fun! Many people went just to see the calliope, a steam organ on wheels. When people heard that familiar sound, they knew the circus was in town. For many years, people in Wisconsin have been able to watch an old-time circus parade that lasts around two hours. Before there were cars and trucks, horses pulled the circus wagons from town to town!

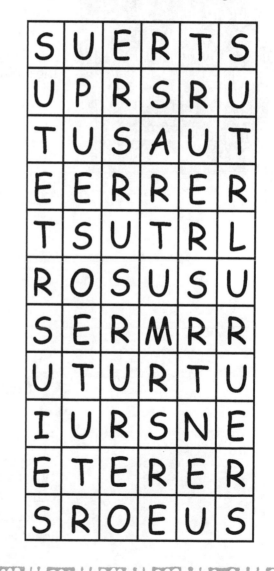

LUV U 4 EVR

What kind of horse is your best friend? To find out, color in the squares that contain the letters that appear three or more times. Read the remaining letters from top to bottom, and left to right.

S	U	E	R	T	S
U	P	R	S	R	U
T	U	S	A	U	T
E	E	R	R	E	R
T	S	U	T	R	L
R	O	S	U	S	U
S	E	R	M	R	R
U	T	U	R	T	U
I	U	R	S	N	E
E	T	E	R	E	R
S	R	O	E	U	S

Fun Fact

Round and Round We Go
Most people think of a carousel as children riding on wooden horses and listening to music. There are also carousel machines that move real horses in a circle for exercise and cooling off after a ride.

The Main Event

Would you believe that the circus is the oldest horse show in history? Its history goes back thousands of years. Horses were and still are the main attraction at a circus. At most circuses, you can see acrobats who do somersaults on the horses' backs or ride on two horses at once. Many of the horses without riders are so well trained that they seem to know what to do and can be directed by just a nod of the head from a person walking around on the ground!

Parading Around

Sometimes the parade part of a circus is the best part! Horses were used to pull all the wagons containing the performers; in the old days, sometimes there were teams of forty horses. How did all those horses keep in step with each other? Sometimes they didn't. Have you ever seen a team of horses where one horse isn't pulling his own share of the load? Horses have been known to kick or nip the lazy horse!

Tomorrow's Horses

Even in small towns, horses and riders still continue to lead the parades or have children riding in wagons pulled by huge horses. If you have a horse or know someone with a horse, you may be able to get permission to ride with him in your local parade. Sometimes, in a big city, the horses may be ridden by a police officer who helps keep order along the parade route.

Bareback and Sidesaddle

Sometimes at the circus or in circus parades, you will see people riding sidesaddle or doing stunts on horses that aren't wearing saddles. Ancient people rode horses without a saddle; saddles weren't even invented until around 2,000 years ago! The rider used the horse's mane as a means to climb up on the horse and many people still grab a handful of hair as they swing themselves up into a horse's saddle. Horses don't seem to mind and some people say there is no sensation in their mane or in the horse's tail, either.

Some riders still go bareback for short periods of time, but it is much safer to ride in a saddle. Bronco riders at the rodeo ride bareback and it certainly looks like it is hard to stay on that horse without a saddle!

If you were a girl and lived many years ago, it was considered unladylike to wear pants and ride with your legs hanging down on either side of your horse. Women were supposed to wear skirts and sit in a special saddle that let them keep both legs on one side of a horse. Imagine a saddle with only one stirrup and a big knob to hook your leg around. It would be harder to control your horse and you wouldn't be able to press with your leg on the right side to tell the horse what to do, so riders must use a little whip and tap it on that side. Some girls still use sidesaddles and wear skirts for certain events.

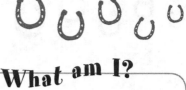

What am I?

Depending on how formal you want to be, you could call me Barbara or Babs. Although I can be found in several other places now, originally I only lived in very warm climates.

What am I?

Barb

Try This

Ride on the Side

If you get the chance, try to ride sidesaddle sometime. To see what it might feel like, try sitting on a chair sideways all through supper, getting up and sitting down, always using only that side.

A New Breed

Do you think they will find a new type of horse as people explore the remote places on our planet? As science has advanced, they have developed new breeds of horses. Scientists and breeders will probably find a way to make a type of horse that has never been seen before! We have several different types of dogs and cats that didn't exist years ago. Maybe they will even find a way to make to make a brand new species if they blend the right kind of animals. Many people already think that a quagga was probably a cross between a horse and a zebra with its striped shoulders and its plain colored body. Maybe we can develop horses that fly or horses with horns!

Brand New Horses

Do you think we will go back to using horses for our work? Police officers have started using them again and so have many of the rangers. If gasoline keeps getting more scarce, many farmers and ranchers may be forced into parking their automobiles and climbing back up on their horses so they can tend to their animals and land. The only fuel a horse requires is food that can be grown by the farmer, like hay and oats.

Many countries still use horses every day for work. How would you like it if you could ride a horse to work or school? As time goes on, there will surely be new horses: bigger ones, smaller ones, and maybe even ones with wings. One thing is certain: The world of the horse is always changing!

Try This

A Good Match

Here's a matching game where you take six horse pictures, tape them on six recipe cards, cut the cards in half and then turn them all face down on the floor. Now try to find two ends that match by looking at any two cards at a time. The person with the most matches at the end wins.

Never Seen Before

Have you ever had a dog that your parents called a mutt? Some horse dealers or trainers will call a horse that is a crossbreed a grade horse or a mutt. The breeds of these horses have been crossed so many times that no one knows for sure what breed it is. Most horses in the everyday world would probably end up in this category of horses. You can always think of these mixed breed horses as one of a kind!

Many of the first crossbreeds occurred when the conquerors of long ago were roaming the world and bringing their new types of horses to these distant lands. Probably the closest thing to a purebred horse in the world is the wild horse called the Przewalski, but the Arabian horse is the domestic horse that most breeders would say is a purebred horse.

Cross-breeding is a way of combining the qualities of breeds of horses like the Arabian, the Morgan, the Thoroughbred, and some other American breeds to create a new breed called the American Saddlebred. Do you look more like one of your parents than the other one? A crossbred horse with a Morgan parent will usually look more like the Morgan breed. The crossbreeding continues with breeders making new combinations from the Arabian and Morgan breeds. Sometimes they even give new names to these combinations like Morab. Would you like to think of some interesting combinations of new breeds and figure out what their new names could be?

Making Your Own Horse

The Nez Perce Indians also created their own breed of horses called the Appaloosas. There are many different markings for these unusual horses and different names for each type of marking. If you could invent your

Words to Know

Crossbreed

A *crossbreed* is an animal that is the result of having a mom that is one kind of horse and a dad that is another—the foal will be a mix of the two! Except for the true original horse, Przewalski's Horse, all of our current breeds resulted from cross-breeding.

Try This

Shoo Fly Pie Kid Style

All you need to make shoo fly pie is a pre-made graham cracker crust, two pints of chocolate ice cream, one jar of caramel topping, and a few chocolate chips for your "flies." To assemble your pie: thaw your ice cream slightly, spread it in the crust, add your jar of topping, sprinkle on a few flies, and freeze.

WALKIE

HORSE

POOCHED

POKE

ICE

SEA

New & Improved

Look at the riddles below. Each animal has been crossed with another to create a compound word or phrase that means something completely different. Use the words around the edge of the page to make the answers. Careful—they will be silly!

EGGS

SWIM

What do you get when you cross...

...a centipede with a parrot?

A WALKIE TALKIE
_____

...a snail with a porcupine?

A
_____

...a goldfish with an elephant?

_____

SLOW

CREAM

...a hen with a dog?

_____

...a dolphin with a pony?

A
_____

TRUNKS

...a penguin with a cow?

_____

TALKIE

400

own horse what would it be? Would it have short hair or long hair? Would it be short or tall?

Horse breeders do select certain horses so that they can choose what the new colt will be like. Will we need heavier, bigger horses for taller people? How about crossing a Clydesdale with a Percheron?

The United States recognizes horses by color as well as breed. We have pink Albinos, blue Grullos, and many shades of red. Do you think we will ever see the red and blue horse types combine to make a purple horse? Points are another word for the color of a horse's muzzle, tips of its ears, and the bottom of their legs. Can you imagine what a purple horse would look like with turquoise points, and maybe even wings or horns? This could be the horse of the future!

Fun Fact

Do Horses Get Married?
When you hear the words "bridle path," you may think it is the aisle that a bride walks down. In the horse world, it is the place you trim in a horse's mane, right behind the ears, where you will want to put the bridle.

Try This

Mobile Horses

You can make your own carousel of horses by using a plastic plate with holes punched around the edges. Then tie several different colors of painted plastic ponies to the plate by tying each one on with yarn or ribbon. Have an adult help you tie one string up through the center and choose a place to hang it.

page 278 • **Show me . . .**

Show me Sir Lancelot's horse...

...and I'll show you a knight mare!

page 293 • **Big Enough?**

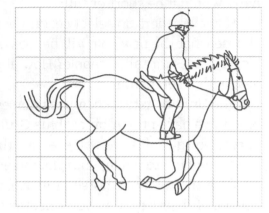

page 283 •
Movie Madness

page 285 • **Pony Express**

page 296 • **Hidden Paint**

402

Puzzle Answers

page 300 • **Horse Work**

```
        G         A
    F A R R I E R R
    J   O         T
  C O W B O Y     I
    C   O         S
    K       V E T T
S T E W A R D
    Y
```

page 307 • **Where's My Horse?**

ADMIRAL

JUMPER

GYPSY

DAPPLE

Pine Street   Pine Street   Pine Street

Maple Street

page 311 • **Apples for All**

```
E L P P A
S E K A E
I A E M H
N P C D T
T P U N L
O L A A L
P E S S A
I E C E T
Y O U C U
```

page 316 • **Where does a sick pony go . . .**

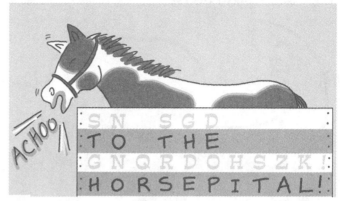

SN SGD
TO THE
GNQRDOHSZK!
HORSEPITAL!

page 320 • **How Many Hands?**

All the horses are exactly the same height! The horse on the right only looks bigger because the pattern of diagonal lines confuses your eyes.

page 323 • **Who is a horses' favorite storybook . .**

1C	2D	3D	4B	5C	6B
W	H	I	N	N	Y

7A	8A	9C
T	H	E

10B	11A	12B	13C
P	O	O	H

A. Not cold.
$\underline{H}_{8}$ $\underline{O}_{11}$ $\underline{T}_{7}$

B. Small horse.
$\underline{P}_{10}$ $\underline{O}_{12}$ $\underline{N}_{4}$ $\underline{Y}_{6}$

C. At what time?
$\underline{W}_{1}$ $\underline{H}_{13}$ $\underline{E}_{9}$ $\underline{N}_{5}$

D. Quick hello.
$\underline{H}_{2}$ $\underline{I}_{3}$

403

page 325 • **Sixth Sense**

page 330 • **How Many?**

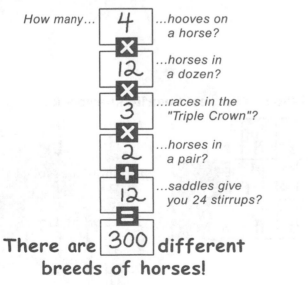

How many...

4	...hooves on a horse?
×	
12	...horses in a dozen?
×	
3	...races in the "Triple Crown"?
×	
2	...horses in a pair?
+	
12	...saddles give you 24 stirrups?
=	
300	

There are 300 **different breeds of horses!**

page 335 • **Horseplay**

1. There are six dappled and painted horses, and eight solid horses with stockings.

2. No. There are five horses with blazes.

3. Ben Blair has the horse with the brand "BB".

page 338 • **In The Shadows**

page 345 • **Growing Up**

H	O	W		D	O		Y	O	U
R	A	I	S	E		A		G	O	O	D
H	O	R	S	E	?		I	N
A	N		E	L	E	V	A	T	O	R	!

page 350 • 'Round and 'Round

HORSE WITH A RIDER

page 353 • Matching Saddles

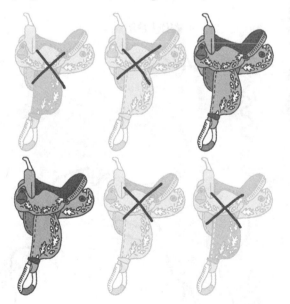

page 362 • Let's Race

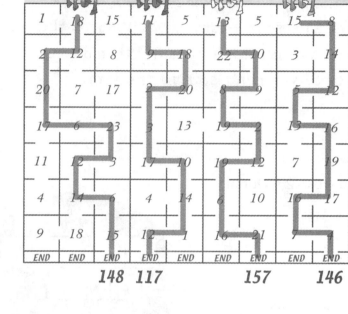

148 117   157   146

page 365 • Lucky Find

page 369 • **Invisible Horses**

1. In the stall, I only talk quietly.
2. Ken rode Opal into town today.
3. Suzy feeds Romeo at six o'clock.
4. It's true — dry hay will not rot!
5. A man eats differently than a horse.
6. Silver can't spin to the left.

page 377 • **Where In The World**

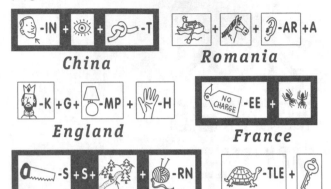

China

Romania

England

France

Australia

Turkey

page 372 • **Ouch!**

A. Causing laughter
F U N N Y
4 23 9 11 22

B. Bucket
P A I L
24 10 13 6

C. Hammer and _____
N A I L
16 5 1 7

D. Short name for pet doctor
V E T
2 3 17

E. Kept in a wire box, like a bird
C A G E D
14 15 18 8 20

F. Past tense of "do"
D I D
12 19 21

|1C|2D|3D| |
|I|V'|E| |

|4A|5C|6B|7C|8E|9A|
|F|A|L|L|E|N|

|10B|11A|12F| |13B|
|A|N|D| |I|

|14E|15C|16C|17D|
|C|A|N'|T|

|18E|19F|20E|21F|22A|23A|24B|
|G|I|D|D|Y|U|P|!

page 382 • **Wild Ride**

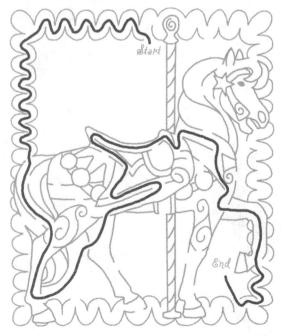

Start

End

page 386 • Can you spot the unicorn?

```
C R N U N C I O R N
U R U N U U U N I C
R O I C N U N U C R
N I C R N N I N O O
I O C N U I C I R C
C C U I N C R C N I
I N R O C I N U U N
O C O R N O U O N U
R C I N U R N R I N
N N R C I N U N C I
```

page 389 • My Crazy Collection

Everyone will end up with a
different story. Here is ours!

I collect only GREEN PLASTIC horses. I have 102 in my collection. I found my favorite horse in OHIO

at a SHOE STORE. It only cost 17 dollars!

page 393 • Time For Some Zzzzz's

page 395 • **LUV U 4 EVR**

page 400 • **New & Improved**

What do you get when you cross...

...a centipede with a parrot?
A WALKIE TALKIE

...a snail with a porcupine?
A SLOW POKE

...a goldfish with an elephant?
SWIM TRUNKS

...a hen with a dog?
POOCHED EGGS

...a dolphin with a pony?
A SEAHORSE

...a penguin with a cow?
ICE CREAM